# ESSENTIALS OF THE LEGAL ENVIRONMENT OF BUSINESS

Applications and Ethical Considerations

**John David Blackburn and Elliot Irwin Klayman**
THE OHIO STATE UNIVERSITY

XanEdu

Printed in the United States of America

ISBN 13: 978-1-97507-686-3





XanEdu

4750 Venture Drive, Suite 400
Ann Arbor, MI 48108
800-562-2147
www.xanedu.com

*Professor Blackburn dedicates this book to*
*his wife,*
*Vita Berezina-Blackburn*
*and their daughter,*
*Iris Mae Blackburn*

*Professor Klayman dedicates this book to Tikkun Olam,*
*his bi-monthly fellowship group that demonstrates*
*the value of a life of sacrifice with a balanced view toward*
*justice and mercy.*

# PREFACE

This book fills the need for quality teaching material for the legal environment of business course. It combines highly readable text with interesting cases and challenging review problems suitable for business students. The book responds to the accreditation standards of the American Assembly of Collegiate Schools of Business (AACSB), as well as those of the Association of Collegiate Business Schools and Programs (ACBSP).

The book surveys the essential fields of the legal environment of business with a goal of helping the student become an executive who is knowledgeable of the legal context in which the business organization operates. The book provides an introduction to American legal institutions, including the sources of law. It presents the basic concepts of public and private law related to business decisions, highlighting the information necessary to train students in good ethical decision-making.

The book consists of eight chapters, organized into four parts:

- *Part One: Law and Ethics in the Business Environment*, covers the interconnection of law and ethics, the nature of law and legal reasoning, and the American legal system .
- *Part Two: Civil Law Foundations of the Legal Environment of Business*, presents the law of property, the law of contractual transactions, and the law of injuries (tort law).
- *Part Three: The Legal and Ethical Environment of Business Organizations*, covers the subjects of agency, partnerships, corporations, and limited liability companies.
- *Part Four: The Legal and Ethical Environment of Business and its Employees*, focuses on equal employment opportunity law.

The thesis of this book is that business law and business ethics are interconnected. The book includes case studies within the Business Application/Ethical Issues boxes, which invite students to determine whether the business practice is ethical. The court cases in the form of appellate court opinions that are included in the book show the intersection of law and business practice. At the conclusion of each chapter are review problems that challenge the student to identify legal and ethical issues, and to consider their resolution.

The goal of this book is for the student to develop a deeper understanding of the social-legal responsibilities of the business community. It is also a goal that the student will set a high standard of ethical decision-making. This book is the authors' contribution toward achieving these goals.

We have had considerable help in writing this book. Joyce Klayman, with her superb library science skills, used her online prowess to locate, and make suggestions for, case and link inclusion. The authors alone are responsible for the views expressed and material used.

**John David Blackburn, J.D.**
**Elliot I. Klayman, J.D.**
**Fisher College of Business**
**The Ohio State University**

# BRIEF CONTENTS

PART I

# LAW AND ETHICS IN THE BUSINESS ENVIRONMENT

CHAPTER 1

# LAW AND ETHICS

## CHAPTER OUTLINE



## LEARNING OBJECTIVES

After learning this chapter the student should be able to:

- Explain the relationship between business ethics and law.
- Recite the fundamental ethical principles reflected in law.
- Describe how businesses address ethics via codes of ethics, compliance programs, by enlisting ethics officers, and by forming creative solutions to ethical problems.

Law consists of rules of human behavior and justice. These rules are often sanctioned by authority. They are often tied to consequences determined by someone empowered to effect them. Law reflects social values. Ethics are rationally justified views about what is right and wrong, moral and immoral, just and unjust. Chapter 1 discusses the relationship of law and ethics.

## LAW AND ETHICS ARE INTERCONNECTED

Many people think of the businessperson as a selfish individual who maintains that it is a dog-eat-dog world where only the fit survive. They consider this view justified by the theory of evolution. This view is not justified by the natural world, human nature, or the world of business.[1]

What separates humans from other animals is that humans are rational creatures. They form communities based on cooperation to live sane lives in safety and security in peace and harmony, seeking fairness, equality, love and compassion. Law is one of the social institutions that human communities rely upon to achieve these goals.

Law is society's way of providing for the safety, security and happiness of its members. It does this by sanctioning rational rules of behavior, and by devising fair ways for resolving disputes. Law works most effectively and efficiently when it is supported by the moral opinion of the members of the community. In harmonious communities, the governmental, educational, religious, economic and social institutions support and are supported by the rule of law.

This book tries to show that business law and business ethics are interconnected.[2] Perceived unethical business behavior often spurs public outcry for increased regulation of business. What is considered ethical business conduct often finds expression as formal law. Contemporarily, law often affects the opinions of individuals and organizations about what conduct is right and wrong, ethical and unethical.

This is not to say that all governmental law is ethical. History supplies examples of unethical governmental laws. The pre-Civil War slave laws in the United States are an example. The slave labor law in Nazi Germany is another. Governments and government officials can commit crimes. People can distinguish governmental laws that promote peace and security among all members of a society from governmental laws that are clever legalisms and subterfuges for doing violence on some, peaceful members of society. You may find more recent examples of governmental laws that do not meet your standards for business conduct and law.

Throughout the book, as seen in this chapter, there are court cases showing the intersection of law and business practice. This book also includes case studies within the Business Application/Ethical Issues boxes. They invite you to determine whether the business practice is ethical and legal. They also invite you to consider what you think should be expressed in the legal environment surrounding the activity. At the conclusion of each chapter there are review problems. These are business fact

---

1 S. I. Hayakawa and Alan R. Hayakawa, *Language in Thought and Action* Ch. 1, "Language and Survival," (Harcourt Brace & Co. 5th Ed. 1990) ("Cooperation within a species (and sometimes with other species) is essential to the survival of most living creatures." at pp. 4–5.).

2 *See*, Thomas W. Dunfee, *On the Synergistic, Interdependent Relationship of Business Ethics and Law*, 34 AM. BUS. L.J. 317 (1996).

patterns. These business problems/cases invite you to identify legal and ethical issues and explain how you think they should be resolved. They are exercises in business application.

You have the ability to understand and form rational opinions about the subject matter content of this book. All you have to do is draw upon the resources that are accessible to anyone. These include your ability to reason as an ordinary rational human being. Included also are your knowledge and experience about facts of the real and practical world. You also understand social life and can consider the most rational organization of it according to present needs.

The goal of this book is that you develop a deeper understanding of the social-legal responsibilities of the business community. It is also a goal that you will set a high standard of business ethics. This book is part of the process of discovery and development of your personal values. Your personal values should guide you toward a happy and productive life as a member of the business/social community. The hope is this book will promote a sane and harmonious world full of freedom, justice, fairness and compassion.

## Business Application/Ethical Issues

Joe, a business student at Go Beyond University, worked as a food server at The Moldau, an upscale restaurant in town. Joe's performance appraisals were superb. Joe left his employment at The Moldau in good standing when he took an internship with Sorata Corporation.

When Joe returned from his internship, he reapplied for an opening as a food server at The Moldau. While Joe was away, a new manager at The Moldau took over the manager's position.

The new manager checked Joe's online social media posts that were available in the public domain. The manager noticed that Joe belonged to groups that promoted passing gun control laws. Joe's social media posts expressed his support for more laws restricting gun ownership and use. The manager was against passing such laws. The manager refused to rehire Joe because of Joe's membership in gun control groups and Joe's social media posts in favor of more restrictive gun control laws.

No law in the city or state where The Moldau is located forbids private, nongovernmental employers from discriminating on the basis of an applicant or employee's political views. There is no federal law in the United States forbidding discrimination on the basis of political expression by private, nongovernmental employers like The Moldau. (The First Amendment of the U.S. Constitution protects political expression—but only from governmental action.)

Do you think the manager's action was ethical? Do you think it should be unlawful for an employer to discriminate on the basis of an applicant's or employee's political views?

# FUNDAMENTAL ETHICAL PRINCIPLES REFLECTED IN LAW

Law and ethics interconnect. What is considered ethical often finds expression in governmental law. Similarly, law may influence the values of individuals and organizations. Often, individuals and organizations look to the law for guidance in deciding what is right and wrong. For example, business people often refer to their fiduciary obligation when deciding what to do in their relations with others. When making company policy, business people often turn to the law for the principles to include in their policy documents. Examples of this include a company code of ethics, or a company's sexual harassment policy.

One result of this law/ethics interaction is that what is considered ethical business conduct often becomes formal law. Another result is the law often influences the values of individuals and companies, affecting the way business is practiced.

This section discusses some legal principles so fundamental that they are part of the everyday vocabulary of business. These legal principles serve as guideposts to business people to determine what is appropriate and ethical business behavior. When encountering situations where you are unsure what to do, the following principles may apply and provide guidance. The principles are:

1. Maintain fiduciary standards to act solely for the benefit of the person whose property or interests you are entrusted
2. Avoid the appearance of conflicts of interest
3. Respect confidential relationships
4. Exercise due care and diligence in the performance of your duties
5. Act in good faith and deal fairly with others

The principles listed above will be discussed at various places throughout this book. For example, the duty of due care is discussed in the chapters on torts and business associations, among others. These principles are well known in the business community and society at large. For example, accountants and psychologists are familiar with the principle of respecting confidential relations. But the following principles are not the only examples of legal principles that have influenced the ethics of the business community. Much of what is practiced by members of the business community is a reflection of what is provided by the law. For example, employment policies, such as sexual harassment policies, reflect the concepts developed in equal employment opportunity law. Much of what is required by law and is considered ethical business practice are two sides of the same coin.

## *Maintain Fiduciary Standards*

The highest legal duty and standard for ethical business conduct is the fiduciary rule. A fiduciary is someone who occupies a position of power, trust and confidence regarding the property of another. Examples of fiduciaries include agents (such as real estate agents), business partners, and directors of corporations. The **fiduciary rule** requires the fiduciary to act solely in the interest of that other person's property and interests.

The following is an excerpt from *Meinhard v. Salmon*, a 1928 decision of New York's highest court. The case involved the duties owed by partners and those engaged in joint business ventures to one another. The excerpt is the most often quoted expression of the fiduciary rule:

> *Joint adventurers, like copartners, owe to one another, while the enterprise continues, the duty of the finest loyalty. Many forms of conduct permissible in a workaday world for those acting at arm's length, are forbidden to those bound by fiduciary ties. A trustee is held to something stricter than the morals of the marketplace. Not honesty alone, but the punctilio of an honor the most sensitive, is then the standard of behavior. As to this there has developed a tradition that is unbending and inveterate. Uncompromising rigidity has been the attitude of courts of equity when petitioned to undermine the rule of undivided loyalty by the "disintegrating erosion" of particular exceptions. Only thus has the level of the conduct for fiduciaries been kept at a level higher than that trodden by the crowd.*

The following is a more recent case. It involves an employee's fiduciary duty to the employer.

**DESIGN STRATEGIES, INC. *v.* MARC DAVIS, ET AL.**
U.S. District Court, Southern District, New York
384 F.Supp.2d 649 (S.D.N.Y. 2005)

Design Strategies, Inc. ("Design") is in the business of providing trained personnel to companies needing technical support on specific projects requiring computer technology services. That aspect of the industry is known as "staffing." Design sued its former employee, Marc Davis ("Davis"), alleging that Davis, while still employed at Design, wrongfully diverted a lucrative business opportunity from Design to Info Technologies Web Solutions ("IT Web"), and subsequently benefitted from that diversion by accepting an offer of employment with IT Web IT Web is a "web solutions" provider. Unlike staffing, web solutions work in the industry involves providing the services of trained personnel employed by the company on its premises and using the computers and other technical equipment supplied at the provider's laboratory on specific projects to design and develop websites for clients in accordance with given specifications. IT Web is a subsidiary of Info Technologies, Inc. ("lnfotech"), a web staffing provider.

The court concluded that Design proved its claim against Davis for breach of fiduciary duties. What follows is the court's opinion, setting forth the court's reasons.

## *Marrero, District Judge*

Davis's work entailed marketing Design's staffing services. He was compensated with a fixed annual salary plus commissions.

Davis left Design in February 2000 to accept a position with IT Web. At the time of his departure, Davis was earning an annual salary at Design of approximately $85,000.

Sometime during the summer of 1999 Davis became aware that Microsoft was involved with a partner, Brill Media, in a venture that would be eliciting companies for a contract worth approximately $10 million. The project, which came to be known as ("Contentville"), entailed establishing a high-profile website using Microsoft software to engage in electronic commerce in books and related products and thus compete with similar businesses operated by Amazon.com and Barnes and Noble.

The services to be provided by the company chosen to work on Contentville involved providing "web solutions" work.

Microsoft awarded the Contentville contract to IT Web in mid-December 1999. IT Web extended an offer of employment to Davis by letter dated December 14, 1999, which Davis accepted.

Davis promoted Design for what eventually became the Contentville contract from the time he learned about it until sometime in November 1999.

In or before early November 1999, Davis ceased attempting to solicit the Contentville contract for Design and, instead, commenced trying to promote IT Web for the contract. He took steps to inform IT Web and Infotech about a business opportunity with Microsoft and to encourage Microsoft to consider IT Web for Contentville.

Under New York law, an employee owes a duty of good faith and loyalty to his employer.

The New York Court of Appeals emphasized the broad nature of this duty in *Elco Shoe Mnfrs., Ins. v. Sisk*: "[N]o man can serve two masters with equal fidelity when rival interests come into existence. Agents are bound at all times to exercise the utmost good faith toward their principals. They must act in accordance with the highest and truest principles of morality."

An employee who is found to have breached his duty of loyalty is generally disentitled to recover his compensation, whether commissions or salary. Disloyal employees may be held liable for their compensation even if the principal suffered no provable damage as a result of the breach of fidelity.

The Court concludes that, even if strictly speaking Design and IT Web were not themselves competitors in the web solutions niche of the computer industry, they had sufficiently conflicting business interests at the relevant time to be deemed competitors in the present context. During the time when Davis attempted to procure Contentville for IT Web, that entity was a division of Infotech and its success directly contributed to Infotech's, which did squarely compete with Design in the staffing business.

Having determined that Davis violated his duty of loyalty to his employer, the Court must consider whether that violation warrants forfeiture of his relevant compensation, and, if so, to what extent.

Forfeiture is warranted because Davis acted "adversely to his employer." Davis's actions aimed at promoting the success of a company that was a division of a direct competitor of Design.

The court finds that the two pay periods from November 11 to December 9, 1999 encompass the time of Davis's disloyal acts. Thus, the Court determines that Davis must forfeit his salary for those two pay periods. For each of these pay periods, Davis received a salary of $3,269.00. The remainder of his compensation during these periods was comprised of commissions. Davis is not alleged to have acted disloyally in relation to any of the Design staffing sales on which he earned those commissions. Consequently, the Court finds that Davis must forfeit $6,538.00 to Design, plus any applicable interest.

**Business Application:** Imagine yourself in Marc Davis's situation. What should you do to avoid liability for breach of the fiduciary duty?

## *Avoid the Appearance of a Conflict of Interest*

A **conflict of interest** exists when your personal interest or duty conflicts with a professional interest or duty. One example is a real estate agent, representing a seller, having an ownership interest in a company wanting to buy the seller's property. Another example would be where a real estate agent represents both the seller and the buyer. In the first example, the agent has a personal interest that conflicts with the agent's duty to the seller. In the second example, the agent's duty to the buyer conflicts with the agent's duty to the seller.

Conflicts of interest create the impression that the person in the conflict situation cannot be fair and impartial. The rule against conflicts of interest is as old as the biblical expression that one "cannot serve two masters." The legal rule stems from the fiduciary rule. It also is rooted in the law of agency (covered in the chapter on business associations). There the rule is that an agent owes a duty of undivided loyalty to the principal (employer). The agent cannot allow his or her personal interests to conflict with that of the principal. The agent cannot deal with the principal as an adverse party.

Someone in a conflict of interest situation has two options: (1) disqualification or (2) disclosure and consent. Disqualification means the person having the conflict avoids the conflict by disqualifying him or herself from the opportunity presented.

In the first example, the real estate agent could disqualify him or herself by either resigning as the seller's agent or selling his or her ownership interest in the company that wants to buy the property. The other way the agent could resolve the conflict is to disclose the conflict to both the seller and the buyer and obtain their consent to continue with the transaction. If the second alternative is taken, a good practice would be to get an independent third party to provide an opinion on the fairness of the transaction. In our example, an independent real estate appraiser could provide an opinion as to the property's value.

Many companies have policies dealing with conflicts of interest. Often these policies are part of a company's code of ethics. (Codes of ethics are discussed later in this chapter.) These policies often require the employee to report a conflict on a company form, which often is available on the company website.

## *Respect Confidential Relations*

When someone receives information "in confidence," or when they are said to be in a "confidential relation," or when they are held to "maintain confidentiality," they are expected to keep information secret. Certain relations and conditions give rise to a legal duty to maintain confidentiality. Examples of relations giving rise to a duty to protect confidentiality are attorney-client, accountant-client, and principal (employer) and agent (employee). An example of a condition creating a duty to maintain confidentiality is where an employee has access to a company trade secret, such as where a company keeps its customer lists or cost information a secret.

Federal law requires confidentiality in certain situations. Federal securities laws make it a crime for those possessing material, non-public information concerning a company to disclose such inside information. (This is explained more thoroughly in Chapter 7 on business organizations.) As a result of federal securities law, many companies have policies providing guidelines to employees, officers and directors for protecting the confidentiality of inside information.

Another federal law (the *Gramm-Leach-Bliley Act*, or *GLB*) requires all financial institutions to safeguard customer information. One purpose of the law is to reduce the risk of identity theft. Financial institutions are defined by the law to include not only banks, but also, among others, credit card companies, securities firms and insurance companies. As a result of this federal law, many companies have customer or client "confidentiality programs" designed to ensure that access to customer or client data is controlled at all times and that data breaches are identified and reported in a timely manner.

Other situations where business people expect information to be kept confidential include instances where one company seeks to buy another, where a company enters into a joint marketing venture with another company, and where employees work with critical company information. It is common in these situations for companies to enter into confidentiality agreements to protect company information.

In the situations described above, and in cases where you enter into a confidential relation or confidentiality agreement with your employer, you should respect that confidentiality. Failing to do so could cost you your job. In the case of violating the securities law, it could result in imprisonment.

## *Exercise Due Care and Diligence*

A principle in the law that is based upon ethical obligation is the requirement to exercise **due care.** Basically, "due care" means that people and companies must be careful not to injure others. A breach of the duty of due care can lead to liability for negligence, which is explained in Chapter 6 in its discussion of tort law. The concept of due care also derives from the law of agency, discussed in Chapter 7 on business organizations, where an agent (employee) is required to exercise skill and care in performing the agent's obligations on behalf of the principal (employer).

The duty of due care requires action at times. For example, it may become necessary to exercise due care and remove a hazard from a store aisle, or to repair the brakes on a company vehicle. As well, the duty of due care may require inaction. An example of this would be a duty to refrain from driving heavy equipment across thick ice, or not working in a construction area without a hard hat.

Due care in business can find expression in the simple statement, "Be careful." It also finds expression as "due diligence" in other areas of law, such as corporate law and securities law (discussed in Chapter 7 on business organizations).

As can be seen from the discussion above, the concept of due care is one that finds expression in several areas of law, and it also is one that is familiar to business people. Your employer will expect you to be diligent, careful, in short, to be competent. Employees who do not exercise due care in performing their jobs do not bring that "added value" to their jobs that employers expect of their employees. Executives who do not perform due diligence functions may create liability for themselves and their employers. The last thing you want to be considered is a liability by your employer.

## *Act in Good Faith and Deal Fairly with Others*

The obligation of **good faith** and fair dealing is fundamental in business. For example, a provision in the *Uniform Commercial Code* (*UCC*), which is law in every state, provides: "Every contract or duty within this Act imposes an obligation of good faith in its performance or enforcement." Another section of the Code provides that "good faith" means honesty in fact in the conduct or transaction concerned."

Included in honesty in fact is telling the truth. The general principle is that it is good to tell the truth. Yet, most would agree that not every lie is wrong. Everyone is familiar with little white lies, such as telling a spouse that what they are wearing looks good. These untruths are exceptions to the general rule to tell the truth, because they are made out of a good faith motivation to not hurt the other person.

Lying under oath, or even on some documents not under oath, for example, tax returns, is punishable as the offense of perjury. Also, it is a crime to lie to an official of the federal government. Martha Stewart, the founder of *Martha Stewart Living Omnimedia*, was convicted of lying to federal prosecutors, and spent time in a federal penitentiary, even though she was found not guilty of insider trading (prohibited by federal securities law) in the same case.

While it is not against the law to lie to your boss, it might get you fired. It is not ordinarily against the law to lie on an employment application, but there may be consequences. If later the employer discovers the lie, the employer can terminate you for cause.

Withholding the truth by silence may also be considered lying. For example, a half-truth regarding a material fact during contract negotiations is considered misrepresentation, making the agreement unenforceable.

Another component of good faith and fair dealing is disclosure. The law requires disclosure in many areas. Four examples are instructive:

1. Federal securities regulation, discussed in Chapter 7, requires full disclosure of the details of a stock offering so investors may be fully informed. It is also fraud under the federal securities laws to make a material misstatement or *omission* in connection with the sale of a security.
2. Most states require that the seller of a house fully disclose any hidden defects which are known to the seller. Additionally, almost every state now requires that the seller provide the buyer with a signed form answering various questions designed to inform the buyer of such hazards or defects as water leakage, the presence of radon gas, mold, and insect problems.
3. The federal Food and Drug Administration mandates labeling disclosure requirements designed to fully disclose to consumers the contents of food, including the calorie, sugar, protein, carbohydrate and fat content. More recently, there has been a push for uniform "green" packaging that would inform consumers that the animals used in producing the food were "antibiotic free," "grass fed," "cage free," "farm raised," "wild caught," or that the food is "fair traded," meaning that the farmers received a fair price. This is an example of ethics driving the law by promoting good faith through full disclosure.

4. The *Federal Trade Commission Used Car Rule* requires that car dealers disclose whether there is a warranty or no warranty; and, if there is a warranty, to make available the written terms. However, the rule only applies to those who sell at least five cars in the previous 12 month period. That means that the rule does not apply to the casual seller of cars.

The obligation of good faith and fair dealing generally arises in the setting of contractual dealings. The contract is essential to a functioning economic system. The law generally enforces contacts. People need to rely upon contractual promises. "A deal is a deal," "You promised," and "freedom of contract," are expressions of the ethical sentiment that promises are binding. While the law enforces contracts, the law does not enforce every promise. When contracts are deemed unconscionable or when they are against public policy, the law employs a form of balancing of the equities to nullify the promise of the party. This is a function of the fundamental obligation of good faith and fair dealing.

In the following case the court applies the implied-by-law obligation of good faith to create an exception to a clause in a lease.

**KNUDSEN *v.* LAX**
City Court of Watertown
842 N.Y.S.2d 341 (2007)

Christopher and Melissa Knudsen, tenants in an apartment building, sued Robert Lax, the landlord, seeking to terminate their lease. The lease provided that if tenants abandoned the premises before the term ended the landlord could "hold the tenant liable for the rent that would have been payable . . . during the balance of the unexpired term." The tenants, parents of three young girls, wanted to move because a registered level three sex offender moved into the adjacent apartment. The tenants vacated the premises after the landlord refused their request to terminate the lease six months before the end of the lease term without paying the remaining rent due.

## *James C. Harberson, Jr.*

The issue in this case is whether a tenant can terminate a lease to protect his family when a level three sex offender moves into the adjacent apartment.

Robert and Barbara Lax (landlords) had the tenants sign a six-page, 33-paragraph lease on August 1, 2006 for a one-year term. The terms of the lease, which the landlords obtained from an Internet site, were not negotiated by the parties before the landlords had the tenants sign it without any input or comment from the tenants.

The lease expressly provided a covenant of quiet enjoyment promising that the tenants "shall . . . peacefully and quietly . . . enjoy said premises for the term." The lease also stated that in the event the tenants abandoned the premises before the term ended the landlord could "hold the tenant liable . . . for the rent that would have been payable . . . during the balance of the unexpired term."

* * *

It is quite clear that in New York it is the public policy of this state to protect potential victims of a sex offender from "the risk of a repeat offense by such sex offender and the threat posed to the public safety" (Correction Law Section

168-l[5]). Once such an assessment is made the sex offender is required on a not less than annual basis to verify his or her address and to notify authorities otherwise whenever the address changes (Correction Law Section 168-f). This information is made available along with other identifying information about the sex offender either by phone (Correction Law Section 168-p) or by an Internet posting (Correction Law Section 168-q) to the public.

* * *

What strikes the court is the emphasis in the notification requirements and the other laws on keeping a sex offender away from the vicinity of children. This reflects the universal concern of society and any parent of a child when a sex offender is found in the proximity of where that child is located.

A reasonable parent or caretaker of a child will either institute heightened vigilance and/or remove the child physically from the zone of danger around the sex offender to reduce the risk to the child of becoming a victim of the sex offender repeating a sexual offense against the child.

In *Dalton v. Educational Testing Serv.* (87 N.Y.2d 384) the Court observed that "implicit in all contracts is a covenant of good faith and fair dealing in the course of contract performance. Encompassed within the implied obligation of each promisor to exercise in good faith are "any promises which a reasonable person in the position of the promisee would be justified in understanding are included" (*Rowe v. Great A. & Pac. Tea Co.*, 46 N.Y.2d 62).

It is clear that neither the landlords nor the tenants at the time the lease was signed contemplated a level three sex offender moving into part of the dwelling rented to other tenants, so when this happened and the tenants brought their concerns to the landlords, the court finds this was a legitimate example of a case where the implied-by-law covenant to act with good faith would apply to the landlords.

* * *

The court finds in this case "a reasonable person in the position of the promisee [tenants] would be justified in understanding" (*Rowe*, 46 N.Y.2d at 69) that the landlords would allow them to terminate the lease in the event a level three sex offender moved into the next-door apartment because neither they nor the landlords would have expected any objection to such an early termination in such an event when the landlords could not force the level three sex offender to vacate the apartment for the safety of the tenants' family.

In this case, the court concludes that the landlords' refusal to allow the tenant to terminate the contract six months before the expiration date, followed by their request under the "abandonment" clause for an additional six months' rent of $2,700, after it was evident that the tenants' right to quiet enjoyment of the apartment was shattered by the level three sex offender moving in next door, was a violation of the covenant of good faith implied in the lease agreement to deal with the situation at the time it was signed.

* * *

This decision will allow a tenant the right to terminate a lease in such case in order to allow the tenant to move to a safe location without liability for future rent.

**Business Application:** What does the obligation of good faith and fair dealing mean to contracting parties when they encounter future unexpected events that require interpreting their contract's performance obligations? That is, when encountering an unexpected future situation, how should a contracting party go about determining what to do? In *Knudsen*, what facts could the landlord have considered when deciding whether to let the tenants terminate their lease without paying the remaining six months rent? If you were the landlord, would you consider the fact that there were susceptible children who would be affected by your decision? Would you consider what are the public policies expressed by laws such as the notification laws for sex offenders? Would you consider what other landlords would do under these circumstances?

## WAYS BUSINESSES ADDRESS ETHICS

How seriously do business organizations and their executives take business ethics? There was a time when the words *business* and *ethics* were thought to be mutually exclusive terms. However, today an executive will not be considered a sophisticated executive if he or she maintains a cavalier attitude toward business ethics. A prominent concern of many U.S. corporations is developing a corporate culture that encourages ethical behavior and discourages unethical behavior. Organizations have developed and enforced codes of ethics, instituted formal ethics training programs, maintained standing ethics committees, hired ethical consultants, and their top managers have actively addressed ethical problems confronting their organizations.

One motivation that companies have for developing corporate ethics codes and compliance programs is to receive favorable treatment under the *Federal Sentencing Guidelines* if their employees are convicted of a federal corporate crime. The *Sentencing Guidelines* make companies responsible when their employees are convicted of federal crimes. The *Sentencing Guidelines* also permit dramatic reductions in penalties for companies that have in place an effective compliance and ethics program to prevent and detect violations of the law. The absence of these programs may be used to increase the punishment a company may receive. In addition to the *Sentencing Guidelines*, the *Sarbanes-Oxley Act*, discussed in detail in Chapter 7, on business organizations, effectively requires a public company to have a **code of ethics** for financial officers and provide mechanisms for protecting whistleblowers who report financial misconduct of the company.

Whatever the motivation, many businesses and their executives take seriously the management of a company's values. Corporate ethics codes and **compliance programs** show that companies are dealing with ethics in a systematic way.

The combination of the *Federal Sentencing Guidelines* and the *Sarbanes-Oxley Act* has provided an incentive for companies to create ethics codes and compliance programs.

### *Ethics Codes*

Securities and Exchange Commission (SEC) regulations set out the requirements of a code of ethics. According to the SEC, a code of ethics means written standards designed to deter wrongdoing and promote:

1. Honest and ethical conduct, including the ethical handling of actual or apparent conflicts of interest between personal and professional relationships.

2. Full, fair, accurate, timely and understandable disclosure in the periodic reports required to be filed by the company.
3. Compliance with governmental laws, rules and regulations.
4. Prompt internal reporting of violation of the code to appropriate persons identified in the code.
5. Accountability for adherence to the code.

## *Compliance Programs*

The *Sentencing Guidelines* set out the seven requirements of an effective compliance and ethics program. They are:

1. The company must establish standards and procedures to prevent and detect criminal conduct.
2. The company's governing authority must be knowledgeable about the content and operation of the compliance and ethics program and exercise reasonable oversight to implement and ensure that it is effective. This means that high-level personnel are assigned overall responsibility for ethics and compliance programs. Specific individuals within the company are delegated day-to-day responsibility for the program and report periodically to high-level personnel on the effectiveness of the program.
3. The company must keep any individual the company knows or should know engaged in illegal acts from serving a high-level position.
4. The company must communicate periodically and in a practical manner its standards and procedures by conducting effective training programs and disseminating information to individual employees that is appropriate to their roles and responsibilities.
5. The company must monitor and audit its program to ensure that it is followed, evaluate periodically the effectiveness of the program, and provide mechanisms for employees to anonymously report violations without fear of retaliation.
6. The company must provide incentives to employees to act ethically and discipline employees who engage in criminal conduct.
7. The company must take reasonable steps to respond appropriately to criminal conduct and to prevent future misconduct.

**Law and Ethics in Business Policies**

The following link is to the *Whirlpool Corporation*'s Code of Ethics. *http://assets.whirlpoolcorp.comlwp-content/uploads/code_of_ethics.pdf*

See "*Support for Our Code of Ethics*" at page 12, and notice the connection with requirement number 5 of the *Sentencing Guidelines*.

## *Ethics Officers*

Business ethicists, sometimes referred to as **ethics officers** or compliance officers, are another level of protection against unethical business practices. They are considered experts in assessing conflicts of interests that arise within the company and outside the company, instituting and monitoring compliance programs, and providing educational programs for the various levels of company executives and employees. Some companies employ the ethicist when the perceived need arises. However, the larger firms hire them in-house.

The *Ethics & Compliance Officer Association* is a professional association for those responsible for assuring ethical best practices (BEP). The *Federal Sentencing Guidelines*, discussed above, have further fueled the employment of ethicists, who often are the ones to testify as experts in corporate fraud cases. The *Sarbanes-Oxley Act* has added still more incentive for the employment of ethics officers.

### *Creative Global Ethics*

In today's global economy, corporations and executives encounter ethical issues that arise when different cultural traditions are confronted. How should U.S. companies and their employees respond when doing business in countries where bribery of political officials is common, or in countries that permit discrimination against certain ethnic groups?

Some argue that cultural relativism, the concept that no culture has better ethics than any other, is the answer. Their position is captured by the old saying, "When in Rome, do as the Romans do." On the other hand, others reject the notion of relativism. They argue that U.S. companies are expected to stand by their values.

When encountering cross-cultural ethical conflict, companies and manager often seek creative solutions to ethical problems. For example, companies can negotiate with their international trading partners regarding concerns about unethical practices. Companies sometimes try to establish international standards through organizations like the *International Chamber of Commerce.* At times, American companies have asked the U.S. government to negotiate treaties to have American ethical standards (e.g., labor standards) of business adopted abroad.

## CHAPTER PROBLEMS

1. Define the following terms:

   *a.* Law
   *b.* Ethics
   *c.* Fiduciary rule
   *d.* Conflict of interest
   *e.* Confidentiality
   *f.* Due care
   *g.* Good faith
   *h.* Code of ethics
   *i.* Compliance program
   *j.* Ethics officer

### *Business Application*

2. David is a research and development chemist employed by Acme Chemical Company. Acme has a range of chemical products marketed strictly in the northeastern region of the United States. David has developed a chemical that he knows will generate a high demand in the United States and, perhaps, worldwide. However, he feels Acme does not have a reputable enough name to market his discovery. David decided to approach a large, western-based chemical corporation. They are willing to hire him, provided they obtain the rights to produce

and market the chemical. In return, David will be given a large block of the corporation's common stock and his salary will be tripled. David is considering the offer. He figures the most Acme will do is give him a bonus for his discovery. Should David accept the offer from the western corporation? Explain. If you were in his position, would you feel obligated to notify Acme of your discovery and not search for alternative companies to market it? Explain.

3. George works for Big Corporation as the manager of one of its departments. He supervises twenty employees. From time to time he has departmental meetings in which he orders food from a local caterer. When the staff works late at night, George often orders pizza for the staff. George's brother has started a restaurant in town. The restaurant sells take-out and makes deliveries. George wants to stop ordering from the caterer and start ordering food from his brother's restaurant for those occasions when he orders food for the department staff. Should George do this? Explain.

4. Matthew Foote was employed by Dow Chemical Company. After learning of billing irregularities by its uniform provider, Cintas, Dow assigned Foote and his co-worker, Mike Hollies, the task of tracking and monitoring uniform charges. At a monthly meeting with Foote, Cintas invited them, as well as other Dow employees, to a Detroit Pistons basketball game. Dow's management approved the attendance at the game. However, Foote believed the attendance at the game presented a conflict of interest. At the time, Foote raised this concern with his supervisor, Dominic Zoeller.

   Around the time that the Dow employees attended the Pistons game, Foote also began a consensual sexual relationship with a direct subordinate Libby Soler. Shortly after beginning the relationship, Foote took steps to remove Soler from his direct reporting line, swapping her for a different employee whose skills were similar. Foote discussed the proposal with Tara Kutchey of Dow's Human Resources Department, and he told Zoeller the details of the situation. Shortly after that, Foote received a letter advising him that his employment was terminated.

   Dow's Code of Business Conduct contains an anti-retaliation policy. Foote believed his termination was in retaliation for his report of his concerns surrounding the Pistons basketball game. He maintained that nowhere in any of Dow's policies is a relationship between employees prohibited.

   Dow asserted that the termination was due to loss of confidence in Foote as a result of his relationship with Soler and the manner in which he handled the situation. Dow pointed to language in its Code of Business Conduct that states: "Nothing in this document constitutes a contract of employment with any individual." It also pointed to the application for employment that Foote completed 19 years earlier, which concludes with the statement, "I understand that I have the right to terminate my employment with Dow at any time without notice and for any reason. I understand that Dow has the same right." Just below that provision is Foote's signature, agreeing that he had read and understood the contents of the application. The employment agreement that followed repeats that statement under the heading of "Employment at Will."

Foote sued Dow for wrongful termination of employment and breach of the employment contract. The court decided the case in favor of Dow. The court explained that Foote's employment arrangement with Dow was an at-will one; therefore, Dow could terminate him for either reason. (*Foote v. Dow Chemical and Zoeller*, 2010 Mich. App. LEXIS 112.)

Do you think Foote acted appropriately? Explain. Do you think Dow acted appropriately? Explain. Do you agree that the law should allow an employer to terminate an employee for any reason where the employer's code of conduct contains a disclaimer stating that the code is not a contract, that the employment relation is an employment-at-will, meaning that both the employer and the employee may terminate the employment relation without notice and for any reason? Explain.

5. Sandra Erwin submitted a prescription to Nichols Pharmacy for a drug that treats a sexually transmitted disease. A pharmacy technician who filled the prescription was aware that Sandra was dating the technician's ex-boyfriend. Concerned for his well-being, the technician informed her ex-boyfriend of Sandra's condition. Did the Nichols Pharmacy employee act appropriately toward Erwin? Explain.

6. Fisheries Incubation Service Health, Inc. (FISH) has been raising fresh water fish on their farms for many years. They cater to a health-minded set of consumers and sell their fish to health food stores across the country. They are government inspected by the local health commission and certified by that state agency as "Superior." FISH has been doing research for years and most recently found that their fish have a mercury and PCB level that makes it unsafe for women of childbearing age to eat more than two servings per month. There does exist a private "Seafood Safe" label that would warn women of this hazard; however, that label has not as yet been adopted by FISH. The law does not require it. You are a clerk in the research and development labs who records the data, and as a result are aware of the findings. You have signed a confidentiality agreement with the company whereby you agree not to reveal any information that you acquire from the job in the research laboratory. What should you do? Explain.

7. Skyhigh Construction Corporation specializes in multifloor office buildings predominately located in major cities throughout the United States. Skyhigh is a much respected firm in the high-rise construction industry. It has the reputation of completing all contracts on time and on budget. Frank Cook, a site supervisor for Skyhigh, comments:

   *Skyhigh employs an average of 240 construction workers per site. For those who work up on the beams, this is a high health-risk occupation. There is a small but considerable number of serious and sometimes fatal accidents at every site before the job is completed. To meet deadlines, I sometimes must send the crew up when weather conditions are not favorable. My crew members are working in a potentially dangerous environment, but they are compensated with attractive wages. If one of them complains about going up every time it gets a little windy, I fire that person. When Skyhigh signs a contract, my job is to ensure completion of it on time!*

   How do you feel about Skyhigh's policy as reflected in Frank Cook's comments?

8. You are a securities broker for Stock & Bond, a major Wall Street firm that is active in a wide variety of financial services. Your firm offers on-line trading. For $10.00 per trade a customer can buy or sell any stocks listed on the national exchanges. You know that one of the customers, Anthony, a family friend, has been committing "economic suicide" by trading recklessly, with the passion of a gambling addict. From time to time Anthony consults with you on mortgage and other securities transactions, seeking your advice. You render full advice to him on these transactions and he pays the full fee. There is a company policy that prohibits you from rendering any advice on less than full service transactions. In fact, an in-house rule states: "Under no circumstances shall a broker render any opinion to a customer who inquires concerning on-line transactions." Anthony comes to you for advice on a full commission stock transaction, and, while engaging in conversation tells you what has been happening in his high risk on-line transactions. You are aware of his financial condition and are alarmed that Anthony is selling off much of his reliable blue-chip stock and real estate holdings in order to support his "on-line habit." You feel compelled to caution against his reckless trading. However, you know that it is against the company's policy to do so, and, if you are caught, you will be fired. What will you do? Explain.
9. Frank Senour is the president of Intercontinental Oil Company. Intercontinental maintains its corporate headquarters in the United States, but also has offices in several Southeast Asian and South American countries, where Intercontinental does much of its business. Intercontinental is looking for a manager of international marketing for its Southeast Asian and South American operations. The position requires that the manager travel to Intercontinental's several Southeast Asian and South American offices and interact with present and prospective customers of the company. Beth Reichman is qualified for the position, has been with the company 12 years, and has been the manager of Intercontinental's marketing operations in the United States for the last four years. She is the only applicant for the position. Frank is aware that according to the practices currently in force in several Southeast Asian and South American countries where Intercontinental does business, many of Intercontinental's customers would prefer to do business with men rather than women. As a result, Frank realizes that Beth will have great difficulty performing the job of international marketing manager. Nevertheless, Beth tells Frank that she can do the job, if given the chance. What should Frank do? Would he be justified in refusing to promote Beth? Explain.
10. Your company is considering selling its product in a foreign country. To do business in this country, your company needs a license from the government. It is accepted practice, and expected by the officials, that to get the license you must hire a certain local individual and pay him $250,000. If payment is not made to this individual, and your company decides to go through proper channels, your company can expect the granting of the license to be delayed by two years. Once the license is obtained, your company can expect to make at least $50 million a year from sales in that country. You are the vice president of marketing for your company. What will be your recommendation regarding making this payment to the foreign individual? Explain.

CHAPTER 2

# NATURE OF LAW AND LEGAL REASONING

## CHAPTER OUTLINE



## LEARNING OBJECTIVES

After learning this chapter the student should be able to:

- Compare and contrast the following conceptions of law: ideal conceptions, positivist conceptions, historical conceptions, sociological conceptions, realist conceptions, economic conceptions, and critical conceptions.
- Describe how the legislature, the executive, the judiciary, and administrative agencies are sources of law.
- Describe the doctrine of stare decisis and why it is important to managers.
- Describe the rule-based rationales, precedent-based rationales, and policy rationales commonly used in legal reasoning, and recognize these rationales when they are used in court opinions.
- Compare and contrast formalistic and purposive methods of interpreting legislation.

This chapter considers the nature of law and legal reasoning. Not everyone would agree on how to define *law.* Therefore, we first examine the various definitions and conceptions of law that have developed over the years. Second, we discuss the sources of law. Finally, we conclude with an examination of legal reasoning, an analytical method distinctive to the legal system.

## THE NATURE OF LAW: WHAT IS LAW?

The simple question, "What is law?" leads to a complex answer that reveals the many-faceted nature of the subject. Each person seems to have his or her own answer to this question. Some think law is a body of rules. Others see it as a means of restricting or directing human conduct. Still others see it as an instrument for protecting basic freedoms. Similar to other basic concepts dealing with human behavior, law is susceptible to many definitions. A historian may regard law as a reflection of a society's mores at a particular time. A sociologist may regard it as a social institution. A theologian may see it as a barometer or moral values.

When defining law, one can refer to several schools of jurisprudence. **Jurisprudence** is the study of legal philosophy. The following discussion outlines several major philosophical conceptions of law, namely:

- Natural Law
- Positivist
- Historical
- Sociological
- Realist
- Critical
- Economic
- Feminist Jurisprudence

### *Natural Law*

Natural law philosophers think law is ordained by nature. For them, law consists of a body of higher principles existing independently of human experience, and it exists as an ideal condition that is either inherent in human nature or derived from a divine source.

According to this conception of law, people cannot create natural law, but they can discover its principles through reasoned thinking. Knowledge of natural law is thus an informed intuition of what is fair and just. The principles of natural law, discoverable by reason, are universally valid. Thus, **natural law** is a body of principles of right and justice existing for all peoples irrespective of time and culture. It transcends human notions of what is right and just.

### *Positivist*

In word-association exercises, the word *law* often evokes the response *rules*, because most people think of law as a body of rules. In jurisprudential terms, this is the positivist conception of law. The *positivist* school of jurisprudence regards law as any body of rules imposed by a sovereign or sovereign body. The term *positivist* stems from the root word *posit*, which means to place, put, or lay down something. A **positive law** is a law laid down by the duly constituted authority. A legal positivist might point to a speed-limit sign as an example of law.

Positivists distinguish between the law as it is and the law as it ought to be. They believe that an immoral command of a duly constituted authority is still law. In this regard, they differ from natural law theorists.

For example, in its early history, the United States enacted the Fugitive Slave Act, requiring the return of escaped slaves to their slaveholders. Positivists regarded the Fugitive Slave Act as law even though it was immoral. Natural law theorists did not regard it as law because it was immoral.

### *Historical*

Those who define law only as the current command of a sovereign may be criticized for ignoring the many rules that bound people in the past. Because law is often older than the state, some argue that the state is an incidental product of more mature legal systems rather than the distinguishing characteristic of all law.

The historical school of jurisprudence defines law as the embodiment of a society's customs. Historical jurisprudence asserts that custom is the chief manifestation of law, and that law evolves with social development. Custom may influence and become the basis of positive law. According to this conception, as customs and cultural values change, so does the direction of positive law. Laws patterned after custom are likely to meet with greater social acceptance.

### *Sociological*

Closely associated with the historical view is the sociological view of law. Sociologists define law in present human conduct. Thus, law is the sum of what the lawbooks permit and what human behavior provides. Under this view, for example, if you wanted to know what constitutes a business contract, you would look at business conduct to ascertain when people in business treat their agreements as binding, as well as when courts would declare such agreements to be contracts. Under this approach, formal law should reflect present human conduct; therefore, it might be necessary to bring about law reforms to have legal rules that reflect human experience.

The similarity between the historical and the sociological conceptions is obvious—both treat human conduct as the source of law. However, the historical conception embodies a long-range perspective, whereas the sociological view focuses on more immediate experience.

The sociological approach to law is not necessarily in conflict with the positivist approach. Positive law may reflect current human conduct. However, where human conduct is not in accord with a formal proposition of law, those adhering to the sociological conception would change the law to bring it into line with human conduct. Stretched to its limits, this logic would reduce formal law to its least influential level if people chose to ignore it.

### *Realist*

A conception of law closely allied to the sociological school is the realist conception. Realism looks beyond logic and reasoning and examines what actually occurs in the legal process. Both sociological and realist jurisprudence view life experiences as affecting the development of law. However, the realist conception focuses primarily on the social influences affecting the judicial decision-making process. It views law as the product of various social influences on official discretion. For example, if a speed-limit sign on a highway stated that the speed limit was 55 mph, but a police officer on patrol would not pull drivers over unless they drove over 65 mph, a legal realist would say that the law was 65 mph.

### *Critical*

A school of jurisprudence called *critical legal studies* is a type of legal realism. Its proponents contend that law is the product of political and sociological judgments made by judges. Critical legal theorists contend that judges make law in such a way as to preserve the existing political and economic order. Critical legal scholars claim that what appear to be legal reforms actually perpetuate the *status quo* by avoiding reconsideration of the basic assumptions behind the economic system.

### *Economic*

The law and economics school of jurisprudence affirms a link between law and economic activity. It contends that good law reflects good economics. It sees law as an instrument by which efficient economic outcomes are achieved. A concern for efficiency is an important, if not overriding, value for those who subscribe to this conception of law. Those belonging to the law and economics school turn to the study of economics in the belief that it can provide a stable basis for legal decisions.

### *Feminist Jurisprudence*

There are three branches of feminist jurisprudence. One branch focuses on traditional legal doctrines of individual rights, exposes ways in which women have not been treated equally with men, and seeks to correct the injustice.

Another branch contends that the law's focus on individual rights reflects a male perspective. It contends that women, primarily due to their roles as bearers and caretakers of children, do not emphasize individualism to the same extent as traditional notions of law; rather, women emphasize a "culture of caring." This branch calls for reevaluating the law in light of this culture of caring. For example, it calls for a reevaluation of the traditional legal rule that a person has no duty to rescue a stranger even though he or she has the ability to do so.

A third branch views women's roles as caregivers as a source of their oppression. It views the law as a means of male dominance that perpetuates the oppression. For example, it considers the First Amendment's protection of pornography not as a guarantee of free speech, but as a protection of violence against women.

## SOURCES OF LAW

It is often said that the legislative branch of the government makes the laws, the executive branch enforces them, and the judicial branch interprets them. Although this is a valid outline of the separation of powers among the three branches of government, it is not entirely accurate. In reality, each branch makes law. Additionally, administrative agencies, which collectively have come to be called the fourth branch of government, often have lawmaking authority. The following discussion focuses on the four primary sources of law, namely:

- The legislature
- The executive
- The judiciary
- Administrative agencies

### *The Legislature*

One source of law is the legislature. A legislature is an organized body of persons having the authority to make laws for a political unit (e.g., Congress). It often exercises other functions, such as the control of government administration (e.g., Congress approves funding for federal agencies and oversees their regulatory efforts).

#### The Legislative Process

Laws created by a legislative body are called *statutes*, *enactments*, *ordinances*, *acts*, or *legislation.* Such law is sometimes called *written law.* The term **legislation** refers either to the process by which a statute is enacted or to the statute itself.

The procedure by which the U.S. Congress enacts a statute is typical of the legislative process. A federal statute begins as a bill introduced in either the House of Representatives or the Senate. Many bills are introduced by sponsors who realize that they have little or no chance of passage. These sponsors use such bills to satisfy constituent demands or to call public attention to particular issues.

After a bill is introduced, it is referred to the appropriate committee. Most bills die in committee from inaction. Those that receive serious consideration result in public hearings and, not infrequently, studies by the committee's staff. The committee then meets in executive session to "mark up" the bill, reviewing it line by line and rewriting it.

Finally, the committee sends the bill to the floor of the house of Congress in which it was introduced. It is accompanied by a committee report detailing the policy reasons for the bill and explaining the bill's intended effect on existing law. A minority report may also be included, if members of the committee disagree with the majority view. Following debate, the bill is voted on. If it receives support, it is sent to the other house of Congress for similar treatment.

When both houses pass similar but different bills, a conference committee consisting of members of both houses is established. This committee develops a compromise bill that satisfies both houses, and then submits it to each house for a vote.

**The Business and Government Interface**

The following link is to the official website for U.S. federal legislative information:

https://beta.congress.gov/

There you can find timely information about the status of bills introduced in Congress, among other matters.

Bills that pass both houses of Congress are forwarded to the president for signature. Pursuant to Article I, Section 7, of the U.S. Constitution, the president may sign the bill into law or return it to the house in which it originated (i.e., veto it). Overriding a presidential veto in such a case requires a two thirds vote in both the House and the Senate. If the president takes no action within 10 days following the bill's transmittal, the Constitution states that the bill becomes law "unless the Congress by their Adjournment prevents its Return, in which case it shall not be a Law." Thus, if Congress adjourns after transmitting a bill to the president, the president may pocket-veto the bill by simply doing nothing.

State laws are enacted through similar procedures, specified in state constitutions.

## *The Executive*

The executive branch of government also makes law, usually by executive orders. However, its lawmaking authority is limited by applicable constitutional provisions. For example, Article II of the U.S. Constitution provides that "the executive Power shall be vested in a President." The executive branch of the government consists of the president, the cabinet, and the agencies and bureaus operating under the president's authority. The president's exercise of official discretion is a source of law. In addition, the Constitution gives the president limited authority to make law in foreign and domestic affairs.

**The Business and Government Interface**

The following link is to the official website for the White House:

http://www.whitehouse.gov/

There you can find timely information about the activities of the President of the United States and the operations of the executive branch of the federal government.

### Presidential Authority over Foreign Affairs

The president's ability to make law regarding foreign affairs derives from the presidential power to make treaties, subject to the advice and consent of two thirds of the Senate. By virtue of the Supremacy Clause in Article VI of the U.S. Constitution, treaties confirmed by the Senate become part of the supreme law of the land, along with the Constitution and congressional enactments. All lawmakers of every state are bound by a treaty, notwithstanding any state law or state constitution to the contrary. The treaty controls whether its ratification precedes or follows the enactment of state law.

Treaties are an important source of law for international businesses. They often determine the type and quantity of goods that may be sold in foreign markets.

### Presidential Authority over Domestic Affairs

The president's authority over domestic affairs is yet another source of law. Article II of the Constitution of the United States provides that the president "shall take Care that the Laws be faithfully executed." Executive lawmaking in domestic affairs is exemplified by the executive orders issued and implemented by presidents throughout U.S. history.

Presidential power to make law has been limited by the Supreme Court's interpretation of the Constitution. For example, during the Korean Conflict, President Harry Truman directed seizure of the nation's steel mills to prevent a threatened strike. The Supreme Court held the seizure unconstitutional for two reasons: first, the Court found no constitutional basis for the seizure; and second, the Congress had refused to confer such authority on the president.[1] The Court stated that the president's power to issue such an executive order must stem from an act of Congress or from the Constitution itself.

**The Business and Government Interface**

The following link is to the official website for the Supreme Court of the United States:

http://www.supremecourt.gov/

## *The Judiciary*

Courts are also a source of law. When a court decides a dispute, it makes law. Through the application of general legal principles to actual controversies, these principles are refined and shaped into a more precise statement of law. A court's application of a statute to a particular case gives meaning to the statute.

Judge-made law is referred to as **common law.** Following the Norman Conquest of England, William the Conqueror sent his court officials throughout the realm to keep the king's peace. William's purpose was to bring the various parts of his newly conquered country under one law. These court officials resolved disputes by applying custom. Thus, there developed in England a body of judicial decisions that constituted the country's common law. As England had no Parliament or written constitution at that time, these decisions became the law of the country. Today, the term *common law* refers to those areas of law that have been developed principally by the courts.

**The Business and Government Interface**

There you can find timely information about the Supreme Court and Supreme Court documents. In addition, the following link is to a popular blog covering the Supreme Court:

http://www.scotusblog.com/

## *Administrative Agencies*

Administrative agencies have the power to affect the rights of private parties. Administrative agencies are housed in the executive branch of government but are created by the legislature. An administrative agency may have functions that are traditionally executive, such as investigating, administering, and prosecuting. It may also have functions that are traditionally legislative or judicial, such as rulemaking and adjudication.

Later chapters discuss lawmaking by administrative agencies in more detail. However, it is helpful to realize that administrative agencies may make law in much the same way that the legislative, executive, and judicial branches. For example, if Congress confers rulemaking authority on an agency, that agency's duly authorized rules and regulations have the same legal stature as if Congress

---

1 72 S. Ct. 863 (1952).

itself had acted on the matters. This area of lawmaking that does not find its origins expressly rooted in the U.S. Constitution is under challenge by certain conservative groupings.

### *Interaction among the Various Sources of Law*

The various sources of law in the United States do not operate in a vacuum. The three branches of government frequently interact. This interaction provides a system of checks and balances in which the branches may aid or block each other. For example, as already noted, a congressional enactment needs presidential approval to become law, and a treaty negotiated by the executive branch needs Senate ratification.

People often think that the judiciary stands isolated from the other two branches and has the final word on any issue. Students often accept appellate court opinions in their casebooks as the final word on the law. In reality, a dynamic interaction occurs between the judiciary and the other branches of government. Congress, for example, can overrule a Supreme Court decision by legislation or constitutional amendment.

The judicial opinions presented in this book should be assessed carefully. You should question not only what the law is but also what it should be.

**Law and Ethics In Business Policies**

Businesses understand the need to be aware of the laws that are being created, especially by administrative agencies. The following link is to *GE's* policy document, *The Spirit and the Letter.*

https://www.ge.com/in/sites/www.ge.com.in/files/TheSpirit&TheLetter.pdf

*See* p 6, "Regulatory Excellence." Note especially *Responsibilities of All Employees*, and *Responsibilities of All Leaders.*

## LEGAL REASONING

The rest of this chapter looks at a method of thinking called *legal reasoning.* Legal reasoning cannot be precisely defined. Because it is a method of reasoning, the most that can be hoped for is a functional description of the process. Indeed, it is ironic but true that generations of law students have been taught to "think like a lawyer" without ever having been told explicitly just what is meant by that statement.

Although the method of reasoning that underlies legal reasoning is not unique to the legal system, we find the method most prominently displayed there. This is due in part to the methods and doctrines developed by courts to guide their decision making. Because courts explain their decisions in written opinions, we turn to court opinions for examples of legal reasoning.

To understand legal reasoning, we must first understand that judicial decision making uses prior cases to decide a present controversy. This method of decision making is referred to as the *rule of precedent*, or more formally, the *doctrine of stare decisis.*

## *The Doctrine of Stare Decisis*

The doctrine of **stare decisis** (Latin for "let the decision stand") is a policy that courts have developed as a general rule; thus, past judicial decisions are applied to decide present controversies. Consequently, a rule of law decided by the highest court of a jurisdiction subsequently binds all lower courts within that jurisdiction. It also generally binds later cases decided by that same court. Unless a court overrules itself, the decision is followed in all future cases presenting the same material facts and legal issues. Thus, a decision is a full-fledged precedent only for future "like" cases, that is, for future cases involving the same material facts.

The decision is not binding on courts in other jurisdictions. However, they may find its reasoning persuasive and follow it when considering similar cases in their jurisdictions. For example, although the Supreme Court of California is not bound by the decisions of the Supreme Court of Pennsylvania, it may adopt the Pennsylvania court's reasoning in a particular case.

Several bases underlie the doctrine of stare decisis. One is fairness. Inconsistent decisions of the same kinds of factual disputes seem unfair. Another basis for the doctrine is predictability. When a court decides a present case the way it decided a similar one before, parties are better able to anticipate and plan for the future.

Although a policy of applying prior cases to decide present controversies appears to look backward, it is important to recognize the way in which the method looks forward. A court's decision today will be tomorrow's precedent. A court, therefore, often carefully considers the future effects of a decision.

### Obiter Dictum

Only the decision of a court is binding on future courts. What a court says and does that is necessary to its decision to settle the parties' dispute has precedential, or binding, effect. However, sometimes a court makes statements by way of explanation that are not really necessary to its decision. These remarks are referred to as **obiter dictum** or **dicta** (in the plural), which is Latin for "a remark by the way." Although these statements lack precedential value, they nevertheless indicate what the court is likely to do in the future. These statements may have some persuasive effect on a future decision of the court.

## *Common Rationales in Support of Legal Reasoning*

Although one of the justifications for the doctrine of stare decisis is that it advances the law's predictability, one quickly discovers decisions of appellate courts in which the judges are divided in their decisions. For example, it is not unusual for the nine justices on the Supreme Court of the United States to be divided five to four over the outcome of a case. If stare decisis works, why are there split votes?

The answer rests in the fact that those cases clearly controlled by precedent are usually either settled before trial or are disposed of routinely by the trial courts. The cases that go to the higher appellate courts involve issues where there are disagreements about the application of precedents or what constitutes sound legal policy.

Just as the parties may disagree about what the rule of law is or should be in a given case, so do judges often disagree. When the court announces its decision, the majority opinion states the court's rationale for reaching its result, and any dissenting judges may register their rationale for their disagreement in dissenting opinions. Although dissenting opinions have no precedential effect, a dissenting judge may register a dissent in the hope of persuading a future court to overrule the present decision. Thus, the majority and dissenting judges may each argue that the other has misread the cases or the rules established by them. This form of argument or rationale relies heavily on rules and precedent.

Judges may also disagree on the probable social effects of their decision. This type of argument or rationale relies heavily on policy. The following discussion describes three of the rationales found in legal opinions: rule based, precedent based, and policy based.[2]

### Rule-Based Rationales

Rationales or arguments that are based on rules deal with the meaning to be given to the words in cases and statutes. (More is said about the interpretation of statutes later in this chapter). Typically, one side asserts that the language of a past case or statute established one rule, while the other side disagrees, asserting that the rule is something else altogether. The reasoning typically falls into one of two broad categories: **formalist reasoning** or **purposive reasoning.**

Formalist reasoning takes the words in a case or statute out of context and defines them without taking into account their purpose, much in the way you would define the words in a sentence by using a dictionary. For example, consider the question of whether the Constitution's First Amendment provision that "Congress shall make no law . . . abridging freedom of speech, or of the press" applies to commercial advertising. A formalist approach to this question might be to look up the definition of the terms *speech*, or *press*, and *advertising* in various dictionaries to ascertain what these words mean. Notice that different meanings can be gleaned depending on whether you use a current dictionary or one from 1791, the year the First Amendment went into effect.

Purposive reasoning, in contrast, attempts to define the meaning of words in a case or a statute by ascertaining the purpose underlying them. Notice that, as with formalist reasoning, different meanings can be derived, depending on how one might characterize the purpose of a given statement. In the example of commercial advertising and the First Amendment, one might assert that the purpose of the First Amendment's free speech clause is to promote an open society with access to all forms of information. Hence, laws forbidding certain forms of advertising would be unconstitutional. On the other hand, one could also assert that the purpose of the constitutional protection of speech is to provide for open communication of political ideas, which is necessary for the functioning of a democratic society. Hence, laws restricting political speech would be unconstitutional, but laws regulating commercial advertising would be constitutional.

As noted earlier, rule-based rationales are found in court decisions where a court is called on to interpret language in its prior cases, as well as in court decisions involving the interpretation of statutes or regulations. In disagreements over the interpretation of language in cases, the formalist approach typically quotes the language of a prior case without elaborating on its context. In contrast, in the purposive approach, the court emphasizes the asserted purpose the court had in mind when it

---

2 Much of this discussion was drawn from J. Boyle, *Anatomy of a Torts Class*, 34 Am. U. L. Rev. 1003 (1985).

decided the earlier dispute. With regard to statutes, the formalist approach tends to focus on the literal language of the statute, while the purposive approach argues that the legislature or Congress had a certain purpose or intent in mind when it wrote the law. This discussion of formalist and purposive rule-based rationales should be reviewed when examining the material on legislative interpretation later in this chapter.

### Precedent-Based Rationales

Rationales or arguments based on precedent involve the basic question of whether an earlier decision applies to the present case, or if it is in some significant way different from the present controversy. If one side wishes to justify a decision on the basis of a past case, it argues that the earlier and current cases have essentially similar facts and issues and concludes that the earlier case controls the current case. The other side may be expected to argue that the cases have essentially different facts and issues, or are distinguishable. Much, therefore, depends on how the two sides characterize the facts and issues of the earlier decision and the current case. Thus, the side that treats the earlier case as similar may give it a broad reading, for example, by drawing analogies. The other side may argue that the earlier case is distinguishable by tying the rule of the earlier case so closely to its facts that it cannot be given a broader application.

A similar form of reasoning involves disagreement over the facts of the current case. The majority and dissent may differ in their descriptions of the facts of the case under consideration. For example, the majority may emphasize facts that the dissent ignores and, in that way, fit the case under consideration into the mold of prior case law. The dissent might emphasize factual characteristics of the earlier case that differ from those of the current case. Of course, the majority may be the side that distinguishes the earlier case, while the dissent may regard it as controlling.

The following U.S. Supreme Court case overruling a long-standing precedent illustrates differing views offered by the majority and the dissent on the application of precedent.

**KNICK *v.* TOWNSHIP OF SCOTT**
Supreme Court of the United States
No. 17-647, 588 U.S._(June 21, 2019)

The Takings Clause of the Fifth Amendment to the U.S. Constitution states that "private property [shall not] be taken for public use, without just compensation." In 1985 the U.S. Supreme Court in *Williamson County v. Hamilton Bank* held that a property owner whose property has been taken by a local government has not immediately suffered a Fifth Amendment violation of his rights. As such, the owner could not bring a federal takings claim action until the state court denied the claim for just compensation first.

Rose Knick owns 90 acres of land in Scott Township, Pennsylvania, which includes a private family cemetery. The town passed an ordinance stating that all cemeteries must be open to the public. Knick filed an action in the federal district court alleging that the ordinance was in effect a violation of the Takings Clause. The district court dismissed the case based upon its precedent in *Williamson County* because she had not exhausted her remedies by pursuing a case for just compensation in state court, first. The Third Circuit Court of Appeals, based upon *Williamson*, affirmed the district court decision, and Rose sought review in the U.S. Supreme Court.

## *Chief Justice Roberts*

The Fifth Amendment right to full compensation arises at the time of the taking, regardless of post-taking remedies that may be available to the property owner. [The Court proceeded to justify overruling Williamson County].

* * *

. . . The fact that the State has provided a property owner with a procedure that may subsequently result in just compensation cannot deprive the owner of his Fifth Amendment right to compensation under the Constitution, leaving only the state law right.

* * *

In sum, because a taking without compensation violates the self-executing Fifth Amendment at the time of the taking, the property owner can bring a federal suit at that time.

* * *

The next question is whether we should overrule *Williamson County*, or whether *stare decisis* counsels in favor of adhering to the decision, despite its error. The doctrine of *stare decisis* reflects a judgment "that 'in most matters it is more important that the applicable rule of law be settled than that it be settled right.'" . . .

We have identified several factors to consider in deciding whether to overrule a past decision, including "the quality of [its] reasoning, the workability of the rule it established, its consistency with other related decisions, . . . and reliance on the decision. All of these factors counsel in favor of overruling *Williamson County.*

* * *

. . . The decision has come in for repeated criticism over the years from Justices of this Court and many respected commentators. [citing a string of sources]

* * *

The state litigation requirement of *Williamson County* is overruled. . . .

*It is so ordered.*

Justice Kagan, with whom Justice Ginsburg, Breyer and Sotomayor join, dissenting.

Today, the Court formally overrules *Williamson County*. . . . But its decision rejects far more than that single case. Williamson County was rooted in an understanding of the Fifth Amendment's Takings Clause stretching back to the late 1800s. On that view, a government could take property so long as it provided a reliable mechanism to pay just compensation, even if the payment came after the fact. No longer. The majority today hold, in conflict with precedent after precedent, that a government violates the Constitution whenever it takes property without advance compensation—no matter how good its commitment to pay. . . . [I]t transgresses all usual principles of *stare decisis*. . . .

* * *

. . . For over a hundred years, this Court has held that advance or contemporaneous payment was not required, so long as the [local] government had established reliable procedures for an owner to later obtain just compensation. . . . The Takings Clause does not demand "that compensation should be made previous to the taking" so long as "adequate means [are] provided for a reasonably just and prompt ascertainment and payment of the compensation." [In *Williamson*] the owner sued in federal court alleging a Takings Clause violation. . . . Consistent with the century's worth of precedent . . . [that] Court found that no Fifth Amendment violation occurred.

* * *

Today's decision thus overthrows the Court's long settled view of the Takings Clause. The majority declares, as against a mountain of precedent, that a government taking private property for public purposes must pay compensation at that moment or in advance [; otherwise the property owner can proceed directly to the federal courts to seek just compensation]. . . . And regardless of how many times this Court has said the opposite before. Under cover of overruling "only" a single decision, today's opinion smashes a hundred years of legal rulings to smitherings.

* * *

. . . When a theory requires declaring precedent after precedent wrong, that's a sign the theory itself may be wrong. The majority's theory is just that.

* * *

And not only wrong on prior law. The majority's overruling . . . will have two damaging consequences. It will inevitably turn even well-meaning government officials into lawbreakers [because they will not know beforehand whether their acts will be considered an unconstitutional taking]. And it will support certain principles of judicial federalism [by bypassing the state courts that are particularly versed in state questions and instead will flood the federal courts with state law issues. . . .]

Everything said . . . Williamson County should stay on the books because of *stare decisis*. Adherence to precedent is "a foundation stone of the rule of law." "[I]t promotes the evenhanded, predictable, and consistent development of legal principles, fosters reliances on judicial decisions, and contributes to the actual and perceived integrity of the judicial process." . . . [I]t is not enough that five Justices believe a precedent wrong. Reversing course demands a "special justification—over and above the belief that the precedent was wrongly decided. . . .

* * *

If that is the way the majority means to proceed . . . we may as well not have principles about precedents at all.

* * *

. . . "Today's decision can only cause one to wonder which cases the Court will overrule next."

**Business Application:** Where is the proper balance to be found between maintaining the stability and rigidity of precedent and overruling it to accommodate a more flexible and logical decision?

### Policy-Based Rationales

Some arguments or rationales in legal opinions involve disagreements over policy rather than precedents. These arguments tend to focus on who should be making policy rather than on the policy issues themselves. However, a careful reading of an opinion reveals the policy choices being made.

One common rationale deals with judicial administration. An opinion, for example, may assert that what is needed is a firm rule, that this rule can be easily administered by the legal system, and any other rule would "open the floodgates of litigation" and bog down the judicial system or otherwise bring about social ruin. In contrast, the competing opinion's view may reason that what is needed is a flexible rule, that the courts are capable of deciding the matter on a case-by case basis, and the public confidence in the judicial system would erode if courts did not assume the responsibility of administering justice.

A similar policy argument deals with institutional competence. One opinion may reason that the rule should be developed by the courts because the judiciary is the only legal institution that combines the capability of determining complex factual issues and the capability of considering changing circumstances. However, another opinion may assert that the issue involves public policy, which should be left to the legislature because it is the governmental body closest to public opinion and best suited for the task of considering the broader social implications.

### Business Application/Ethical Issues

Howard Ross is a sales representative for the Page Printing Company. Page's employee handbook provides a progressive discipline procedure for employees. Under this procedure, if an employee violates the rules contained in the manual, he or she receives harsher penalties for each new violation. The company can discharge an employee after three violations of company rules.

The county prosecutor indicted Ross for rape. Ben Johnson, Ross's supervisor, suspended Ross from his duties pending the outcome of his criminal case. Johnson told Ross, "You will have your job back if there is a satisfactory outcome to your case."

The jury in Ross's trial could not reach a verdict, so the judge dismissed the indictment against Ross.

Ben Johnson went to see Donald Altai, Page's vice president of human resources, and asked what to do about Ross. Altai contacted Page's attorney, Anne Penn, who wrote an opinion letter.

Penn's letter concluded that under present state law, Page could fire Ross and disregard the employee manual and Johnson's statement. Her letter also mentioned that the law in this area was dynamic. Some states had recently declared employment manuals and supervisor's statements binding on the employers. Even under these views, it is unclear whether Page would have to honor the statements in the manual or those made by Johnson.

What are the ethical issues? What would you do?

## *Legislative Interpretation*

Legal reasoning is not confined to the interpretation of case law; it is also used to interpret and apply legislation to legal disputes. Thus, the meaning of a statute is not fully known until the statute is interpreted by the courts.

In interpreting statutes, the courts begin by attempting to determine the legislature's intent, which may be expressed explicitly in the statute. However, the legislature may not have envisioned the particular controversy before a court, so legislative intent may be nonexistent. In such cases, the court attempts to determine how the legislature would have wanted the statute applied in the given case. The most obvious indirect indication of the legislative intent is the statute's language. Where the language is clear, a court does not go beyond the plain meaning of its words to determine what a statute means. This is known as the **plain meaning rule.** A court will not apply a statute literally, however, where doing so produces an absurd result or renders the statute unworkable.

In examining the statutory context, a court considers the statute as a whole, not merely the particular clause at issue in the case. In this way, the court avoids considering a particular statutory clause out of context. Thus, courts do not divorce a single phrase or section of a statute from its other portions.

Where the context of the statutory language does not reveal legislative intent, courts frequently consider the statute's legislative history. This includes the social conditions that gave rise to the legislative response and any documents, such as committee reports, proceedings, and records of legislative debates. This approach aims at arriving at the purpose of the statute.

In the following case the majority and the dissent interpreting the same portion of the Gun Control Act come to opposing views.

**ABRAMSKI *v.* UNITED STATES**

Supreme Court of the United States

134 S. Ct. 2259 (2014)

Bruce Abramski (Abramski) offered to purchase a handgun for his uncle. The form that federal regulations required Abramski to fill out asked whether he was the "actual transferee/buyer" of the gun, and clearly warned that a straw purchaser (namely, someone buying a gun on behalf of another) was not the actual buyer. Abramski falsely answered that he was the actual buyer. Abramski was convicted under a federal statute for knowingly making false statements "with respect to any fact material to the lawfulness of the sale" of a gun, and for making a false statement "with respect to the information required . . . to be kept" in the gun dealer's records. The Fourth Circuit Court of Appeals affirmed the conviction. Abramski appealed to the U.S. Supreme Court. He argued that his false statement was not "material."

The Supreme Court affirmed the lower court decisions. What follows is the Supreme Court's majority opinion, delivered by Justice Kagan and joined by justices Kennedy, Ginsburg, Breyer, and Sotomayor. The Court's majority opinion is followed by the dissenting opinion, filed by Justice Scalia and joined by justices Roberts, Thomas, and Alito.

### *Justice Kagan*

At its core, [Abramski's] argument relies on one true fact: Federal gun law regulates licensed dealers' transactions with "persons" or "transferees," without specifically referencing straw purchasers. Section 922(d), for example, bars a dealer from "sell[ing] or otherwise disposing] of" a firearm to any "person" who falls within a prohibited category—felons, drug addicts, the mentally ill, and so forth.

But that language merely raises, rather than answers, the critical question: In a straw purchase, who *is* the "person" or "transferee" whom federal gun law addresses? Is that "person" the middleman buying a firearm on someone else's behalf? Or is that "person" instead the individual really paying for the gun and meant to take possession of it upon completion of the purchase? In answering that inquiry, we must (as usual) interpret the relevant words not in a vacuum, but with reference to the statutory context, structure, history, and purpose. All those tools of divining meaning—not to mention common sense, which is a fortunate (though not inevitable) side-benefit of construing statutory terms fairly-demonstrate that § 922, in regulating licensed dealers' gun sales, looks through the straw to the actual buyer.

. . . [T]he statute establishes an elaborate system to verify a would-be gun purchaser's identity and check on his background. It also requires that the information so gathered go into a dealer's permanent records. The twin goals of this comprehensive scheme are to keep guns out of the hands of criminals and others who should not have them, and to assist law enforcement authorities in investigating serious crimes. And no part of that scheme would work if the statute turned a blind eye to straw purchase—if, in other words, the law addressed not the substance of a transaction, but only empty formalities.

* * *

No piece of information is more important under federal firearms law than the identity of a gun's purchaser—the person who acquires a gun as a result of a transaction with a licensed dealer. Had Abramski admitted that he was not that purchaser, but merely a straw—that he was asking the dealer to verify the identity of, and run a background check on, the wrong individual—the sale here could not have gone forward. That makes Abramski's misrepresentation material under § 922(a)(6). And because that statement pertained to information that a dealer must keep in its permanent records under the firearms law, Abramski's answer also violated § 924(a)(1)(A). Accordingly, we affirm the judgment of the Fourth Circuit.

## *Justice Scalia, dissenting*

Contrary to the majority's assertion that the statute "merely raises, rather than answers, the critical question" of whether Abramski or his uncle was the "person" to whom the dealer "[s]old" the gun, the statute speaks to that question directly. Giving the text its plain, ordinary meaning, Abramski, not his uncle, was that "person." That being so, the Government has identified no reason why the arrangement between Abramski and his uncle, both of whom were eligible to receive and possess firearms, was "material to the lawfulness of" the sale.

* * *

The only thing which can justify [the majority's] leap is the false imperative to make the statute as effective as possible, rather than as effective as the language indicates Congress desired.

[P]erhaps Congress drew the line where it did because the Gun Control Act, like many contentious pieces of legislation, was a compromise among highly interested parties attempting to pull the provisions in different directions. Perhaps those whose votes were needed for passage of the statute *wanted* a lawful purchaser to be able to use an agent.

* * *

We must accept that Congress, balancing the conflicting demands of a divided citizenry, wrote the statute it wrote—a statute going so far and no further.

**Business Application:** How might a consumer gun lobby have proposed a modification to the statute in order to satisfy the dissent that the majority is correct?

## CHAPTER PROBLEMS

1. Define the following concepts and terms:
   *a.* Jurisprudence
   *b.* Natural law
   *c.* Positive law
   *d.* Legislation
   *e.* Common law
   *f.* Stare decisis
   *g.* Obiter dictum
   *h.* Formalist reasoning
   *i.* Purposive reasoning
   *j.* Plain meaning rule

### *Business Application*

2. What conception of law is embodied in the following statement from the Declaration of Independence?

   When in the Course of human events, it becomes necessary for one people to dissolve the political bonds which have connected them with another, and to assume among the powers of the earth, the separate and equal station to which the Laws of Nature and of Nature's God entitle them, a decent respect to the opinions of mankind requires that they should declare the causes which impel them to the separation. We hold these truths to be self-evident, that all men are created equal, that they are endowed by their Creator with certain unalienable Rights, that among these are Life, Liberty and the pursuit of happiness.

3. In 1973, the U.S. Supreme Court was called on to decide the constitutionality of a state statute making it a crime to obtain an abortion. In deciding that the statute was unconstitutional, the Court stated:

   > We forthwith acknowledge our awareness of the sensitive and emotional nature of the abortion controversy, of the vigorous opposing views, even among physicians, and of the deep and seemingly absolute convictions that the subject inspires. One's philosophy, one's experiences, one's exposure to the raw edges of human existence, one's religious training, one's attitudes toward life and family and their values, and the moral standards one establishes and seeks to observe, are all likely to influence and to color one's thinking and conclusions about abortion. . . . Our task, of course, is to resolve the issue by constitutional measurement free of emotion and predilection.

   Which conception of law best describes the Court's statement? Do you think that the Court can resolve the issue "by constitutional measurement free of emotion and predilection?" Explain.

4. Martin Luther King, Jr., once wrote: "I think we all have moral obligations to obey just laws. On the other hand, I think we have moral obligations to disobey unjust laws because non-cooperation with evil is just as much a moral obligation as cooperation with good." Lewis F. Powell (retired associate justice of the Supreme Court of the United States), when he was president of the American Bar Association, deplored the doctrine "that only just' laws need to be obeyed and that every man is free to determine for himself the question of 'justness.'" He added, "An ordered society cannot exist if every man determines which laws he will obey." Which conception of law was Justice Powell expressing? Which position was Dr. King espousing? Explain. With which position do you agree? Explain.
5. The federal Equal Pay Act (EPA) forbids sex-based wage discrimination. It states, "No employer shall discriminate between employees on the basis of sex by paying wages to employees at a rate less than the rate he pays employees of the opposite sex for equal work on jobs the performance of which requires equal skill, effort, and responsibility, and which are performed under similar working conditions." Congress took the terms, "equal skill, effort and responsibility" and "similar working conditions" from the language of job evaluation system, developed in the field that was then called industrial relations/human resource management (IR/HRM). What conception of law is reflected in Congress's use of the language of IR/HRM when writing the EPA? Explain.
6. The Uniform Commercial Code (UCC) is a statute, enacted in part in all states, that provides rules regulating many types of commercial transactions. Section 1-102 of the UCC states the following: "(1) This Act shall be liberally construed and applied to promote its underlying purposes and policies. (2) Underlying purposes and policies of this Act are (a) to simplify, clarify and modernize the law governing commercial transactions; (b) permit the continued expansion of commercial practices through custom, usage and agreement of the parties, and (c) to make uniform the law among the various jurisdictions." Which conception of law does Section 1-102 of the UCC reflect? Explain.
7. Explain the role of legal precedents in the development of the law.
8. The president of the United States concludes a commercial treaty with Russia. The treaty is subsequently ratified by the U.S. Senate. After ratification, a group of citizens files a lawsuit in a federal court attacking the treaty as unconstitutional. Will the citizens win? Explain.
9. The Federal Trade Commission, a federal agency, brings action against Conglomerate Car Company as a result of a complaint filed with the commission by Bigdome Car Company. After reviewing the complaint, the commission concludes that Conglomerate is guilty. The commission's opinion provides its reasons for reaching this conclusion. Is the commission's opinion law? Explain.
10. Arthur and Ava Strunk have two sons, Tommy, age 28, and Jerry, age 27. Tommy is married, employed, and a part-time college student. He suffers from a fatal kidney disease and is being kept alive by frequent dialysis treatment, a procedure that cannot be continued much longer. Jerry is incompetent and has been legally committed to a state institution for the mentally retarded. He has an IQ of approximately 35, which corresponds to a mental age of approximately six years. He is further handicapped by a speech defect that makes it difficult for

him to communicate with people who are unacquainted with him. When it was determined that Tommy would need a kidney transplant to survive, doctors looked for a donor. Possible donors include cadavers as well as live persons. Because of compatibility of blood type and tissue, the only acceptable live donor is Jerry. The parents petitioned a court for authority to proceed with the operation. There are no statutes or prior case law to guide the court's determination. How should the court decide?

CHAPTER 3

# THE AMERICAN LEGAL SYSTEM

## CHAPTER OUTLINE



## LEARNING OBJECTIVES

After learning this chapter the student should be able to:

- Recognize when a business should consult an attorney and how to select one.
- Determine whether particular communications are protected by the attorney-client privilege.
- Evaluate whether a firm not directly transacting business in a state is likely to be subject to suit in that state.
- Recognize the different stages of the litigation process and their importance to a firm facing possible litigation.
- Determine in particular settings the advantages and disadvantages of using alternatives to litigation for settling disputes.

Businesses come into contact with the legal system under a variety of circumstances. Disputes with suppliers or customers may result in lawsuits that bring the manager face to face with the legal system and its process. Contact with the judicial system creates a need for legal advice.

This chapter begins by explaining the attorney-client relationship. The next sections describe the judicial system. Finally, the chapter surveys alternatives to litigation (the traditional way to resolve disputes).

## THE FIRM AND ITS ATTORNEY

Businesses call on lawyers to assist them through the red tape of government regulation. In the past, a business usually did not contact lawyers until a problem arose—for example, when it was sued or when a distributor would not pay an outstanding debt. However, now more and more businesses are concerned with preventive law. By contacting lawyers early and following their legal advice, companies may avoid the consequences that accompany uninformed business practices. Business managers today have more of an ongoing relationship with lawyers than in the past; hence, they need to know more about lawyers.

Lawyers have a common base of education: law school. There, law students receive generalized training that enables them to adapt to a wide range of tasks. The average person thinks that lawyers know the law. It is more accurate to say that lawyers are versed in general legal principles and methods. They are trained to find the relevant law and to apply it to particular circumstances.

### *Corporate Legal Strategy*

A long-standing tension has characterized the relationship between lawyers and business managers. Lawyers tend to be conservative in their advice and often dampen a business's desire to do creative things. Many business executives believe that attorneys should be consulted only to find out what cannot be done. Because they use attorneys only on an *ad hoc* basis, they do not know how to incorporate them into their business organization charts.

Some businesses, however, recognize the need to develop a comprehensive corporate legal strategy. This corporate strategy may appear in any of several forms. A *preventive* strategy employs attorneys to review new programs and documents with an eye to avoiding legal problems. An *enforcive* strategy uses legal activity to protect a company against patent infringement and other violations of its rights. A *creative* strategy employs legal counsel to help formulate corporate goals. An *active* strategy brings the manager and the attorney together to explore various ways of achieving those goals, through, for example, a merger with another corporation, legal loopholes, or lobbying for a change in the law. The preventive, enforcive, creative, and active corporate legal strategies may be used together, depending on the circumstances that confront the company.[1]

---

1 This discussion of corporate legal strategy is derived from F. Sturdivant and C. Green, *Building a Strong Corporate Strategy*, College of Administrative Science, The Ohio State University, Working Paper Series 83–70 (October 1983).

## The Lawyer's Roles

Lawyers play many roles in relation to the business firm. They counsel the firm's managers regarding transactions, compliance with regulations, and similar matters. They draft and review legal documents. Their primary goal as counsellors and drafters is to prevent legal problems from developing.

Lawyers also represent their clients as advocates. They negotiate to settle disputes with other parties on terms favorable to their clients. They represent their clients before courts, administrative agencies, and arbitrators. As advocates, their duty is to present the facts and argue the law in the light most favorable to the client. Counsel for opposing parties will do the same for their clients. Lawyers serve as partisan advocates in a legal system that is based on an adversarial model.

To perform their various roles, lawyers often must investigate relevant facts. Because of the need to investigate, communication between a firm and its attorney is very important.

## Communicating with Lawyers

A person needing a lawyer's services should contact counsel early, before the problem intensifies. It is better to have a lawyer draft a contract than to call in a lawyer to solve a problem caused by a contract poorly drafted by the client.

The client should fully disclose the facts relevant to the question at hand. If an attorney's opinion is based on less than full information, the opinion is incomplete. A general understanding of the law affecting the business helps a client detail the material facts and avoid irrelevancies when communicating with a lawyer. Understanding the lawyer's role also facilitates communication.

The client should actively assist the lawyer's search for solutions. Also, the client should inform the lawyer of the company's goals so that the lawyer seeks solutions compatible with those goals. Finally, the client should expect high-quality service from counsel and should communicate that expectation. After all, the client is paying the bill.

### The Attorney-Client Privilege

The law protects confidential communications between the attorney and client from disclosure to a third person. Without the client's permission, the attorney may not divulge communications made during the attorney-client contact. The client may, however, waive the privilege and authorize the attorney to make disclosure. The privilege applies only to confidential communications; it does not include statements made to an attorney in the presence of third parties other than the client's or attorney's agents or employees.

A corporation communicates with its lawyers through its employees. The courts have grappled with the question of which employees speak for the corporation so that their statements are protected by the privilege. Some states limit the privilege to statements from senior management who guide and integrate the firm's operations.

In federal court, however, the Supreme Court has refused to limit the privilege to the senior managers who control the firm.[2] The Court applies the privilege on a case-by-case basis, inquiring:

- Was the employee directed by his or her superiors to speak with counsel?
- Was the communication to enable the firm to get legal advice?
- Did the communication concern matters within the scope of the employee's job?
- Did the employee know the reason for the communication?
- Was the communication confidential?

The attorney-client privilege protects only the communication between the client and the attorney. The communication must be for the purpose of obtaining legal advice. The underlying information is not protected. A client cannot hide information just by telling it to the attorney.

The reason for the attorney-client privilege is to promote compliance with the law. The purpose of seeking legal advice is to avoid violating the law. A client who trusts the attorney not to reveal communications between them should be forthcoming with the facts needed by the attorney in forming a legal opinion.

Exceptions to the attorney-client privilege exist when there is an overriding public policy. For example, an exception allows an attorney to disclose communication where the client is trying to use the lawyer's services to commit a crime or fraud.

### Work Product Doctrine

A doctrine akin to the attorney-client privilege is the work-product doctrine. Any materials that have been prepared in anticipation of a lawsuit fall under this doctrine, and are privileged. Neither the attorney nor the client can be compelled to disclose these materials. The doctrine covers not only materials that have been prepared by the client or the attorney, but also any materials prepared by, for example, consultants.

In some cases a party to a lawsuit may obtain these materials if there is a substantial need and there is no other way to obtain them without undue hardship. However, even in this case the court will still protect against disclosure of the mental impressions, conclusions, opinions or legal theories of an attorney or other representative of the party concerning the litigation.

## *Professional Conduct Rules for Attorneys*

Every state has ethical rules of conduct governing lawyers' professional behavior. Lawyers have certain responsibilities to their clients, to the legal system, and to their own consciences. These responsibilities often result in ethical dilemmas. To guide attorneys and bodies that regulate their conduct, the American Bar Association (ABA), a national organization of attorneys, has approved The Model Rules of Professional Conduct (usually known just as the Model Rules). Most states have adopted the Model Rules, with variations from state to state. Lawyers who violate the Rules of Professional Conduct may be disciplined or disbarred.

---

2 Upjohn Co. v. U.S., 449 U.S. 383 (1981).

The Model Rules require the lawyer to provide competent representation to a client. According to the Model Rules, competent representation "requires the legal knowledge, skill, thoroughness and preparation reasonably necessary for the representation." The lawyer must act with reasonable diligence and promptness in representing a client. This must be accomplished while abiding by the client's decision regarding the objectives of the representation and while exercising candor to the tribunal hearing the case.

The Model Rules provide that lawyers may not represent clients whose interests conflict with those of other clients, unless each affected client gives informed consent, confirmed in writing. The Model Rules require lawyers to adopt reasonable procedures to determine whether there are any conflicts of interest.

Under the Model Rules, a lawyer must keep confidential all information relating to the representation, unless the client consents to its disclosure. This rule does not apply if a lawyer knows that a client intends to commit a crime that would result in death or substantial bodily harm. A client has the right to discharge a lawyer with or without cause.

**The Business and Government Interface**

The following link is to the ABA's *Model Rules of Professional Conduct* for attorneys:

http://www.americanbar.org/groups/professional_responsibility/publications/model_rules_of_professional_conduct.html

They have been adopted as law in most states. Clicking *Model Rules Table of Contents* takes you to the rules. Clicking *Rule 1.6, Confidentiality of Communications* gives you the full rule on this aspect of the lawyer-client relation. Clicking *Rule 1.5 Fees* takes you to a rule most potential clients find interesting.

# THE COURT SYSTEM

The judicial system in the United States includes the federal system and the judicial systems of the 50 states. Separate federal court systems exist for the District of Columbia and U.S. territories such as Puerto Rico, the Virgin Islands, and Guam. This means there are more than 50 distinct judicial systems. It is not unusual for a firm to do business in a number of states and, hence, to be subject to the judicial processes in many jurisdictions. The business manager therefore needs a general understanding of the workings of federal and state judicial systems.

## *Jurisdiction*

**Jurisdiction** is the power of a court to hear and decide a case. To exercise this power, a court generally must have jurisdiction over both the subject matter of, and the parties to, the dispute.

Jurisdiction over the subject matter is accomplished by selecting a court that has power to hear the type of case. State courts of general jurisdiction are usually empowered to hear any type of case. The federal courts, as discussed in the next section, have limited subject-matter jurisdiction.

Jurisdiction over the person may be accomplished by serving the defendant with notice of the suit within the state in which the court is located. The notice is called a *summons.*

The requirement that the process be served on the defendant in the state in which the court is located poses a severe limitation. Suppose a defendant who resides in Alaska strikes a pedestrian while driving a car in Florida. If the Alaskan resident returned home, the injured pedestrian might be forced to sue in Alaska. To combat this shortcoming, states enacted long-arm statutes. A **long-arm**

**statute** is a means of gaining service over an out-of-state defendant. Most states have longarm statutes that subject an out-of-state defendant to the jurisdiction where the defendant is doing business or has committed a civil wrong. Long-arm statutes must comply with the Constitution's requirement of due process. In *International Shoe Co. v. Washington*, the U.S. Supreme Court held that the U.S. Constitution requires a defendant, if not present within the state, to have certain minimum contacts with the state where the suit is filed.[3]

## Venue

Jurisdiction must be distinguished from venue. *Venue* is concerned with the geographic locality within the jurisdiction where an action should be tried. Venue is specified by statute; it may require that the case be heard in the county where the defendant resides or where the property that is the subject of the action is located. When the location of a trial would result in an inconvenience and a hardship, the doctrine of **forum non conveniens** permits a defendant to transfer the case to another geographic location where venue is proper.

## The Federal System

The federal judicial system derives from the U.S. Constitution. Article III provides that "the judicial Power of the United States shall be vested in one supreme court, and in such inferior courts as the Congress may from time to time ordain and establish." Pursuant to Article III, Congress has created 14 circuit courts of appeal and 94 district courts (*see* Figure 3-1).

**FIGURE 3-1 Federal Court System**

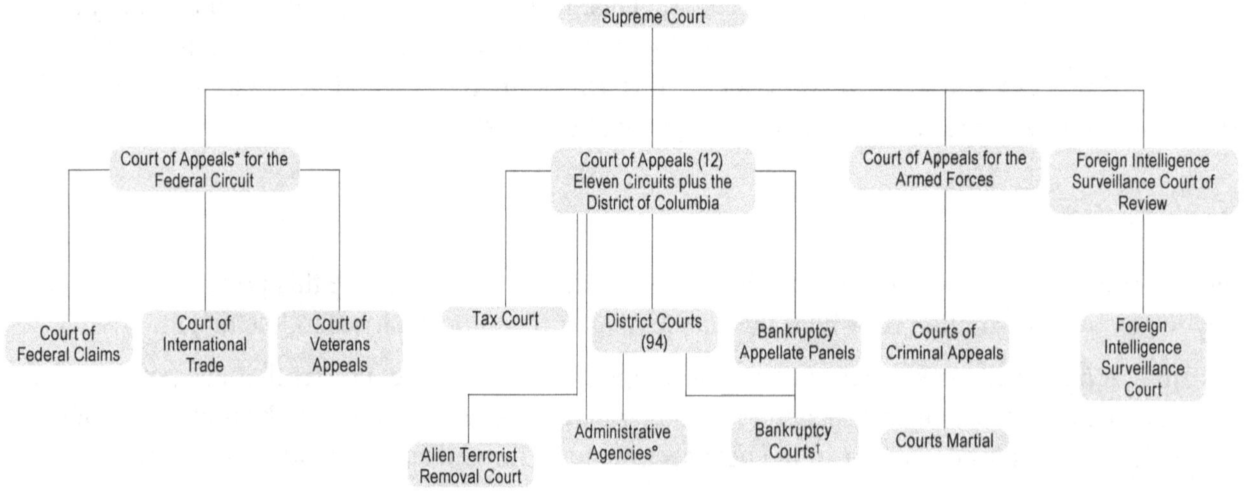


*Cases involving patents, trademarks, copyrights, and contract claims against the United States are reviewed by the Court of Appeals for the Federal Circuit

†Some appeals proceed to the Bankruptcy Appellate Panel; others go directly to the District Court.

°Most appeals are reviewed by the Court of Appeals; some are reviewed de novo in the District Court.

3 326 U.S. 310 (1945).

## District Courts

The basic federal trial court is the U.S. district court. There is at least one district in every state and territory. Many states are divided into more than one district, depending on size, population, and number of lawsuits filed. District courts also hear appeals from a few federal agencies, such as the Social Security Administration.

The district court has subject matter jurisdiction only if a statute gives it jurisdiction. The two broadest statutes give district courts jurisdiction over cases involving a federal question and diversity of citizenship.

**The Business and Government Interface**

The following link is to the United States Courts website:

http://www.uscourts.gov/Home.aspx

There you will find information, including videos, podcasts, statistics and other information about the federal courts.

**Federal question jurisdiction** cases include any claim arising under a federal statute, a treaty, or the U.S. Constitution. Cases involving robbery of federal banks, federal antitrust violations, and interpretations of U.S. treaties with foreign nations are all properly heard by a federal district court because they present federal questions.

U.S. district courts also have **diversity jurisdiction** over cases between citizens of different states where the amount in contest exceeds $75,000. A corporation is considered a citizen of the states in which it is incorporated and in which it has its principal place of business. A partnership, even a limited partnership, is considered a citizen of every state in which a partner is a citizen. There must be complete diversity of citizenship; no plaintiff (the party who initiates the suit) may be a citizen of the same state in which any defendant (the party who is sued) is a citizen. If there are multiple plaintiffs, each must claim, in good faith, damages exceeding $75,000 (not counting interest or court costs).

For example, assume that four individual plaintiffs sue Chemical, Inc. because wastes it dumped into a waterway ultimately polluted the plaintiffs' property. Each seeks more than $75,000 in damages. Three of the plaintiffs are citizens of Ohio, and the fourth is a citizen of Michigan. Chemical, Inc. is incorporated in Delaware and has its principal place of business in Michigan. Here, diversity of citizenship is not present because a plaintiff and a defendant are citizens of Michigan. If the Michigan plaintiff were eliminated from the suit, then diversity jurisdiction would be present.

The federal district court sitting in a diversity case hears and resolves the case according to the law of the state in which it sits. This is known as the *Erie Doctrine*, named after a case in which this principle was first announced.[4] The court does, however, apply its own procedural rules, such as rules of evidence and rules of conduct regarding the administration of the trial.

Plaintiffs are not required to sue in federal district court, even though that court would have jurisdiction. In most cases, they may elect instead to file suit in a proper state court. The district court has concurrent jurisdiction, with the state courts, as opposed to exclusive jurisdiction. However, if plaintiffs sue in a state court, the defendant may have the case removed to the federal court as long as the case could have originally been brought in that court.

4 Erie Railroad Co. v. Tompkins, 304 U.S. 64 (1938).

### Court of Appeals

Appeals from the district courts are heard by the U.S. circuit courts of appeals. There are 11 numbered circuit courts of appeal, the District of Columbia circuit, plus the Courts of Appeals for the Federal Circuit and for the Armed Forces. They also hear appeals from the Tax Court and review most administrative agency actions. The Tax Court hears disputes involving tax deficiencies assessed against a taxpayer.

### U.S. Supreme Court

Sitting atop the federal legal system is the U.S. Supreme Court. Review in the Supreme Court is not automatic. Parties seeking review must request that the Court hear the case by filing a petition for **certiorari.** The Court has absolute discretion to grant or deny certiorari, and it rarely gives a reason for a denial. Certiorari is granted if any four of the nine Supreme Court justices are in favor of it. Certiorari is likely to be granted when a constitutional issue of national importance is posed or when an issue has been decided in a conflicting manner by the circuit courts of appeals.

## *The State System*

State trial courts consist of courts of general and limited jurisdiction (*see* Figure 3-2). A court of general jurisdiction is one that can hear any type of case unless specifically prohibited by statute. Some cases, such as admiralty, bankruptcy, and patent infringement actions, may be brought only in federal court. Most state trial courts of general jurisdiction are organized at the county level. Their names vary from state to state. The most popular names are circuit court, court of common pleas, and superior court.

State trial courts of limited jurisdiction are those that can hear only specific types of cases. A probate court, for example, cannot hear a divorce case; a small claims court cannot try a felony case. Some courts are limited in that they can only hear disputes up to a maximum monetary ceiling.

**The Business and Government Interface**

The following link is to the website of the Supreme Court of Ohio & The Ohio Judicial System:

http://www.supremecourt.ohio.gov/

This is provided as an example of a typical state court system.

Many states have an intermediate court of appeals, similar to the federal circuit court of appeals. Following a decision by the court of appeals, review may be sought in the state supreme court; similar to the U.S. Supreme Court, it reviews most cases by certiorari. In the smaller and less populous states, which lack intermediate courts of appeals, appeals from trial courts are taken directly to state supreme courts.

A state supreme court is the highest authority on the law of its state. The U.S. Supreme Court has no power to decide issues of state law. State supreme court decisions interpreting federal statutes, treaties, and the U.S. Constitution are, however, subject to U.S. Supreme Court review.

**FIGURE 3-2 Typical State Court System**

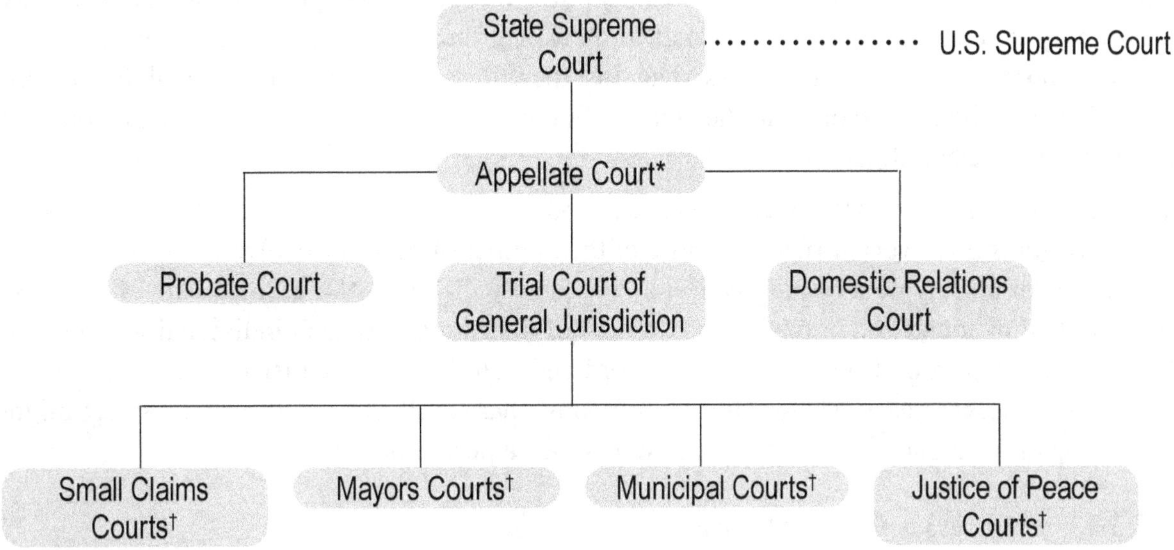


*Not present in the system in smaller, less populous states.

†In some cases, appeals are made directly to the Appellate Court.

# THE CIVIL PROCESS

A dispute must involve a case or controversy before a court will decide it. Courts do not act when there is no real dispute.

Courts are best equipped to decide cases when the parties have a personal stake in the outcome. Under these circumstances, the parties have the incentive to expend their best efforts in prosecuting or defending a case. This is the adversary system. In this adversarial environment, courts are in the best position to examine the arguments, find the truth, and apply justice.

When an event triggers a dispute, the potential for a lawsuit exists. A lawsuit is a civil case. Table 3-1 contrasts civil and criminal cases. The civil process is the sequence of events from the beginning of the suit to the final appeal. It consists of four stages: the *pleading stage*, the *discovery stage*, the *trial stage*, and the *appellate stage* (*see* Figure 3-3).

## *The Pleading Stage*

The *pleadings* are the documents that tell each party's claims or defenses against the other parties. *See* Table 3-2 for a summary of the pleadings.

### Class Action Suits

Under certain circumstances, a person may bring a suit on behalf of a class of people who have been similarly injured. This is known as a **class action suit.** For example, assume that many members of the public have been injured as a result of illegally inflated utility prices. It may not be feasible for every injured person to sue the utility company individually, and not everyone may be aware of the illegal activity. The cost of maintaining the suit also may discourage people from suing, especially if the amount of potential recovery is too small to be worth the effort. The law in these cases may permit one or more persons to undertake a suit against the utility company on behalf of all the injured customers. By consolidating in one suit the claims of many, the class action suit avoids the potential for repetitious, inefficient litigation.

Class actions have involved thousands and even hundreds of thousands of people. The administration of a class suit is often very difficult because of the number of persons involved. The distribution of the proceeds of a settlement or judgment may be equally difficult. Not all members of the class may be identified or found. Additionally, the amount of distribution to each individual may be disputed. Some courts, aware of this problem, have ordered that damages be distributed to benefit the public. For example, in a case where a utility company charges illegally high rates, a court might order the company to reduce its rates to all consumers for a period of time.

**TABLE 3-1 Civil versus Criminal Cases**

| | *Civil* | *Criminal* |
|---|---|---|
| Who institutes the action? | Individual or business enterprise | Sovereign |
| Who has been wronged? | Individual or business enterprise | Society |
| What is the burden of proof? | Preponderance of the evidence* | Beyond a reasonable doubt† |
| What is the remedy? | Damages, injunction, or other private relief | Punishment (fine and/or imprisonment) |

*By the greater weight of the evidence.

†To satisfy this burden the trier of the facts (judge or jury) must have an abiding conviction amounting to a certainty of the guilt of the accused. This is a greater burden of proof than "preponderance of the evidence."

**FIGURE 3-3 The Civil Process**

| Pleading stage | → | Discovery stage | → | Trial stage | → | Appellate stage |
|---|---|---|---|---|---|---|
| Complaint<br>Answer<br>Reply | → | Deposition<br>Written interrogatories<br>Request for production of documents<br>Request to inspect premises<br>Request for admissions<br>Request for physical examination<br>Request for mental examination | → | Selection of jury<br>Opening statements<br>Cases in chief<br>Closing arguments<br>Instructions to jury<br>Verdict<br>Judgment | → | Review by appellate court |

In a class action lawsuit, one or more members of a class sue as representative parties on behalf of all members of the class. The court must determine whether to certify the action as a class action. The requirements for certification as a class action include that questions of law or fact must be common to the class, and the claims of the representative parties must be typical of the claims or defenses of the class. When the court certifies a lawsuit as a class action, it defines the class, the claims or defenses, and appoints counsel to represent the class. The court directs that notice be given to all members of the class who can be reasonably identified. The notice states that absent class members may enter an appearance through an attorney, or request exclusion from the class action (which permits the absent member to bring an individual lawsuit). The notice also states that any class judgment is binding on all members of the class.

**TABLE 3-2 Pleadings**

| *Pleading* | *Who Files against Whom* | *Purpose* |
|---|---|---|
| Complaint | Plaintiff against defendant | States the factual basis for the claim. |
| Answer | Defendant against plaintiff | Admits or denies the allegations of the complaint; may also raise affirmative defenses. |
| Counterclaim | Defendant against plaintiff | States basis for claim by defendant against plaintiff. |
| Reply | Plaintiff against defendant | Answers counterclaim. |
| Cross claim | Defendant against another defendant | States basis for claim. |
| Impleader | Defendant against a nonparty | Defendant adds another party to the lawsuit. |
| Intervention | Nonparty against a party | Another party seeks to join the lawsuit. |
| Interpleader | Plaintiff or defendant against two parties | Forces the court to determine the rightful holder of monies. |

### Motions

During the pleading stage it is not unusual for a party to file a **motion to dismiss** or a **motion for judgment on the pleadings.**

A motion to dismiss may attack any number of deficiencies in a pleading. It may be used, for example, by a defendant questioning whether the court has jurisdiction over the defendant or over the subject matter. Or, it may allege that the matter should be dismissed because the Complaint fails to state facts that would constitute a reason for the Plaintiff to win the lawsuit. In effect this motion says, "So what. Even if you prove what you said, the law does not recognize this as actionable." For example, in a jurisdiction where a surrogate mother contract is not recognized, a complaint seeking relief under such a contract should be dismissed for failure to state a cause of action.

A motion to dismiss will also be warranted when it is clear on the face of the Complaint that the statute of limitations has run. In a jurisdiction where the statute of limitations for a wrongful discharge of employment is four years, for example, a motion to dismiss should be granted if it is clear from the Complaint that it was not filed within that time period. Finally, there are consequences when the defendant fails to answer the Complaint in a timely manner, or the Plaintiff fails to Reply to the Counterclaim within the time specified by law. In such a case a motion for default judgment may result in the movant winning.

A motion for judgment on the pleadings may be filed by either party. It is similar to the motion to dismiss, however it alleges that on the basis of an examination of all the pleadings, the movant should prevail. For example, assume that the plaintiff alleges in its complaint that defendant owes it a sum of money. Defendant, in his Answer, pleads poverty, but does not deny the debt. Based on these pleadings a motion for judgment on the pleadings should be granted in Plaintiff's favor.

## *Remedies*

Most people sue for money damages, but in some cases a plaintiff asks the court for an **injunction**—an order compelling the defendant to do something or to refrain from doing something. The plaintiff is not entitled to a permanent injunction until the end of the case. In a proper case, however, the plaintiff may obtain a preliminary injunction by demonstrating that: (1) the plaintiff is very likely to win on the merits of the case, (2) the plaintiff will suffer irreparable harm if the preliminary injunction is not issued, (3) the injunction will not be unjustly harsh on the defendant, and (4) the injunction is in the public interest.

## *The Discovery Stage*

**Discovery** refers to the process where each party attempts to learn what the other party knows. Each party may direct written questions, known as *interrogatories*, to the other party, who must provide written answers under oath. Each party may also ask the other parties to produce and allow the requesting party to inspect documents or electronically stored information, or the premises. Each party may ask the other parties to admit or deny specific facts, or submit to a physical or mental examination. Parties may also take each other's deposition, a procedure whereby individuals are questioned under oath before a court reporter.

The discovery process contributes substantially to the costs of litigation. In an effort to control these costs, the Federal Rules of Civil Procedure impose on parties a duty to disclose to the other party, without being asked, the following:

- names, addresses and phone numbers of individuals with knowledge relevant to disputed facts alleged with particularity in the pleadings
- copies or descriptions of documents, electronically stored information, and tangible things relevant to disputed facts alleged with particularity in the pleadings
- computations of all monetary damage claims
- copies of liability insurance policies covering the dispute
- names and copies of reports by expert witnesses
- names of witnesses the party plans to call

The Federal Rules rely on automatic disclosure as the primary means of discovery.

### Litigation Holds

A litigation hold is where a company suspends its usual document retention and preservation policy and directs its employees to preserve documents and electronically stored information (ESI) in anticipation of future litigation. The duty to preserve documents and ESI arises when litigation is anticipated. The duty is often triggered by a "litigation hold letter" the company receives from a potential adversary's attorney. However, the duty also arises when management is aware of potential litigation from other sources, such as when supervisors are overheard talking about harassment of employees.

The company's management, or its attorney, will usually direct employees to retain documents and ESI, putting a hold on all evidence that may be relevant to future litigation. The hold can extend to employee cell phones, text messages, and home computers that access the company network. The purpose of the hold order is to preserve evidence and protect against spoliation of evidence.

Failure to preserve relevant evidence can result in court ordered "discovery sanctions." These include court orders that: prevent the disobedient party from introducing certain evidence, that dismiss the disobedient party's claims and defenses, or award a default judgment against the disobedient party. Discovery sanctions can also include an order that the disobedient party pay the opposing party's attorney fees.

### Motions

During the discovery stage, it is common for parties to file a **motion for summary judgment.** This motion is not confined to an examination of the pleadings. It calls attention to the discovery materials, and may include additional sworn statements not part of the discovery. It is not unusual for both parties to file a motion for summary judgment and seek a favorable ruling based upon the sworn facts as applied to the law. Movants are required to file a memorandum that argues why the court should rule in its favor, based upon the uncontroverted facts, as applied to the law.

In a motion for summary judgment, the court is required to construe the facts in the light most favorable to the party against whom summary judgment is sought. Hence, if the question is whether the traffic light was red or green, and there is sworn testimony to both versions, then the court will overrule the motion since these facts are contested.

The following case involves issues of when a duty to preserve evidence arises, the consequences in litigation of a party's spoliation of evidence, and whether a motion for summary judgment should be granted.

**FREIDIG *v.* TARGET CORPORATION**

United States District Court for the Western District of Wisconsin

329 F.R.D. 199 (2018)

Carla Freidig was walking through an empty checkout lane at a Target store when she slipped on a puddle and fell.

After the fall, Target employees came to help Freidig. An employee inspected the area where Freidig fell and found a puddle of clear liquid that was about the size of a basketball.

Target investigated the accident and took a formal, recorded statement from Sarah Raemisch, a Target employee. Raemisch said that she had walked through that area 10 to 15 minutes prior to Freidig's fall. She did not notice any liquid on the floor, but she only "sometimes" looks for spills and hazards. She said that "to [her] knowledge," she was the last person to walk through the area before Freidig. She was facing away from the checkout lane at the time of Freidig's fall.

Freidig's slip and fall were captured on Target's security camera. Target had a policy to preserve video recording of accidents in its stores, including from 20 minutes before the accident to 20 minutes after. But for reasons unexplained, Target preserved video beginning only six seconds before Freidig's accident. So the recording did not show Raemisch's walk through the area or show how the puddle was formed.

Freidig received treatment for wrist pain, culminating with surgery. She sued Target under Wisconsin's safe-place statute, Wis. Stat. Section 101.11. The safe-place statute required employers and owners of public buildings to "adopt and use methods and processes reasonably adequate" to maintain and repair their buildings and to "do every other thing reasonably necessary to protect the life, health, safety, and welfare of . . . employees and frequenters." Wis. Stat. Section 101.11(1). The duty to repair or maintain a building arose when the defendant had actual or constructive notice of an unsafe condition.

Target moved for summary judgment, contending that Freidig could not show that Target had actual or constructive notice of the puddle that Freidig slipped on.

## *James D. Peterson, District Judge*

Summary judgment is appropriate only if there is no genuine dispute as to any material fact. In ruling on a motion for summary judgment, the court views all facts and draws all inferences in the light most favorable to the non-moving party. Summary judgment will not be granted unless the record taken as a whole could not lead a rational trier of fact to find for the non-moving party.

Target contends that Freidig cannot show that it had actual or constructive notice of the puddle. In response, Freidig filed a motion for relief contending that Target failed to take reasonable steps to preserve video of the checkout lane. Freidig argues that if Target preserved video of the lane prior to Freidig's fall, it would have shown whether the puddle was on the floor long enough to give Target constructive notice.

There is no evidence that Target had actual notice of the puddle, but Freidig could prove that Target had constructive notice if she can show that the puddle existed a long enough time for a reasonably vigilant owner to discover and repair it.

Freidig contends that the puddle was present at least 10 to 15 minutes prior to her fall, when Target's employee, Sarah Raemisch, walked through the area. Freidig construes Raemisch's statement to mean that she was the last person to walk through the area. Because the puddle could not have formed on its own, Freidig argues that it follows that the puddle was present for at least 10 to 15 minutes if no one else was in the area to cause the spill after Raemisch and before Freidig.

But Raemisch's statement does not unequivocally establish that no one was in the area after Raemisch walked through. Raemisch said that "[t]o her knowledge" she was the last person through the area before the fall. But Raemisch did not say that she was monitoring the area, or that she even remained in the area throughout those 10 to 15 minutes. And even though Raemisch was nearby when Freidig fell, Raemisch was facing a different direction and had to turn around to see what happened.

Target argues that Freidig has no evidence to corroborate Raemisch's equivocal statement, so she cannot establish that Target had constructive notice of the puddle. The court does not agree. Target is entitled to summary judgment only if it can establish that Freidig does not have evidence sufficient to support a reasonable verdict in her favor. Raemisch's statement is somewhat equivocal, and her credibility might be impeached based on her lack of definitive knowledge of what happened before the fall. But Freidig does not have to prove her case on summary judgment. A reasonable jury could find, based on Raemisch's statement that to her knowledge no one else walked through the area of the fall, that no one did walk through that area.

And there is another factor to consider: the missing video. Freidig contends that if Target had followed its video preservation policy and preserved the 20 minutes of video footage prior to Freidig's accident, then Freidig could have used that footage to show whether any other person walked through the area after Raemisch. So Freidig asks for relief for Target's spoliation of the video.

When a party is aware of an accident that it knows is likely to cause litigation, it triggers the party's duty to preserve evidence.

Target also should have been aware that the lead-up to the fall itself was relevant to a potential suit from Freidig. Target has a policy to preserve 20 minutes of footage before and after an accident. Although this policy does not itself create a duty to preserve, it does show that Target is aware, as a general matter, that footage prior to an accident is commonly relevant to litigation. That is especially true in this case because Target's investigator took a statement from Raemisch that she had walked through that area 10 to 15 minutes prior to Freidig's fall and had not noticed a puddle. So even without the policy, a reasonable party in Target's position would have realized that footage of those 10 to 15 minutes was relevant to how the puddle was formed.

In this case, the only evidence of the content of the missing video is Raemisch's statement and it suggests that the missing video would have helped Freidig's claim. Raemisch said that she did not notice the puddle, and that to her knowledge, no one else walked through the area after she did. Target has no evidence at all to suggest that, contrary to Raemisch's statement, someone else made the puddle after Raemisch walked through. So the available evidence suggests that the lost recording would have been helpful to Freidig.

Freidig is prejudiced because she cannot corroborate Raemisch's statement that no one walked through the area after Raemisch. So, for the purposes of summary judgment at least, the court will credit Raemisch's statement that she was the last person to walk through the area. Accordingly, the court concludes that Freidig has adduced sufficient evidence that the puddle was there at least 10 to 15 minutes before Freidig's fall, and that the puddle was there when Raemisch walked through the area.

Under the safe-place statute, Target had constructive notice of the puddle if it existed a long enough time for a reasonably vigilant owner to discover and repair it.

This is typically a question of fact left to the jury, and it includes considerations of the surrounding facts and circumstances, including the nature of the business and the nature of the defect. Wis. Stat. Section 101.11(l). Target has not shown that 15 minutes is not long enough to meet this standard or that Target missed the puddle despite procedures that were reasonably vigilant. So drawing all inferences in the light most favorable to Freidig, a reasonable jury could conclude that Target had constructive notice of the puddles before Freidig's fall.

Because a reasonable jury could conclude that the puddle was on the floor long enough to give Target constructive notice, and that Freidig's slip and fall injured her wrist, the court will deny Target's motion for summary judgment on Freidig's safe-place claim.

**Business Application:** What policies, procedures, and practices should a business have in place and follow when customers and employees are injured on the business premises?

## *Pretrial Conference*

The judge is interested in an efficient trial. Toward that end, the court will seek out ways to decrease the length of the trial. Parties will be asked to mark their exhibits beforehand and to provide the opponent a copy. Stipulations of evidence whereby the parties agree to the admission of certain documents, or to certain findings, is another way to streamline the trial. The number of witnesses should be realistic and duplication of testimony by different witnesses should ordinarily be avoided.

The court is also interested in the status of settlement negotiations, and will strongly encourage settlement. Of course, settlement will avoid the time and the risk of trial. Usually, the court will be proactive in moving the parties to agreement, and may even suggest or require ADR.

## *The Trial Stage*

If the plaintiff is seeking monetary damages (known as *legal relief*), the parties are ordinarily entitled to a trial by jury. They may, however, waive this right and try the case to the court. If the plaintiff is seeking equitable relief, such as an injunction or other court order, the parties are not ordinarily entitled to a jury trial.

In most civil cases, the plaintiff has the burden of proving the case by a preponderance of the evidence. Preponderance of the evidence means by the greater weight of the evidence. To sustain that burden of proof, the plaintiff must convince the judge or jury that the facts are probably as the plaintiff alleges. If at the end of the case the trier of the facts is undecided, then the defendant wins.

After selection of the jury (if a jury trial is proper and not waived), counsel for the plaintiff makes an opening statement, explaining what he or she intends to prove. Defense counsel may make an opening statement immediately thereafter, or reserve opening statement until the close of plaintiff's case. Plaintiff then presents a case in chief by calling witnesses who testify and by presenting other evidence, such as business records, photographs, or other tangible objects, called *exhibits.* The defendant is given the opportunity to cross-examine the plaintiff's witnesses. The judge decides on the admissibility of the evidence, based on the law. The plaintiff rests after completing the case in chief.

The defendant then proceeds with an opening statement, if previously reserved, and presents his or her case in chief. When the defendant rests, the plaintiff may offer evidence to rebut the defendant's case in chief. The defense may follow with surrebutal.

When all of the evidence is in, the parties' lawyers deliver their closing arguments. If the case was tried without a jury, the judge makes findings of fact and conclusions of law. In jury trials, the judge instructs the jurors on the relevant law; they then deliberate and reach a verdict.

### Motions

At the trial stage two motions are common: motion for directed verdict and motion for judgment notwithstanding the verdict. Both motions basically say the same thing, but come at different times during the trial.

The **motion for directed verdict** may sound like this in the voice of the attorney moving for it:

> Your Honor, based upon the evidence that has been presented, reasonable minds cannot differ. There is nothing to send to the jury because the evidence is clear, and as a matter of law, your Honor must find for my client.

The motion requesting that court direct a verdict in the movant's favor is customarily made by both parties at the end of the opponent's case in chief. Of course, if either party's motion is granted, that ends the case.

The **motion for judgment notwithstanding the verdict** is ordinarily made by the losing party after the return of an unfavorable verdict. It states in essence that the case should never have been sent to the jury because reasonable minds could not differ on the facts, and as applied to the law, the movant should win. In effect this gives the judge another opportunity to rule in favor of the movant, whose motion for directed verdict was previously overruled. It is rare that the court would upset the jury verdict and enter a judgment notwithstanding the verdict, but it does happen from time to time.

## Business Application/Ethical Issues

Burger Town, Inc. is a chain of hamburger stands with 20 establishments located in 15 towns in Kentucky. Big Time Burgers, Inc. is an international hamburger restaurant chain with over a thousand restaurants located throughout the United States, Canada, and Europe. Last week Burger Town started running full-page ads in newspapers stating: "Burger Town hamburgers and fries are healthier than Big Time's Burgers. An order consisting of a Burger Town hamburger and french fries contains less saturated fat than a Big Time hamburger and fries."

John Killbuck is the vice president of operations for Big Time Burgers, Inc. Killbuck's department includes the legal department. Teresa Vermilion, an attorney in the department, has informed Killbuck that Big Time could bring a lawsuit against Burger Town for false advertising. However, the success of the lawsuit would depend on the evidence presented in court.

Big Time cooks its hamburgers and fries in beef tallow. It is quite likely that a Big Time hamburger and fries contain more saturated fats than Burger Town's, if Burger Town cooks its hamburgers and fries in vegetable oil.

Killbuck knows that Burger Town is a small, regional chain and cannot withstand the expense of a lengthy lawsuit. However, Big Time's financial and legal resources could enable it to sue and tie up Burger Town in costly litigation for years. Killbuck is considering filing a lawsuit against Burger Town and immediately seeking to negotiate a quick settlement. Killbuck tells Vermilion, "Teresa, if I were in Burger Town's shoes, I would settle the case quickly even if it cost me several thousand dollars rather than face us in court with all the expense that would involve. Also, suing Burger Town would teach those small fries who's the boss of burgers."

What are the ethical issues? What would you do?

### *The Appellate Stage*

Once the trial court makes a final judgment in the case, the losing party may not institute a new suit against the same parties involving the same issues. This would be barred by a doctrine called *res judicata* (the matter has been decided), which bars a second suit involving the same parties and the same issues.

However, the legal system provides an opportunity for a party to ask a higher court to review a case for error committed by the trial court judge. The basis for such a request might be that the judge's ruling on a motion was wrong, the judge improperly admitted or excluded evidence, or the judge's instruction to the jury misstated the law. The courts that review trial court decisions are called *appellate courts.* An appellate court does not hold a new trial, nor does it hear additional evidence; it merely reviews the record of the trial and listens to the arguments of the party (called the *appellant*) claiming some serious error in that trial. The appellate court also listens to the arguments of the opposing party (called the *appellee*), who may be claiming that no serious error occurred.

After reviewing the record of the trial and the arguments of the parties involved, the appellate court has several alternatives. It can: (1) affirm the verdict of the trial court, that is, accept it as is and change nothing; (2) reverse the verdict, that is, decide that the outcome of the trial was wrong and enter judgment for the appellant; (3) modify the legal remedy provided by the trial court; or (4) reverse and remand the case to the trial court for further proceedings.

### *Abuse of the System*

In recent years, courts and legislatures have tried to curb parties from abusing the judicial system. Rule 11 of the Federal Rules of Civil Procedure is typical of these efforts. It requires that a party or lawyer sign every document filed in the lawsuit and attest that to the best of the signer's knowledge, after reasonable inquiry, the document is well grounded in fact and law and is not being filed for an improper purpose. If the other party believes the rule was violated, it must so advise the alleged violator. If the violator fails to withdraw the offending document, the lawyer and client may be liable for the other party's expenses, including reasonable attorney's fees. Additionally, many states by statute or common law permit parties who have been subjected to frivolous lawsuits to sue for attorney fees and costs, and other damages.

## ALTERNATIVE DISPUTE RESOLUTION

Two problems plague our civil justice system: delay and expense. These problems result from the heavy volume of lawsuits and the formalities and technicalities of the discovery and motion practice. Consequently, parties and courts have developed a number of alternative dispute resolution (ADR) techniques for resolving legal disputes.

### *ADR Techniques*

Most legal disputes never actually go to trial. Instead, they are settled. A variety of procedures have developed to assist the parties in settling disputes. If the parties are unable to settle, they can avoid court by agreeing to one of the many alternatives to litigation.

#### Mediation

**Mediation** involves an intermediary to assist the parties in resolving the conflict. The mediator has no power to force a solution; his or her job is to persuade the parties to come to agreement. A skillful mediator helps the parties understand their opponent's perspective; grasp the strengths of their opponent's case and the weaknesses of their own; and assess the benefits of settlement and the costs of continuing to fight. Often, the success of mediation turns on the mediator's ability and the parties' desire to settle.

## Arbitration

**Arbitration** replaces the judge and jury with a private arbitrator, who holds a hearing and decides the dispute. Many associations, such as the American Arbitration Association, and the Better Business Bureau, provide arbitration services.

Disputants may voluntarily agree to use one or more ADR techniques, either on their own or at the suggestion of a court. Arbitration is the most extensively used voluntary ADR technique. Ad hoc arbitration occurs when the parties agree to submit a particular dispute to arbitration. Increasingly, however, parties are agreeing, before any disputes arise, that all disputes will be arbitrated. These blanket arbitration agreements are standard practice in some industries, such as construction, securities, and commodities.

**The Business and Government Interface**

The following link is to website of the American Arbitration Association:

www.adr.org

In voluntary arbitration, the parties control the procedures, the timing, and even the identity of the arbitrator. Thus, arbitration provides greater flexibility than litigation and can solve the problems of delay, cost, and lack of expertise. For example, the parties can require that the arbitrator hear and decide the case by a specified date. If the arbitrator is unable to do so, they can select a different arbitrator. The parties can agree to limit or eliminate the formal discovery process. This can save a great deal of time and expense. Parties can also save money in appropriate cases by limiting or eliminating transcripts and briefs.

The parties can require that the arbitrator have expertise in the technical matters involved in the dispute. This can save the parties the time and money they would spend on educating a generalist judge and jury. It would also provide for a more informed decision.

In addition, the parties can also control whether the arbitration is public. They can agree to exclude the media and to keep the record confidential.

On the other hand, arbitrators do not have the same powers that judges have. Judges have the power to swear witnesses and issue subpoenas. Judges can hold witnesses who refuse to obey subpoenas in contempt and jail or fine them until they agree to comply.

More than three fifths of the states and the District of Columbia have adopted the Uniform Arbitration Act (UAA). The UAA gives arbitrators the power to swear witnesses and issue subpoenas. But an arbitrator has no contempt power. If a witness refuses to obey a subpoena, the parties must sue the witness in court. If the court orders the witness to obey and the witness persists in refusing, the court can then hold the witness in contempt.

An arbitrator's decision is called an *award.* The award may order a party to take action, such as paying money to the other party. However, an arbitrator has no power to enforce the award. As with subpoenas, a party must sue in court if the other party refuses to comply with the award.

Arbitrators have the power to award compensatory damages. There is considerable uncertainty, however, over whether an arbitrator has power to award punitive damages, attorney fees, or equitable relief. The trend in court decisions is to recognize broad arbitrator authority, but the law in this area is still developing.

Courts will not overturn arbitration awards for errors of law or fact. Arbitrators need not give reasons for their decisions. A court will only overturn an award if it displays a manifest disregard for the law.

In the following case, the Supreme Court decided that arbitration agreements are to be treated by the courts like any other contract.

**AT&T MOBILITY LLC *v.* CONCEPTION**
Supreme Court of the United States
563 U.S. 321 (2011)

Vincent and Liza Concepcion entered into an agreement for cellular phone service with AT&T Mobility. The deal was advertised as including free phones, which they got from AT&T. The contract contained a clause requiring arbitration of all disputes between the parties in the parties' "individual capacity, and not as a plaintiff or class member in any purported class or representative proceeding." This clause prohibited the Conceptions from participating in class action lawsuits.

AT&T charged the Conceptions $30.22 sales tax for the phones. The Conceptions filed suit against AT&T in federal district court in California. They alleged that AT&T had engaged in false advertising and fraud by charging sales tax on phones it advertised as free. The suit was consolidated with a class action lawsuit. AT&T moved the court to compel arbitration under the terms of its contract with the Conceptions.

The district court denied AT&T's motion, relying on a California Supreme Court case, *Discover Bank v. Superior Court*, (*Discover Bank*), which decided that under California law arbitration clauses that disallowed class-wide proceedings were unconscionable and therefore unenforceable. The federal court of appeals for the Ninth Circuit affirmed the district court decision.

The Supreme Court of the United States reversed the lower courts. The Supreme Court held that the Federal Arbitration Act (FAA) preempted state law, and the FAA required enforcement of the arbitration clause. What follows is the Supreme Court opinion.

## *Justice Scalia*

Section 2 of the Federal Arbitration Act (FAA) makes agreements to arbitrate "valid, irrevocable, and enforceable, save upon such grounds as exist at law or in equity for the revocation of any contract."

We have described this provision as reflecting both a "liberal federal policy favoring arbitration," and the "fundamental principle that arbitration is a matter of contract."

The "principal purpose" of the FAA is to "ensur[e] that private arbitration agreements are enforced according to their terms." This purpose is readily apparent from the FAA's text. Section 2 makes arbitration agreements "valid, irrevocable, and enforceable" as written (subject, of course, to the savings clause); § 3 requires courts to stay litigation of arbitral claims pending arbitration of those claims "in accordance with the terms of the agreement"; and § 4 requires courts to compel arbitration "in accordance with the terms of the agreement" upon the motion of either party to the agreement (assuming that the "making of the arbitration agreement or the failure . . .

to perform the same" is not at issue). In light of these provisions, we have held that parties may agree to limit the issues subject to arbitration, to arbitrate according to specific rules, and to limit *with whom* a party will arbitrate its disputes.

The point of affording parties discretion in designing arbitration processes is to allow for efficient, streamlined procedures tailored to the type of dispute. It can be specified, for example, that the decisionmaker be a specialist in the relevant field, or that proceedings be kept confidential to protect trade secrets. And the informality of arbitral proceedings is itself desirable, reducing the cost and increasing the speed of dispute resolution.

California's *Discover Bank* rule interferes with arbitration. Although the rule does not *require* classwide arbitration, it allows any party to a consumer contract to demand it.

[T]he switch from bilateral to class arbitration sacrifices the principal advantage of arbitration—its informality—and makes the process slower, more costly, and more likely to generate procedural morass than final judgment. In bilateral arbitration, parties forgo the procedural rigor and appellate review of the courts in order to realize the benefits of private dispute resolution: lower costs, greater efficiency and speed, and the ability to choose expert adjudicators to resolve specialized disputes. But before an arbitrator may decide the merits of a claim in classwide procedures, he must first decide, for example, whether the class itself may be certified, whether the named parties are sufficiently representative and typical, and how discovery for the class should be conducted. A cursory comparison of bilateral and class arbitration illustrates the difference. According to the American Arbitration Association (AAA), the average consumer arbitration between January and August 2007 resulted in a disposition on the merits in six months, four months if the arbitration was conducted by documents only. As of September 2009, the AAA had opened 283 class arbitrations. Of those, 121 remained active, and 162 had been settled, withdrawn, or dismissed. Not a single one, however, had resulted in a final award on the merits. For those cases that were no longer active, the median time from filing to settlement, withdrawal, or dismissal not judgment on the merits was 583 days, and the mean was 630 days.

Because it stands as an obstacle to the accomplishment and execution of the full purposes and objectives of Congress, California's *Discover Bank* rule is preempted by the FAA. The judgment of the Ninth Circuit is reversed, and the case is remanded for further proceedings consistent with this opinion.

**Business Application:** How do you think many businesses will write their contracts as a result of the Court's decision?

# CHAPTER PROBLEMS

1. Define the following terms and concepts:
    *a.* Jurisdiction
    *b.* Long-arm statute
    *c.* Federal question jurisdiction
    *d.* Diversity of citizenship jurisdiction

*e.* Certiorari

*f.* Class action suit

*g.* Discovery

*h.* Injunction

*i.* Mediation

*j.* Arbitration

## *Business Application*

2. Plastic Corporation manufactures plastic containers sold to bottling companies. The bottling companies fill the containers with liquid and secure them with leakproof caps. John T. purchased from Ace Hardware a bottle of Prevention Plus, a sulfuric acid-based liquid drain unstopper. While carrying the bottle home, it leaked, causing severe bums to John T.'s body. The container was manufactured by Plastic Corporation and the Prevention Plus was bottled by Sure Bottle Company. John T. threatens to sue. Plastic Corporation seeks to hire an attorney. How should Plastic Corporation select an attorney? As a managerial executive in Plastic Corporation, what is your objective in this conflict? Assume that your lawyer informs you that John T. is willing to settle the case for $10,000. What other information do you need to determine whether to settle or not?
3. Al Ladin, attorney for Spray Lawn, Inc., suspected that two of Spray Lawn's lower-echelon employees were diverting the corporation's funds to their own use. Ladin confronted the employees with his suspicions, and they both confessed. At Ladin's insistence, the employees wrote a detailed account of their activities involving the diversion of company funds. Their employment was then terminated. Subsequently, the IRS conducted an audit of Spray Lawn, Inc. and issued a summons for the written statements in Ladin's possession. Must Ladin produce the statements? Explain. Could the IRS derive the information in any other way?
4. Your company is being sued by Tantalus Corporation for breaching a contract to build an air compressor which was to meet specifications contained in the contract. You claim that the air compressor meets the specifications. Tantalus claims that it does not. During discovery, Tantalus subpoenas all your documents and electronically stored information relating to the construction of the air compressor. You have a confidential hardcopy memo from one of your engineers that indicates that certain shortcuts were taken to reduce the cost of constructing the air compressor. Can you turn the memo over to your attorney and then successfully resist Tantalus's discovery request by claiming attorney-client privilege? Explain.
5. UHF, Inc., a citizen of the state of California, manufactured weather insulation. It sold the insulation to contractors who installed it in buildings throughout the United States. The insulation was found to be hazardous to health. Thousands of people suffered injury as a result of being exposed to it. Hundreds of thousands more have been exposed to the insulation, but have no symptoms at this time. What are the potential consequences to UHF, Inc.? Explain.

6. Helicopteros Nacionales de Colombia (Helicol) is a Colombian corporation that has its principal place of business in the city of Bogota. It provides helicopter transportation services for oil and construction companies in South America. Four U.S. citizens were killed when one of Helicol's helicopters crashed in Peru. The crash victims were working for Consorcio/WSH at the time of the crash. Consorcio/WSH was building a pipeline in Peru and needed helicopters to move personnel, materials, and equipment to and from the construction area.

   About two years before the accident, the chief executive officer of Helical traveled to Houston, Texas, and conferred with representatives of Consorcio/WSH. They negotiated a contract later signed in Peru. It stated that controversies arising out of the contract would be decided by the Peruvian courts. It also provided that Consorcio/WSH would make payments to Helicol's bank account with Bank of America in New York. More than $5 million in payments received in these accounts were drawn on a Texas bank. Over an approximately seven-year period, Helicol purchased helicopters and spare parts for more than $4 million from Bell Helicopter Company in Fort Worth. Helical sent pilots for training to Fort Worth. It also sent management and maintenance personnel to visit Bell Helicopter in Fort Worth. Are there sufficient contacts to confer personal jurisdiction over Helicol in Texas? Explain.

7. Asahi Metal Industry, a Japanese manufacturer of tire valve assemblies, sold them to Cheg Shin Rubber Co. in Taiwan. Cheng Shin used the assemblies in making tires, which it distributed worldwide. Asahi knew that its assemblies would be incorporated into tires sold in California and other states.

   Gary Zurcher sued Cheng Shin in the Superior Court in California for injuries he sustained allegedly caused by a defective motor cycle tire manufactured by Cheng Shin. Cheng Shin, through the use of the California long arm statute, sought to add Asahi to the lawsuit, alleging that the valve assembly was defective. Are the contacts with California sufficient for the California court to exercise jurisdiction over Asahi? Why or why not?

8. Professor Ephriam Cross is employed by New York University to teach French, Spanish, and Romance linguistics. He and his wife sailed from New York for France via Portugal, Morocco, Algeria, and Italy. On arriving in Marseilles, they split up. Mrs. Cross continued to tour, and Mr. Cross, though not pursuing a formal course of study, visited schools, courts of law, churches, book publishers, and restaurants; read magazines; listened to radio broadcasts; conversed with students and teachers; and attended political meetings. Cross and his wife returned to New York in time for Cross to resume his teaching schedule at NYU. Cross filed his income tax return and deducted the full cost of the trip he and his wife took to Europe.

   The IRS objected to the deduction and brought suit against Cross, demanding payment of the amount he allegedly underpaid. Cross contended that the deduction was pursuant to the Internal Revenue Code provision that allows deductions for all expenses incurred in carrying on a trade or business. Cross presented affidavits of other professors that indicated the desirability and necessity of foreign travel for a professor of foreign languages. He then moved for summary judgment. Cross contended that the summary judgment was appropriate under the circumstances. Do you agree? What is the criterion for granting a summary judgment? What if Cross listed separately the expenses incurred by his wife and himself and sought to deduct only his own expenses? Would additional information still be required? Explain.

9. Stanford University had a contract with Volt Information Sciences, Inc. to install electric conduit as part of a construction project. The contract contained a broad arbitration clause. Volt billed Stanford for extra work. When Stanford refused to pay, Volt demanded arbitration. Stanford filed a lawsuit against Volt and two companies that designed and managed the construction project. The suit accused Volt of fraud and alleged that the other two companies were responsible for the extra costs and should indemnify Stanford. Stanford's contracts with the other two companies did not have arbitration clauses. Should Stanford be forced to arbitrate the Volt claim? Why or why not?

10. XYZ Corporation is negotiating a contract with Computer Consultants, Inc. (CCI). Under the contract, CCI will provide customized computer programming, software support, and hardware consulting for five years. XYZ will pay an hourly fee. CCI has proposed that the contract require submitting all disputes to arbitration. Should XYZ agree to this? Explain.

PART II

# CIVIL LAW FOUNDATIONS OF THE LEGAL ENVIRONMENT OF BUSINESS

CHAPTER 4

# THE LAW OF PROPERTY

## CHAPTER OUTLINE



## LEARNING OBJECTIVES

After learning this chapter the student should be able to:

- Define property.
- Categorize property as real or personal.
- Compare and contrast lost, stolen, and mislaid property.
- Identify the types of bailments.
- Identify a fixture by applying the appropriate tests.
- Compare and contrast patents, copyrights, and trademarks.
- Differentiate between those processes that are patentable and copyrightable from those that are not.

All around us we are surrounded by "things." From the smallest seed in the ground to the most distant star in the sky, these things occupy our existence. Things have certain properties. They are made up of molecular structures. However, property, in the legal sense, is concerned with relationships—the relationship between a thing and a person. This chapter deals with the law of property. It highlights the definition of property, and then focuses on personal property, real property, and intellectual property. The chapter concludes with an observation about property rights in other countries.

## DEFINITION OF PROPERTY

Property can be thought of as a bundle of rights. This bundle of rights includes the right to possess, use, sell, donate, lease, improve, and destroy property. A distant star does not fit this definition; however, a house, a car, and a patent do.

Property may be real or personal. **Real property** is the land and anything that is permanently attached to land. In contrast, **personal property** is property that has no fixed site but is moveable. Personal property may be further divided into tangible and intangible property. Tangible personal property, such as clothing, frying pans, and airplanes, may be touched. Intangible personal property has no physical being and, as such, may not be touched. It includes stocks, bonds, patent rights, and copyrights.

## PERSONAL PROPERTY

We are dependent upon personal property for our existence. The food we eat, the clothing we wear, and even the bed we sleep in are all personal property. Personal property may be acquired in a number of ways, and may be entrusted to another. The law regarding the acquisition and entrustment of personal property follows.

### *Acquiring Personal Property*

The normal way of acquiring personal property is by purchase. The purchase may be by cash or by credit. However, some acquisitions do not involve an exchange of money. They occur as a matter of law, as, for example, when property is abandoned, lost, stolen, mislaid, or gifted.

#### Abandoned Property

Abandonment occurs when the owner voluntarily and intentionally surrenders property. When this occurs the property is unowned. The next person to appropriate the property owns it. By example, assume that someone places a stuffed animal and a sofa on the curb by the street with the intent of surrendering possession and control. The first person to retrieve them owns this abandoned property.

#### Lost Property

Lost property is property that is involuntarily left somewhere. One who finds lost property has good title to the property against anyone in the world except the true owner. The finder, in fact, has an obligation to return the property to the known owner. Many states have statutes governing the disposition of lost property. Under these statutes, the finder usually becomes the absolute owner of the property after the find is made public, a certain period of time elapses, and the owner fails to claim the property.

### Stolen Property

Property that is stolen is ordinarily treated as lost property. The owner of the property has superior title to the world. A thief does not gain title to the property stolen. However, there is at least one instance where the Uniform Commercial Code (UCC) holds that one who acquires property from a thief becomes the absolute owner.

> **UCC § 2-403(2)**
>
> Any entrusting of possession of goods to a merchant who deals in goods of that kind gives him [or her] power to transfer all rights of the entruster to a buyer in ordinary course of business.

Assume that on Monday, Romeo and his girlfriend Juliet go to Badunov's Jewelry Store to size an engagement ring that was previously purchased by Romeo. Badunov tells them to come back in one week to pick up the ring. On Tuesday, Dick and Liz come into Badunov's in order that Dick may buy Liz a diamond to celebrate their engagement to be married. Badunov sells them Juliet's ring. It fits Liz's hand perfectly. Dick pays for the ring and takes it out of the store. Juliet and Liz, who have been friends since childhood, decide to go out for dinner Saturday night to celebrate their engagements. During dinner, Liz proudly displays her new engagement ring, and Juliet quickly discovers that Liz is wearing Juliet's ring. Between Juliet and Liz, who owns the ring?

Badunov is a thief, and, under common law, cannot convey good title to the ring. Normally, Juliet would be entitled to a return of her ring. However, under Uniform Commercial Code, section 2-403(2), which controls in cases involving the sale of goods, as here, Liz would be the owner of the ring. Naturally, Badunov would be subject to criminal liability, and civil liability to Juliet.

Note that this provision applies only to merchants—those who customarily deal in a particular type of good, including pawn shops. The provision would not apply to the street vendor from whom one would buy a stolen watch. Consumers expect to obtain clear title to items they buy in a store. If a consumer could not have that expectation, retail sales could suffer greatly. The rights of the consumer have been balanced against the rights of the person entrusting goods to merchants. The balance is clearly in favor of the consumer knowing that he or she is getting good title when purchasing an item.

### Mislaid Property

Mislaid property is property that is left somewhere and forgotten. The finder of mislaid property must surrender it to the owner of the premises where it is found. The reason for this requirement is that the owner of mislaid property will eventually remember where he or she left it and return to the premises. The owner of the premises holds the property in trust for the true owner. Finding statutes, in some states, specify the rights and obligations of the true owner, the finder, and the owner of the premises.

### Gifts

Property may also be acquired by gift. A gift occurs when one individual or entity gives something to another person or entity without any value given in return (consideration). Gifts come in a variety of forms. An *inter vivos*, or living gift, is made by a person when the donor is alive and has no expectation of imminent death. When three necessary elements occur, the gift is completed, and irrevocable. First, the donor (or gift giver) must intend to make a gift to a donee (gift receiver). Second, that gift must be delivered to the donee or the donee's agent. Delivery must be either physical, by turning over control of the item to the donee, or may be achieved by giving the donee some evidence of title. For example, a gift of an automobile may be completed by handing over an endorsed certificate of title and the keys, even if the automobile is located elsewhere at the time. Unless the element of delivery is present, there is no gift. Finally, the donee must accept the gift.

A gift *causa mortis* is a gift in contemplation of death in the near future. In this type of gift, intent, delivery, and acceptance are still necessary. However, even when these three elements are present, the gift may still be revocable by the donor. Consider the situation where Carlos is to have major surgery, and has been told that he has only a 30 percent chance of recovering. Carlos gives his watch to his close friend Bruce, telling Bruce he wants him to have the watch if the surgery is unsuccessful and Carlos dies. If Carlos recovers, he can invalidate the gift. He can also revoke the gift for any reason before he dies, and the gift is invalid if the donee (in this case, Bruce) dies before the donor.

A gift may be complete subject to a condition. Under the common law, for example, an engagement ring is a gift to the bride-elect, conditional upon the marriage taking place. Consequently, if the marriage does not occur because of the actions of the bride-elect, no gift occurs and the man gets the ring back. Because of a spate of litigation, many states have now adopted specific statutes that alter the common law rule regarding the status of gifts made in anticipation of marriage.

## *Entrusting Personal Property*

The law governing the entrustment of personal property is known as the *law of bailments.* **A bailment** occurs when one person (the bailor) transfers personal property to another (the bailee) with instructions to return it or otherwise dispose of it. For example, assume that Freda takes her car to a mechanic to have it repaired. Here, a bailment is formed. After the repair, the mechanic is obligated to return the car to Freda. Title to property does not pass by a bailment.

### Types of Bailments

Most bailments are voluntary. However, an involuntary bailment may arise as, for example, when someone finds property that is lost. The finder becomes an involuntary bailee who holds the found property in trust for the owner. An involuntary bailee owes the owner a slight duty of care, and is only liable for damages caused by intentional misconduct or gross negligence.

Another way of classifying bailments is by examining who benefits. Some bailments are solely for the benefit of the bailee. These bailments, sometimes referred to as *gratuitous bailments*, occur when, for example, one person lends a friend a car. Here, the bailee must return the car in the same condition and is liable for damages caused by even slight negligence. The duty here upon the bailee is to exercise extraordinary care. Other bailments are solely for the benefit of the bailor. These occur when a bailee takes possession of property without pay or benefit, but as an accommodation to the bailor, as, for example, when a friend agrees to temporarily store furniture. The bailee here will not be liable for damage to the property unless grossly negligent.

Finally, mutual benefit bailments are the most common. A mutual benefit bailment usually involves a contract for hire, for example, entrusting property to another for repair. Here, the bailor would benefit from having the item repaired, and the bailee would benefit by receiving compensation for the repair. The bailee will be liable for damages that result from a lack of ordinary care.

**Business and Government Interface**

These links, the first from an FTC site and the second from a law firm site, contain information on the compliance standards for representing that a product is made in the USA, and the associated dangers.

http://www.business.ftc.gov/documents/bus03-complying-made-usa-standard

http://www.frostbrowntodd.com/resources-123.html

## Rights and Duties

The rights and duties under a bailment may be part of a contract, express or implied. Any damages that occur as a result of a breach of the agreement may result in liability. However, bailees are often prone to include within the contract an exculpatory clause. An exculpatory clause limits or relieves liability for damages. Courts are apt to strike down such clauses when they are deemed to be against public policy—when there is an unequal bargaining position between the parties. For example, assume that Vera entrusts to Hank's Vehicle Repair a car for the purpose of fixing the brakes. A clause within the contract states that Hank's is not liable for any damage to the car while in its possession. One of Hank's employees negligently rams the car into the gas pump island and damages the front end. Assume further that all the garages in the neighborhood have a similar exculpatory clause within their contracts. A court most likely would strike down the clause and hold Hank's Vehicle Repair liable for the damage due to its employee's negligence.

Generally, in absence of specification, the bailee is entitled to reasonable compensation for the work done or for storage. The bailor is entitled to a return of the goods in substantially the same condition as when first received.

## Special Bailments

Innkeepers, common carriers, and warehousers are deemed professional bailees, and, in addition to the ordinary rules of bailment, are subject to special rules. Innkeepers operate inns, hotels, motels, and lodges. At the common law, innkeepers were strictly liable for the loss or damage to personal property of their guests. This rule has been modified in many states that place a limit on liability, for example, $1,000.

**Understanding the Private Law Sector**

This Michigan State University link to an article highlights an inconsistency in the law of bailments when pets are delivered to their veterinarian for treatment.

https://www.animallaw.info/article/bailment-and-veterinary-malpractice-doctrinal-exclusivity-not

A common carrier is in the business of transporting goods. Common carriers must serve the public on a nondiscriminatory basis and are strictly liable for damage or loss of goods. The common carrier is, in that sense, an insurer of the property. There are some exceptions: acts of God, of war, or of public authorities; the bailor's negligence; or the natural spoilage or deterioration of the goods. Additionally, by clear terms in a contract, common carriers may limit their liability.

A warehouse company stores property for others. It is usually subject to extensive state and local fire, health, and safety regulations. Like the common carrier, it may limit its liability.

**Business Application/Ethical Issues**

Heart Felt is the President of Hi-Fly, Inc., which owns a plant in the United States that produces high performance stunt kites. They come in various styles, shapes, colors and aerodynamic models. Their packaging says, "Made in the USA." In fact, the entire kite is assembled and packaged in a plant in Hope, Arizona. Of the 27 parts that comprise their Model 5X kite, 25 are manufactured in the Hope plant. Two small rings situated on the bridle of the kite can adjust the performance of the kite by moving the rings closer or farther from the nose. These rings are ordered from a U.S. supplier who purchases them from Taiwan. The total cost of the kite's parts is $89.00 and it sells for $199.00. The two rings cost $.14 each.

Every state that has a law concerning labeling of products "Made in USA," except California, requires only that the product be substantially made in the United States. California requires that all parts of any product that bears a "Made in the USA" representation must be made wholly in the United States.

Hi-Fly's in-house attorney informs Felt about the California law. Consequently, Felt orders his production manager to come into compliance with the law. In the meantime he is hoping that the company will not be caught with the inventory already in the stores in California. He feels it is an unfair law to require 100% compliance. Yet, he is intent on complying, and says, "If we get caught in the meantime, then we will do the right thing and pay the fine."

What are the ethical issues? What are Felt's alternatives?

## REAL PROPERTY

Real property is comprised of land and every thing that is attached to land. As such, it consists of air, surface, and subsurface rights. The old theory was that a landowner owned from his or her property straight up to the heavens and straight down to the center of the earth. With the advent of air transportation and modem methods of excavation, this theory was not very pragmatic and, hence, fell into disuse, in favor of the reasonable use theory. The property owner owns everything above and below the land that he or she may reasonably use. This is an attempt to balance the competing interests of members of society.

This section considers the law of fixtures (which is a way of determining whether an article is personal or part of the real estate), the law of estates and of concurrent interests in an estate.

### *Fixtures*

A **fixture** is personal property that has been affixed to the realty in such a manner as to become part of the realty. For example, a kitchen sinktop is personal property when it is carried into the kitchen to be installed. After installation, it is considered a fixture and it is part of the real estate.

Fixtures pass with real estate by deed whereas personal property does not. It is also important to distinguish between fixtures and personal property for purposes of insurance claims. For example, assume that an insured house burns to the ground. If the carpeting is a fixture, it will be covered for real property insurance purposes; but, if it is personal property, then it would not. Additionally, there is a difference in taxing of the property, depending upon whether it is deemed personal or real.

The controlling test of whether an item is a fixture is the intent of the attacher. The law has three tests to determine this intent—annexation, adaptation, and relation tests.

### Annexation

When an item is attached to the real estate in such a manner that it would cause damage to sever it or leave it in an unfinished condition, then it is probably a fixture. Built-in medicine cabinets, wall-to-wall carpeting, light fixtures, antennas, and permanent fences are examples. Throw rugs, davenports, and stacked timber do not meet this definition, and are probably personal property.

### Adaptation

When an item that is not physically attached nonetheless is specifically adapted to the real estate, it is deemed a fixture. Hence, rugs that are not tacked down but are custom cut would be considered a fixture under the adaptation test. Custom-made storm windows or an air conditioner specially modified to accommodate a window meet the adaptation test and hence are fixtures.

### Relation

In cases where it is difficult to come to a conclusion based upon the annexation and adaptation test, the relation test may tip the balance. Under the relation test, the law prefers purchasers over sellers and tenants over landlords. For example, consider an air conditioning unit, installed by the owner, that has been occupying a window for several years. Assume further, the owner sells the house. In favoring the buyer the law presumes that the intent of the seller when affixing the unit was that it be part of the house. The air conditioner, hence, would pass to the buyer by the deed, as it would be considered a fixture. However, in the event that a tenant installed the same air conditioner in an apartment, the law would favor the interpretation that the tenant did not intend for the air conditioner to become a fixture. As such, the tenant would be entitled to remove and retain it after the termination of the lease. As in most cases a written agreement clearly characterizing the item goes a long way to avoid ambiguity.

**Decision Making in the Legal Environment**

This link from a Chicago Tribune article contains practical information about the law of fixtures in relation to what is included in the sales price of a home and what is not.

https://www.chicagotribune.com/news/ct-xpm-1996-11-09-9611090182-story.html

## *Trade Fixtures*

The law of fixtures relating to business use of property is different than it is for residences. Often, a business must make significant improvement to a property in order to be able to use it effectively. A pizza parlor, for example, must install ovens, bolting them to the floor and venting them through the roof, creating a hole in the roof. A restaurant may install a walk-in cooler that attaches to the floor and/or walls. If the law of fixtures were to be applied in the same manner to both businesses and residences, businesses could be at a severe disadvantage in trying to do business, knowing that if they change location they lose all their business fixtures. Business fixtures are known as *trade fixtures*, and the business tenant is allowed to remove them prior to the expiration of the lease. The business tenant does have the obligation, however, to restore the property to its original condition once the personal property has been removed. For instance, the pizza parlor owner would have to repair the ceiling and roof once the pizza ovens were removed.

## *Estates and Interests*

Estates are interests in real property. Some, like the fee simple absolute, fee tail, life estate, and leaseholds are possessory estates, while easements, profits and licenses are nonpossessory interests. Each is discussed.

### Fee Simple Absolute

The **fee simple absolute** is the greatest quantum of interest that one may own in real property. The owner of a fee simple absolute estate may use the property as he or she sees fit, subject to local zoning laws, nuisance laws, and other laws of the municipality and state in which the property is located. One who owns a fee simple has the fullest interest in the bundle of rights, and, as such, has the power to sell, lease, improve, destroy, and pass the property to heirs. The fee owner may transfer less than the fee interest in the property to other entities without giving up the whole fee simple interest. For example, Tom purchases a parcel of property with a building on it. He gives the right to farm the land to his brother-in-law and he leases the building to Ichabod's Insurance Company for three years, but he still owns the fee. Most property today is owned in fee simple absolute.

### Fee Tail

The fee tail passes the property from lineal generation to generation. It promotes family wealth, since the property is kept in the family. A transfer in fee tail is accomplished by transfer "to the grantee and the heirs of his or her body." This would continue the property to the lineal descendants. The property is not very marketable as a result. Hence, most states have abolished the fee tail or have afforded ways where it may be converted to a fee simple absolute.

### Life Estate

A life estate is an interest in land. It is a right of use and enjoyment of land as measured by the life of that person or another person. At the death of the person whose life determines the length of the estate, the fee simple interest reverts to the grantor or to others, known as *remaindermen*. Holders of life estates may not do any act to damage or cause a decrease in the value of the land.

### Leaseholds

A leasehold is an interest in land created by a contract called a *lease*. The tenant, or lessee, obtains the right to use the property for a specific purpose, usually for a specified period of time, in return for a periodic cash payment, known as *rent*, paid to the landlord, or lessor. A lease may apply to a residential unit or to commercial property. Lease provisions vary widely. For example, a residential lease may require the lessor to make all repairs and the lessee to pay a specified fee in dollars per month for rent. A commercial lease may provide that the tenant makes all repairs, and may further provide that the tenant pay a percentage of the real estate taxes on the leased property. In a commercial lease, other provisions may specify that the lessee must stay open for business a given number of hours each day, and that the lessee must pay a specified percentage of gross sales to the lessor, in lieu of rent, or in addition to a base rent.

Leases terminate at the expiration of the term. If no term is stated and rent is payable periodically, the lease is terminable upon giving one full period's notice. When the lease ends, possession of the property reverts to the owner.

### Easements

An easement gives a right to use the land of another for a specified purpose, but not to possess the land. As an example, Paul may give Art an easement to drive across the back of Paul's paved parking lot so that Art may have access to another street. Easements may be bought or sold, or may be created at the time of transfer of the fee from one owner to another. Easements can also be implied by law. Assume, for example, that Ginger sells half of her land to Fred, and that Fred's portion of the land has no access to a street. The law will imply an easement allowing Fred the right to gain access to the street by driving over Ginger's property.

### Profits and Licenses

A profit gives one a right to remove something from another's land, such as trees or oil. While a profit is an interest in the land, a license is not. A license is a right to enter land for a particular purpose. For example, a license may grant an individual a right to play 18 holes of golf on the owner's course or to watch a movie in a theater.

## *Co-Ownership of Property*

Ownership of real property is often shared by two or more individuals or other entities such as partnerships, corporations, or trusts. There are various methods of holding concurrently. They include tenancy-in-common, joint tenancy and tenancy by the entireties, community property, condominiums, and cooperatives. Each is discussed.

### Tenancy-in-Common

In a tenancy-in-common, each co-owner has an undivided fractional interest in the property. The potential interests need not be equal. Each tenant-in-common has a right to possess the property. One tenant-in-common may sell his or her share to another entity without affecting the existence of the tenancy-in-common.

Tenancies-in-common may also be used in time sharing agreements, where property is shared by a number of people, each having the right to use that property for a defined period each year. For example, 52 people may each have the right to use of an estate in Palm Beach, Florida, for one week each year. These people are tenants-in-common. They may sell their interests without disturbing the tenancy-in-common.

When a tenant-in-common dies, his or her share passes to heirs. If disputes arise as to the benefits from, or use of, the property among the co-tenants, a *partition* action may be undertaken in the courts. In such an action the court will either physically divide up the property among the co-tenants, or will order the sale of the property, with proceeds to be divided among the co-tenants according to their proportional share of ownership. If no particular type of relationship between co-tenants is specified in the deed, the law will ordinarily imply the existence of a tenancy-in-common.

### Joint Tenancy and Tenancy by the Entireties

Each joint tenant owns an equal undivided share in the property. Upon the death of one joint tenant, his or her share passes to the other joint tenants. A joint tenancy will be terminated if one joint tenant conveys all or a part of his or her interest to another party, or if that interest is sold by a creditor to satisfy a debt. In either of those events, the remaining owners will then be tenants-in-common.

A form of joint tenancy, between husband and wife, called a *tenancy by the entireties*, is allowable in some states. This tenancy, like a joint tenancy, has a right of survivorship feature, so that when one spouse dies, the other immediately becomes sole owner of the property. Unlike the joint tenancy, however, neither party may sell his or her share without the consent of the other, nor may a creditor sever the tenancy to satisfy the debt of one of the spouses. Should the husband and wife sever the marriage relationship, the tenancy by the entireties ceases to exist. Because of a couple's ability to shield their real property from creditors through the tenancy by the entireties, many states have abolished this type of co-ownership.

### Community Property

Some jurisdictions, including California, Texas, and a number of southern states, are community property states. Under this type of ownership, each spouse owns half of all property, real or personal, acquired by the efforts of either spouse during the marriage. Property owned by a spouse prior to marriage, or acquired with the proceeds of separate property owned by that spouse, remains the individual property of that spouse.

### Condominiums

In a condominium, individuals own units of a larger parcel in fee simple, and are tenants-in-common with other owners in the parcel as to common areas such as elevators, swimming pools, and land. The individual owners also share the costs of maintaining the common areas. Since owners own their units in fee simple, they have the right to mortgage their property interests or the right to transfer title to their units.

The developer of the condominium records a Declaration of Condominium, which describes the land on which the condominium is to be developed, and includes rules for how the condominium is to operate. For example, the bylaws may provide that all owners must be at least 55 years of age, and that no individual under 18 years of age is allowed to live in the condominium more than a specified number of days each year. Once a certain number of units are sold, the unit owners form their own condominium association which governs the affairs of the condominium.

### Co-Operative

A co-operative, or co-op, is usually established for an apartment or office building. The building in question is owned by one entity, such as a corporation. Individuals purchase shares in the corporation, which allows them the right to lease units in the co-operative. The bylaws of the corporation establish the rights and duties of tenants, and control the rights these shareholder-tenants have to sublease their unit or transfer their share in the corporation to others. A share in the co-operative is not an ownership interest in land; consequently, the shareholders cannot obtain a mortgage loan to finance the purchase of their units.

### Timeshares

Timeshares are a popular form of ownership whereby multiple individuals share rights to use the resort property; each will be allocated a time slot, for example a fixed week during the year. Timeshares come in all types of variations. The time units may be for one week every other year; may change pursuant to a rotating schedule each year; be fractional parts of the week; or other creative time divisions depending upon the particular timeshare program. The purchaser may hold the timeshare in fee simple absolute; it may be a lease; or a right to use only for a fixed number of years, with no ownership interest. Other forms of timeshares may be held in perpetuity.

**Understanding the Private Law Sector**

This link to a Washington Post article examines the differences between condos and cooperatives.

http://www.washingtonpost.com/realestate/condos-vs-co-ops-whats-the-difference/2013/04/25/f673e29c-a5e6-11e2-b029-8fb7e977ef71_story.html

In an attempt to meet the flexible needs and objections of the buyer, the points program has become very popular. The purchaser buys a time unit and depending upon the location and the size earns points. These points may be exchanged for timeshare units in any number of locations or even for airfare and auto rentals.

There are secondary markets where timeshares are resold. Because of the increasing costs of maintenance and management fees, many purchasers wind up with buyer's remorse; or tire on the financial drain and the pressure of utilizing the property at time-fixed intervals. As such, timeshares are sold on the secondary market at greatly reduced prices; and some sell for as little as $1.00, with the proviso that the purchaser pays all the periodic fees.

The resale market opens up the opportunity for brokers to market timeshares for those who want out and to find buyers who want in. As the next case illustrates timeshare resales may be the target of fraudulent activity.

**UNITED STATES OF AMERICA *v.* FREEMAN**

Seventh Circuit Court of Appeal

No 16-1419 (7th Cir. Ct of Appeal 2016)

Gilbert Freeman pleaded guilty to five counts of wire fraud based on his participation in a large-scale scheme that bilked hundreds of people out of their savings by pretending to assist them in selling their Mexican-based timeshare properties. The scheme was built upon multiple fictitious companies, including some that purportedly worked with corporate buyers, and a fake escrow company. The timeshares were never actually sold, and none of the costs or fees extracted from the timeshare owners were ever refunded. More than 1,400 victims were defrauded out of more than $4.8 million. Dozens of people contributed to the fraudulent activities, with as many as 15 employees actively working at one time. Freeman, charged with 13 counts of wire fraud, pleaded guilty to five of those counts pursuant to a plea deal. He admitted that his role in the scheme included obtaining lists of timeshare owners, helping to create websites and advertising for the fake companies, and opening bank accounts for these companies into which victims would transfer money.

At sentencing evidence was presented showing that Freeman, along with another person named Moe, led the scheme. The evidence included email conversations between co-schemers, grand jury testimony from co-defendants and other former employees, and statements in co-defendants' plea agreements. This evidence showed that Freeman presented himself to others as being in charge of the organization and that employees viewed him as their boss. It suggested that he handled employee complaints and adjusted employee pay. The evidence also showed that Freeman had the power to recruit employees, hire contractors, direct employees' actions, and approve inter-office procedures. Freeman and Moe received the largest cut of the profits.

In the Presentence Investigation Report (or PSR), the probation officer recommended a four-level enhancement under the sentencing guidelines based on Freeman's role as "an organizer or leader of a criminal activity that involved five or more participants." That enhancement contributed to raising Freeman's sentencing guideline range from 135 to 168 months to 210 to 262 months. In Freeman's initial sentencing memorandum (prepared by former counsel), he agreed that he had been a leader in the scheme. Later Freeman obtained new counsel and retracted his earlier acceptance of the leadership characterization.

In the sentencing hearings the TRIAL judge found that Freeman was a leader; as support for that finding, she also deemed it significant that Freeman previously had agreed that he was the co-leader. The judge also noted that she had looked into the issue further and concluded that "there is certainly plenty of evidence to support the probation office's conclusion that [Freeman] does merit the leadership enhancement." After she settled on the proper guidelines range, the judge considered the factors outlined in [the statute] and sentenced Freeman to 240 months' imprisonment.

### *Diane P. Wood, Chief Judge and William J. Bauer, and Diane S. Sykes, Circuit Judges*

* * *

On appeal Freeman challenges only the court's decision to apply the leadership enhancement. . . . The evidence was unreliable, he says, because it consists primarily of grand jury statements and plea agreements of "biased" co-defendants and is . . . "unsubstantiated hearsay without corroboration." Neither of those points goes anywhere. A court may use any evidence at sentencing, as long as it is sufficiently reliable, even if it would be inadmissible at trial. A defendant is entitled to challenge the information's reliability, but if he offers only a bare denial of that information with nothing more (which is all that Freeman has done), then the government has no obligation to bolster its reliability. Freeman also argues that he was deprived of the chance to show that the information was unreliable because he could not cross-examine the co-defendants about their statements. That would concern us more if Freeman had offered any reason to doubt the reliability of the co-defendants' testimony. But he has not, and without such evidence, the district court was free to rely on those statements. As the government points out, the statements of the various co-defendants were not inconsistent, and some of the information was corroborated by other evidence, including emails and statements of other employees.

Next Freeman argues that the evidence was insufficient to establish that he was a "leader" as that term has been interpreted under [the sentencing guidelines]. He contends that a defendant must exercise control and authority over others for the leadership adjustment to apply and that no evidence shows that he had any ability to coerce or direct any other participant in the scheme. . . . While the question of a person's control over others is an important factor in determining whether the person is a leader, the focus of the inquiry is on the relative culpability of the defendant as compared to others involved in the scheme. A more culpable defendant "ought to receive the harsher organizer/leader enhancement. In evaluating a person's role in a scheme, the court may consider all of the factors . . . including the exercise of decision making authority, the nature of participation in the commission of the offense, the recruitment of accomplices, the claimed right to a larger share of the fruits of the crime, the degree of participation in planning or organizing the offense, the nature and scope of the illegal activity, and the degree of control and authority exercised over others.

. . . Freeman made decisions about company management; he used his name for many of the fake companies and bank accounts required to run the scheme; he recruited other members; he and Moe received the largest share of the profits; he was included in many emails about top management decisions; he participated in the scheme over the course of several years and across international borders; and he was viewed by others in the scheme as having control. Substantial evidence showed that Freeman exercised actual control over other people. He controlled aspects of employee payment, gave employees specific tasks to complete, and, along with Moe, held veto power over operating procedures. "[A] defendant exercises control and authority over another when he 'tells people what to do and determines whether they've done it.'"

Because Freeman has failed to show either that the evidence supporting the leadership adjustment was insufficient or unreliable, or that there were any procedural flaws in the sentencing process, we AFFIRM the judgment of the district court.

**Business Application:** In assessing whether Freeman was a "leader," discuss which comports better with business realities: the "control" or "relative culpability" tests.

# INTELLECTUAL PROPERTY

Intellectual property deals with rights of individuals and businesses in applied ideas. For example, an author's idea may be translated into, and published as, a novel. The law of intellectual property does not protect the physical book itself. Stealing the book does not violate the author's intellectual property rights. Use of the plot and characters of the novel in a movie, however, does constitute misappropriation of the author's intellectual property.

Intellectual property is a form of intangible personal property. It includes several rather distinct areas of the law. Patents, copyrights, and trademarks are traditional areas of intellectual property rights. Each is discussed.

**Business and Government Interface**

From the World Intellectual Property Organization (WIPO) this link imparts a summary of what you need to know about intellectual property rights.

http://www.wipo.int/about-ip/en/

## *Patents*

> **U.S. Constitution, Art. I § 8**
>
> Congress shall have the power: "To promote the Progress of Science and useful Arts, by securing for limited Times to Authors and Inventors the exclusive Right to their respective Writings and Discoveries."

**Patents** are authorized by the U.S. Constitution. A patent is a limited monopoly to make, use, and sell an invention, granted by the government. To encourage innovation and technology, the government generally grants an inventor a 20-year monopoly on an invention, provided an application is filed, making public disclosure of the details of the invention.

### Patentable Subject Matter

Patents are obtainable on an invention that is novel and useful, and that falls under one or more classes listed in the federal statute. Specifically, the statute authorizes patents for any processes, machines, manufacture, composition of matter, or improvement on one of these classes. In addition, specific statutory provisions authorize patents on designs, asexually reproduced plants and even genetically engineered bacteria.

The following case takes up the question of whether the process of cloning sheep is patentable.

**IN RE: ROSLIN INSTITUTE (EDINBURGH)**
United States Court of Appeals
750 F. 3d 1333 (Fed. Cir. 2014)

Keith Henry Stockman Campbell and Ian Wilmut successfully produced the first mammal ever cloned from an adult somatic cell: Dolly the Sheep. The cloning method Campbell and Wilmut used to create Dolly constituted a breakthrough in scientific discovery. Known as somatic cell nuclear transfer, this process involves removing the nucleus of a somatic cell and implanting that nucleus into an enucleated (i.e., without a nucleus) oocyte. A somatic cell is any body cell other than gametes (egg or sperm). An oocyte is a female gametocyte (an egg cell prior to maturation), and a nucleus is the organelle that holds a cell's genetic material (its DNA).

Once the nucleus of a somatic, donor cell is removed, that nucleus is fused with an oocyte, which develops into an embryo. The embryo can then be implanted into a surrogate mammal, where it develops into a baby animal. The resulting cloned animal is an exact genetic replica of the adult mammal from which the somatic cell nucleus was taken.

Campbell and Wilmut obtained a patent on the somatic method of cloning mammals, which it assigned to Roslin Institute of Edinburgh, Scotland. The examiner issued a nonfinal rejection of Campbell's and Wilmut's patent claims because she found that they were directed to nonstatutory subject matter under 35 U.S.C. § 101. The Patent Board affirmed the examiner's rejection of Campbell's and Wilmut's claims. It concluded that the claimed subject matter was ineligible for patent protection under § 101 because it constituted a natural phenomenon that did not possess "markedly different characteristics than any found in nature."

Roslin Institute appealed the decision of the Patent Board. The Federal Circuit Court of Appeals affirmed the Board decision.

### *Circuit Judge Dyk*

* * *

. . . [N]aturally occurring organisms are not patentable.

* * *

Accordingly, discoveries that possess "markedly different characteristics from any found in nature," . . . are eligible for patent protection. In contrast, any existing organism or newly discovered plant found in the wild is not patentable.

* * *

While Roslin does not dispute that the donor sheep whose genetic material was used to create Dolly could not be patented, Roslin contends that copies (clones) are eligible for protection because they are "the product of human ingenuity" and "not nature's handiwork, but [their] own." Roslin argues that such copies are either compositions of matter or manufactures within the scope of § 101. However, Dolly herself is an exact genetic replica of another sheep and does not possess "markedly different characteristics from any [farm animals] found in nature. Dolly's genetic identity to her donor parent renders her unpatentable.

* * *

However, Roslin argues that its claimed clones are patent eligible because they are distinguishable from the donor mammals used to create them. First, Roslin contends that "environmental factors" lead to phenotypic differences that distinguish its clones from their donor mammals. A phenotype refers to all the observable characteristics of an organism, such as shape, size, color, and behavior, that result from the interaction of the organism's genotype with its environment. A mammal's phenotype can change constantly throughout the life of that organism not only due to environmental changes, but also the physiological and morphological changes associated with aging.

Roslin argues that environmental factors lead to phenotypic differences between its clones and their donor mammals that render their claimed subject matter patentable. . . . Contrary to Roslin's arguments, these phenotypic differences do not confer eligibility on their claimed subject matter. Any phenotypic differences between Roslin's donor mammals and its claimed clones are the result of "environmental factors."

Second, Roslin urges that its clones are distinguishable from their original donor mammals because of differences in mitochondrial DNA, which originates from the donor oocyte rather than the donor nucleus. . . . Mitochondria possess their own DNA, which is distinct from the DNA housed in the cell's nucleus. In the cloning process, the clone inherits its mitochondrial DNA from its donor oocyte, instead of its donor somatic cell. Therefore, Dolly's mitochondrial

DNA came from the oocyte used to create her, not her donor mammary cell. Roslin argues that this difference in mitochondrial DNA renders its product claims patent eligible.

. . . Roslin's patent application does not identify how differences in mitochondrial DNA influence or could influence the characteristics of cloned mammals. . . .

There is nothing in the claims, or even in the specification, that suggests that the clones are distinct in any relevant way from the donor animals of which they are copies. . . . To be clear, having the same nuclear DNA as the donor mammal may not necessarily result in patent ineligibility in every case. Here, however, the claims do not describe clones that have markedly different characteristics from the donor animals of which they are copies.

Finally, Roslin argues that its clones are patent eligible because they are time-delayed versions of their donor mammals, and therefore different from their original mammals. But this distinction cannot confer patentability. As the Board noted, "[t]he difficulty with the time-delayed characteristic is that it is true of any copy of an original." Thus, we affirm the Board's finding that Roslin's clones are unpatentable subject matter under § 101.

AFFIRMED.

**Business Application:** How might Roslin now seek to protect his "invention" outside of patent protection?

### Procedure to Obtain a Patent

The process for obtaining a patent can be long and expensive. An inventor must prepare and file an application in the United States Patent Office. To comply with the Constitutional mandate, the application must fully describe the invention. The description must have sufficient detail such that upon expiration of the inventor's limited monopoly the invention may be reproduced by others.

The Patent Office examines the application to be sure that it is new and useful, and that it falls within one of the statutory classes. Not every development by an inventor rises to the level of an "invention." The Patent Office over the years has developed the objective test of **non-obviousness.** The question posed is, would the development described in the application have been obvious to the ordinarily skilled worker in the art at the time the "invention" was made? If it would have been obvious, the development is not patentable. Only those developments that represent a real step forward rise to the level of invention.

The Patent Office is an administrative agency under the Department of Commerce. An applicant dissatisfied with any decision by the patent examiner is entitled to an appeal within the agency to the Patent Office Board of Appeals, and, if dissatisfied with the decision of the board, may appeal to the Court of Appeals for the Federal Circuit, a special appellate level federal court that has jurisdiction in all patent matters.

### Patent Owner's Rights

The patent statutes give the owner of a patent the exclusive right to make, use, and sell the invention. The application for a patent must be filed by the individual who made the invention. However, the inventor may assign (transfer ownership) all or any part of the patent rights to another individual or entity. Employees of a company, who work in technical areas, generally sign, at the time of employment, an agreement surrendering to their employer all rights to any inventions made during the course of their employment.

A license involves the transfer of rights under a patent, without transferring ownership. The owner of a patent may license one company to manufacture the patented product, while retaining the right to sell the product. Or, in the reverse, the inventor may manufacture the product and license someone else to sell the product.

Licenses may be either exclusive or nonexclusive. Under an exclusive license, only a single person or entity has the exclusive right; not even the inventor or patent owner retains a right to manufacture. A nonexclusive license, on the other hand, gives the patent holder the right to invest other entities, including itself, with similar rights under the patent.

The owner of a patent may enforce patent rights through a suit for patent infringement filed in the federal courts. If successful, the patent owner is entitled to statutory damages, which include actual damages (at least in the amount of a reasonable royalty), which may be trebled, and attorney fees, as well as an injunction ordering the infringing party to stop the infringing activity.

## *Copyrights*

A **copyright,** like a patent, is a limited monopoly that finds its origin in Article I, Section 8 of the U.S. Constitution. While the Constitution speaks in terms of writings and authors, copyright protection today covers a very broad span of business and the creative arts. Copyright law is governed exclusively by a federal statute.

The statute lists specific classes of copyrightable works, for example, literary works; musical works; dramatic works; choreographic works; pictorial, graphic, and sculptural works; motion pictures and other audiovisual works; sound recordings; and architectural works. At the same time, the statute expressly excludes copyright protection for any idea, procedure, system, method of operation, concept, principle, or discovery.

### Procedure to Obtain a Copyright

The procedure for obtaining a copyright is very different from the procedure involved in patenting an invention. Copyright protection is obtained by publication of the work with the statutory notice, which is the word *copyright*, its abbreviation *copr.*, or the international copyright symbol ©, followed by the year of first publication, and the name of the owner of the copyright. The copyright is perfected by filing an application to register the copyright, along with copies of the work, in the copyright office in Washington, D.C.

### Copyright Owner's Rights

The statute provides that the copyright owner has the exclusive right to do and to authorize reproduction of the copyrighted work, distribution of copies or phonorecords of the work to the public, and public performance or display of the work. The major limitation upon the exclusive rights is the doctrine of fair use, which permits limited use of the copyrighted work for purposes such as criticism, news reporting, teaching, or research.

Licensing of copyrights is very much like assignment and licensing of patents. Like patents, the various rights granted by the statute may be divided up in licensing arrangements.

The copyright statute provides one major exception to the general rules of licensing. Specifically, if the owner of a music copyright permits a recording to be made and distributed, then anyone is free to make their own recording, provided the copier pays the royalty provided by statute. These are known as the *compulsory licensing provisions* of the copyright law.

The statutory remedies for copyright infringement include actual damages to the copyright holder, punitive damages, profits of the infringer, temporary and permanent injunctive relief, and impoundment and disposition (usually destruction) of the infringing articles.

## *Trademarks*

While patents and copyrights have their origin in the U.S. Constitution, and are both the exclusive domain of federal statutory law, **trademarks** originate in the common law, and involve both federal and state law. Federal involvement with trademarks is limited to cases affecting "interstate commerce."

The federal law of trademarks is codified in the Lanham Act, which defines a trademark as "... any word, name, symbol, or device or any combination thereof adopted and used by a manufacturer or merchant to identify his goods and distinguish them from those manufactured or sold by others." For example, look at the following list of trademarks: Old Spice®, Kool Aid®, Tylenol®, Kleenex®, Q-tips®, and Listerine®. These are immediately recognizable.

These trademarks are identifiable, and carry with them some concept of quality and performance. Even if people do not know the specific manufacturer, they buy the brand because of its known reputation for quality. Thus, the trademark is the basis for the purchase decision.

At the state level, trademark laws vary rather widely. Many states have adopted broad protection for trademarks, while other states offer more limited protection. Obviously, state protection is operative only within the bounds of a given state, and hence all but local companies opt for federal trademark protection. The balance of our discussion of trademarks will be limited to the Lanham Act and the federal law of trademarks.

**TABLE 4-1 Trademarks**

| *Trademark* | *Product* | *Owner* |
|---|---|---|
| Old Spice® | Deodorant | Shulton |
| Kool Aid® | Powdered drink mix | General Foods |
| Tylenol® | Pain medication | McNeil PPC |
| Kleenex® | Facial tissues | Kimberly-Clark |
| Q-tips® | Cotton-tipped swabs | Chesebrough |
| Listerine® | Mouthwash | Warner Lambert |

### Classification of Trademarks

Trademarks may be categorized in several ways. They may be classified by form (word marks, symbol or design marks, or composite marks), by use (use on a product, use on a service, or use as a certification), or by relative strength. It is this last classification that is most important to the businessperson in understanding the nature and scope of trademark protection.

A *generic* mark is one employing the common descriptive name for a product. For example, the term *carbonated* is the generic term for a beverage having carbonation. This is the weakest of marks. No one is permitted exclusive rights in a generic term.

A *descriptive* mark is one that merely describes the product or qualities of the product to which it is applied. For example, a bakery might employ the trademark "Oven-Fresh" on its goods. Because the term *oven-fresh* is simply descriptive of the qualities of baked goods, it would be unfair to permit any one merchant to develop exclusive rights in the mark. Thus, anyone in the bakery business is free to use this descriptive term. A merchant can use such a phrase as a trademark, but will be unable to develop any exclusive rights in the mark.

A *suggestive* mark is one that may suggest the product or the qualities of the product to which it is applied, but yet is not merely descriptive of that product. If a term requires imagination, thought, or perception to reach a conclusion as to the nature of the goods, it is "suggestive." For example, the Second Circuit Court of Appeals held that "Roach Motel" was a suggestive mark when used on an insect trap. Hence, suggestive marks are stronger than descriptive ones.

A trademark is considered *arbitrary* if it is a new word, or if it is a common word that has no relation whatsoever to the product to which it is applied. For example, the well-known trademark Kodak® is arbitrary. It is a combination of five letters that has no independent meaning at all. A more subtle example would be Ivory®. You can look in any dictionary and find a number of standard definitions for the word *ivory.* However, as applied to soap, the mark is considered "arbitrary." In the trademark sense, arbitrary trademarks are the strongest.

The federal statute that is controlling provides that a mark that is not arbitrary may be registered only if it can be shown that ". . . the mark has become distinctive of applicant's goods in commerce." Such a showing is called **secondary meaning.** In reality, it means that through widespread, continuous, and exclusive use, a particular mark has developed a new or secondary meaning in which it serves to identify the specific goods of a particular merchant. One such example would be "Apple," of which the primary meaning is a type of fruit but a secondary meaning relates to a brand of computers.

### Federal Registration and Remedies

Under the common law, trademark rights were acquired by adopting a mark and applying it to goods sold in the trade. As originally codified in the Lanham Act, use of the mark in commerce was required before an application could be filed to register the mark.

The Lanham Act provides for registration of trademarks in the United States Patent Office. An application for registration is filed, and examined by the Patent Office to be sure that all statutory conditions are met. Specifically, the Patent Office ensures that generic marks are not registered, and that nonarbitrary marks are registered only if an appropriate showing of secondary meaning is provided.

**Business and Government Interface**

This United States Patent and Trademark Office link helps the student understand the trademark protection process.

http://www.uspto.gov/trademarks/process/index.jsp

When the examiner is satisfied with the application, the mark is published for opposition. An official publication of the United States Patent Office lists all marks that have been passed by the trademark examiners, and anyone who may be damaged by registration of the mark is entitled to file an opposition. This is a contested administrative proceeding, adjudicated by the Patent Office. The amendments to the Lanham Act in 1988 provided for the first time an opportunity to register a mark based upon "intent to use." This provision had been widely sought by major corporations who wished to establish their trademark position prior to actually putting a product on the market with a new trademark.

Registration provides many major advantages to the trademark owner. First, it provides constructive notice throughout the entire country of the trademark user's claim to rights in the mark. In other words, if a small firm starts operations in the Pacific Northwest, registration will give the firm nationwide protection for its mark. Second, after six years of continuous use following registration, the mark becomes "incontestable." This incontestability gives the trademark owner significant procedural advantages to enforce rights in the mark. And finally, the statutory remedies become available in enforcement.

**Business and Government Interface**

This link, an excerpt from a U.S. Department of State publication, contains a concise guide to international property rights treaties and protection.

http://iipdigital.usembassy.gov/st/english/publication/2008/04/20080429214132myleen5.741519e-02.html#axzz3AQRfLzFz

Under the Lanham Act, the trademark owner may bring an action for infringement seeking the statutory remedies of treble damages, attorney fees, and destruction of infringing labels. The fundamental issue in a trademark infringement action is likelihood of confusion. Where the marks are the same, and the goods on which they are used are the same, the issue is clear. However, when either the marks or the goods are different, the issue becomes much more difficult, and takes into account the strength of the mark, the similarity of the marks, the similarity of the goods upon which the marks are used, the similarity of the channels of distribution, and evidence, if any, of actual confusion. For example, Coca-Cola was able to stop a competitor from using the mark "LaCoq" on soft drinks. Even though the marks look different, they sound very similar, and Coke® is a very strong mark. The owner of the mark Johnny Walker® for whiskey was able to stop use of the identical mark on shoes. Again, the court found the mark to be very strong and accorded protection, even though the goods were very dissimilar.

## INTERNATIONAL PROPERTY RIGHTS

With the increase of multinational companies—those doing business in more than one country—there is a concomitant concern about protecting intellectual property. Patents, copyrights, and trademarks are afforded great protection in this country; however, not every country's laws are as protective. Some countries do have adequate protection. The United States does have patent, trademark, and copyright treaties with a number of nations. Some are nondiscrimination treaties. Others provide for limited protection, while others provide for protection upon registration. Still others give automatic protection without registration. Companies need to be wary of those nations that have a reputation for pirating intellectual works and either not deal in those nations when their property rights are at risk or take special precautions to protect those rights. Currently, serious problems exist with countries that are lax on enforcement of intellectual property laws, including India and China. The United States has the power to impose trade restrictions on those nations.

# CHAPTER PROBLEMS

1. Define the following terms and concepts:
   *a.* Real property
   *b.* Personal property
   *c.* Bailment
   *d.* Fixtures
   *e.* Fee simple absolute
   *f.* Patent
   *g.* Non-obviousness
   *h.* Copyright
   *i.* Trademark
   *j.* Secondary meaning

## *Business Application*

2. Karen Ray worked as a receptionist at Flower Hospital. One evening she noticed a soft-shell eyeglass case on the top of the information desk. It contained rings, earrings, and other jewelry. What should Ray do? Why?
3. Johnson played a round of golf at the Firestone Country Club. Prior to teeing off at the first hole, he took off his Rolex watch and placed it in the front compartment of the golf cart he had obtained from the club. At the end of the game one of the players drove the cart to the pro shop and dropped it off. About 20 minutes later, Johnson realized that he was not wearing his watch and remembered that he had left it in the cart. The watch was never found. What should Johnson do, and why?
4. The Premonstatensian Fathers (Fathers) owned a one-story building that was insured. The Fathers leased out the building to a tenant that used it as a supermarket. A major fire damaged the building. The insurer refused to pay for the damage to five Hussman walk-in coolers situated in the building, contending that they were personal property installed by the tenant. The construction of the coolers was as follows:
   *a.* The exterior walls of the cooler, in four instances, constituted the interior wall of another room.

*b.* In the two meat coolers, a meat-hanging-and-tracking system was built into the coolers. These tracks were used to move large cuts of meat from the cooler area into the meat preparation areas, and were suspended from the steel girders of the building structure by means of large steel bolts. These bolts penetrated through the roof of the cooler supporting wooden beams, which, in turn, supported the tracking system. The tracking in the coolers was a part of a system of tracking throughout the rear portion of the supermarket.

*c.* The coolers were attached to hardwood planks that were, in turn, attached to the concrete floor of the supermarket. The attachment of the planks to the floor was accomplished through the use of a ramsetting gun. The planks were laid on the floor, and the bolts were driven through them into the concrete floor, where they then exploded, firmly fixing the coolers into place. There was a material placed on the planks that served as both an adhesive and an insulation.

*d.* The floor of the coolers was specially sloped during the construction of the building so that the slope would carry drainage into a specially constructed drain in the concrete. In addition, four of the coolers were coated with a protective coating to seal the floors. In the freezer, a special concrete buildup was constructed in the nature of a trough, the purpose of which was to carry away moisture as frozen chickens melted.

*e.* A refrigeration unit was built into each cooler. The unit was suspended from the ceiling of the cooler, and tubing was run through the wall of the cooler to compressors located elsewhere in the store.

*f.* Electric lights and power receptacles were built into each cooler and were connected by electrical wiring through the walls and the ceiling of the cooler to the store's electrical power supply.

*g.* The walls of the cooler were interlocked and set into the splines, and the hardwood planks ramset into the concrete floor, in tongue-and-groove fashion.

Are the Fathers entitled to be compensated for the damage to the coolers? Explain.

5. John, Mary, and James owned real estate in fee simple absolute as "joint tenants with the right of survivorship." John died, leaving Candy and Rollins as heirs. Then Mary sold her interest to Van. Who has what, and why?

6. John Moore was diagnosed with hairy-cell leukemia. Dr. David Golde, a physician attending Moore at the University of California-Los Angeles (UCLA) Medical Center, removed Moore's spleen to slow down the progress of the disease. Dr. Golde was aware of the scientific and commercial value of blood components from Mr. Moore as a result of his specific disease. In follow-up sessions, Dr. Golde withdrew blood and bodily fluids from which he was able to grow a culture to produce lymphokines on a continuous basis (cell line). Lymphokines are proteins that regulate the immune system, and they have particular therapeutic value. Dr. Golde and UCLA obtained a patent on the cell line.

   Genetics Institute has made Dr. Golde and UCLA an attractive financial offer for the exclusive access to the materials and research performed on the cell line and products derived from it. They are contemplating the offer.

   What are the ethical issues? What should the result be?

7. Universal (respondent) owned the copyrights on a variety of television programs that were broadcast over the public airwaves, and brought suit against Sony (petitioner) for copyright infringement. Sony manufactured and sold the Betamax home video tape recorders, called at the time *VTRs.*

   Universal argued that customers who had purchased the VTRs had used them to unlawfully record copyrighted programs, and that Sony, because of its marketing of the device, was liable for copyright infringement. Both parties conducted surveys that showed that the primary use of the machine for most owners was "time-shifting"—the practice of recording a program to view it once at a later time, and thereafter erasing it. Both surveys also showed, however, that a substantial number of interviewees had accumulated libraries of tapes. Has Sony infringed? Is the practice fair use? Explain.

8. Kinko photocopied excerpts of several copyrighted books, without permission and without payment, compiled them into course "packets," and sold them to college students. The owner of one of the copyrights sued for copyright infringement. Kinko defended by asserting that its copying was a "fair use" of the copyrighted material for educational purposes. Argue the case for the copyright owner. Who do you think should prevail, and why?

9. Rolls Royce, a British company that has a worldwide reputation as a producer of luxury automobiles and jet engines, obtained a U.S. registration of the words "Rolls Royce" as a trademark for its products. Alexander Knockoff formed a small company and began producing a low-cost reproduction of a roll-top desk that he called "The Rolls Royce." What action, if any, would you recommend that Rolls Royce take? Explain.

10. Owings-Corning Fiberglass Corp (OCF) filed an application to register the color "pink" as a trademark for the company's fibrous glass residential insulation. It uses the color in advertising, employing the "Pink Panther" in a cartoon-type animation in connection with the rolling out of pink insulation.

    Do you think that OCF will be able to obtain a trademark registration for the color pink? Explain.

CHAPTER 5

# THE LAW OF CONTRACTUAL RELATIONS

## CHAPTER OUTLINE



## LEARNING OBJECTIVES

After learning this chapter the student should be able to:

- Determine whether a promise is legally enforceable.
- Determine whether particular promises require writings to be enforced and the legal significance of reducing a contract to writing.
- Evaluate whether particular promises are not enforceable because of a party's status or conduct or because of the substantive provisions of the promise.

- Evaluate the effects of unforeseen changes in circumstances on a party's duty to perform under a contract.
- Assess the remedies a court is likely to award for a breach of contract.

Most people associate the word *contract* with formal written documents, such as a contract to purchase real estate, a contract in a complex business transaction, or a professional athlete's employment agreement. The legal term *contract* is far broader than that, however; a contract is a promise that the law will enforce. The definition suggests that the law does not enforce every promise.

Most contracts consist of exchanges of two or more promises. In the typical case, the *promisee*, that is, the party to whom one of the promises was made, is attempting to enforce that promise against the *promisor*, the party who made it. At its core ethical and economic considerations drive the law's policy of enforcement of certain types of agreements. This chapter explores the factors that determine whether the law will enforce particular promises.

## SOURCES OF CONTRACT LAW

The basic law of contracts is common law, that is, it is judge-made law. However, the National Commission on Uniform State Laws believed that some common-law rules did not serve the commercial community as well as they could, and tried to write new rules that more closely reflected how most people conducted business. These new rules were codified in the Uniform Commercial Code (UCC). The UCC consists of nine articles, governing such commercial transactions as security interests in property, checks, drafts and other commercial paper. The UCC has been enacted as a statute in 50 states and the District of Columbia. (Louisiana has enacted part of the UCC, but not Article II.)

Article I of the UCC contains general provisions. Article II governs contracts for the sale of goods. A *good*, as the term is used in the UCC, is a tangible commodity capable of being moved from place to place. Pens, books, desks, appliances, cars, factory equipment, and office supplies are examples of goods. Real estate, services, stocks, bonds and other securities, and intangible property—such as patents and copyrights—are not goods.

When a contract involves the sale of goods, the UCC applies. The UCC's influence on the law of contracts has not been limited to contracts for the sale of goods; at times, courts considering contracts outside the UCC view the UCC changes positively and adopt them into common law.

## INTENT TO CONTRACT—THE OBJECTIVE THEORY OF CONTRACTS

Every day, people make promises they do not intend to carry legal consequences. Many of these are social obligations, such as a promise to meet for lunch or to study together; and family obligations, such as a promise to visit parents next month. Companies often sign nonbinding letters of intent, expressing their expectations that after negotiations, agreements will be reached, but providing that neither party will be obligated until an agreement is reached. Additionally, some promises are simply just made in jest. If the parties do not intend to be legally bound, their promises are not legally enforceable.

Intent to contract does not refer to a party's subjective state of mind. Contractual intent is determined objectively by examining the parties' observable behavior—their words and conduct. The relevant legal inquiry thus becomes whether a reasonable person in the position of the promisee would conclude that the promisor intended to be legally bound.

For example, assume that Smith, a farmer, and Jones, the owner of a retail store, are enjoying a beer at their favorite tavern and discussing the low prices farmers are receiving for their crops. Jones says to Smith, "If you're fed up with farming, I'll buy your farm from you for $600,000." Smith thinks that Jones is joking and decides to play along. In a serious tone of voice he says, "You have a deal." Jones replies that he will need time to obtain financing. Smith still thinks the discussion is a joke, but discusses details of the transaction with Jones for a half hour and writes all the details on a piece of paper that Smith and Jones sign. Subjectively, Smith did not intend to sell the farm to Jones, rather thinking that the matter was a joke. Nevertheless, a reasonable person in Jones's position would conclude that Smith intended to sell. Therefore, Smith would be legally bound to sell the farm to Jones.[1]

## THE BARGAIN THEORY OF CONTRACTS

The law of contracts is the backbone of business. It enables parties to transact business with the knowledge that if one party fails to live up to the agreement the other party can seek redress from the courts. It is a primary guarantor of transactional integrity.

There are many reasons why parties would keep their promises even if the courts did not enforce them. For example, if a business developed a reputation for not abiding by its agreements, others would be very reluctant to do business with it.

The basic type of promise that a court enforces is one that is part of a bargained-for exchange. The elements of a bargained-for exchange are offer, acceptance, and consideration.

### *Offer*

An **offer** is made by the *offeror* and gives the *offeree* the power to bind the offeror by accepting the offer. The objective theory is used to determine whether an offer has been made. The test is whether a reasonable person in the position of the offeree would interpret the offer as signifying the offeror's intent to be bound.

Offers must be distinguished from invitations to negotiate. Parties frequently send out announcements that they are seeking to do business and invite others to deal. These announcements may be contained in circulars, price quotes, catalogs, and advertisements. They are frequently indefinite concerning quantity and other terms. Most important, they usually do not identify the offeree.

---

1 Lucy v. Zehmer, 196 Va. 493; 84 S.E. 2d 516 (1954).

There are some exceptions to the rule that an advertisement does not constitute an offer. The first are the reward cases. For example, Kelley promises a reward of $100.00 to the person who locates Duchess, her chihuahua dog. This promise is an effective offer, and is enforceable should someone accept the offer by locating and returning Duchess to Kelley.

An offer is not effective unless it is communicated to the offeree. For example, assume that John offers a $500 reward for the return of an antique watch he lost. Sarah, unaware of the offer, finds the watch and turns it over to the police, who return it to John. Sarah learns of the offer two days later. Sarah is not entitled to the reward because her acceptance, that is, her return of the watch, occurred before the offer was communicated to her.

### Termination of an Offer

Offers do not last forever but expire at a time depending on the circumstances. An offer may specify its expiration date. If it does not do so, the offer terminates after passage of a reasonable time. Death of the offeror also terminates an offer.

Also, a rejection by the offeree terminates the offer. A counteroffer is both a rejection and a new offer. It terminates the original offer.

The most common method of terminating an offer is by **revocation**. A direct revocation occurs when the offeror advises the offeree that the offer is revoked. An indirect revocation occurs when the offeree receives truthful information from a reliable source that is inconsistent with the offer remaining open. For example, Susan offered to sell her house to James. The next day James learned from Carol that Susan had just sold her the same house. A sale to Carol is inconsistent with a possible sale to James. If the statement from Carol is truthful, the offer to James has been indirectly revoked.

### Irrevocable Offers

If an offeror states that the offer will remain open until next Tuesday, the offeror usually can revoke prior to that time. Next Tuesday simply fixes the offer's expiration date in the event there are no intervening circumstances that cause termination of the offer. Even if the offeror promised not to revoke, the offeror could still revoke it unless the offeree gave money or other value for the promise. If the offeree gives value, such as the payment of money, the offer would be part of an option contract and would be irrevocable.

Under the UCC, a merchant's firm offer is irrevocable. A merchant is a party who regularly deals in, or otherwise has expertise in, the goods involved in the transaction. A firm offer must be in writing and must be limited to a reasonable period of time, not to exceed 90 days.

## *Acceptance*

An **acceptance** consists of words or actions by which an offeree signifies his or her intention to be bound by the offer. Acceptance binds the offeree and the offeror. Acceptance must occur before the offer is terminated.

An offer may only be accepted by the offeree. For example, assume that Ace Widget Co. writes Deuce Gizmo Co., offering to sell Deuce 100 widgets for $200. The president of King Gizmo Co., while visiting the president of Deuce, sees the offer on the desk. The King president writes to Ace, "We hereby accept your offer of 100 widgets for $200." There is no contract between King and Ace. Because King was not the offeree, King cannot accept the Ace offer. King's letter is merely an offer to Ace, which Ace is free to accept if it wishes to do so.

An acceptance must signify the offeree's clear intent to be bound. Ambiguous actions or statements, such as "sounds like a good deal," are not acceptances. An offeror cannot declare that an ambiguous action will be treated as an acceptance. For example, assume Jack says to Jill, "I offer to sell you my car for $1,500. You may accept by taking the business law final exam next week." If Jill takes the final exam she will not have accepted Jack's offer because her action is ambiguous. She may be taking the final because she wishes to accept the offer, or she may be taking the final because it is required for the course.

Usually, silence by the offeree is ambiguous and cannot serve as an acceptance. Silence in the context of a prior course of dealings or silence plus acceptance of the benefits of the offer is not ambiguous and can serve as an acceptance.

### The Mirror Image Rule and UCC 2-207

At common law, the acceptance must mirror the offer. If it adds new terms or changes any terms, it is not an acceptance but a counteroffer.

In commercial transactions, buyers and sellers frequently use printed forms with terms that do not agree, sometimes referred to as "the battle of the forms." Under the mirror image rule, each form exchanged is a counteroffer, even though it may be intended as an acceptance. The terms of the last form sent by either party govern the transaction when that counteroffer is accepted by the other party's shipment or acceptance of the goods.

Section 2-207 of the UCC changes this common-law rule. It provides that a document intended to be an acceptance is an acceptance even though it has terms different from or in addition to those in the offer. The acceptance creates a contract on the offeror's terms. The new terms found in the acceptance are proposals to add to the contract. Unless both parties are merchants, the new terms only become part of the contract when both parties expressly agree to them.

If both parties are merchants, the new terms automatically become part of the contract unless one of three conditions is met: (1) the offer expressly limited acceptance to the terms of the offer; (2) the offeror notifies the offeree of its objection to the new terms; or (3) the new terms materially change the contract.

For example, assume that Buyer sent Seller an offer to purchase 100 widgets for $200 on Buyer's printed order blank. The terms on the order blank included statements that full warranties apply and that the goods were to be delivered by Speedy Delivery Service. Seller responds with a printed acknowledgement form, promising to ship the widgets on the requested date. Seller's form specifies delivery via Quick Delivery Service and limits the warranty to replacement of defective widgets. Seller ships the widgets, Buyer accepts them, and two weeks later a defective widget causes $5,000 damage to Buyer's equipment. To determine the contents of the contract under the common law and the UCC, *see* Table 5-1.

### Acceptance by Promise or Performance

Most offers contemplate contracts in which promises are exchanged for promises. For example, Owner offers to pay Roofer $1,500 for reroofing Owner's house. If Roofer accepts, the contract consists of Owner's promise to pay the money and Roofer's promise to do the work. This is called a *bilateral contract.* Roofer may accept by promising to do the job or by actually starting. If Roofer begins performance, Roofer is impliedly promising to do the entire job.

Sometimes the offeror is not interested in the offeree's promise, but is only concerned with full performance. For example, if a company offers a reward for the return of some lost documents, it is not bargaining for someone to promise to search for the documents; the company is only interested in the documents. The offeree can accept only by producing the documents. This is called a *unilateral contract.* Because the offeree makes no promise, the offeree is not obligated to perform; but if the offeree performs, the offeror is bound to perform.

**TABLE 5-1 The Mirror Image Rule and UCC 2-207**

| | *Common Law* | *UCC (At least 1 party is not a merchant)* | *UCC (Both parties are merchants)* |
|---|---|---|---|
| Buyer's order | Offer | Offer | Offer |
| Seller's acknowledgment | Counteroffer because of the delivery and warranty terms | Acceptance; changes in delivery company and limitation on warranty are proposals to change the contract | |
| Buyer accepts the goods | Acceptance of Seller's counteroffer | Irrelevant | Irrelevant |
| Change in name of delivery company | Part of contract as Buyer accepted Seller's counteroffer | Not part of contract as Buyer did not agree to it | Part of contract because Buyer did not specify in its offer that acceptance must be limited to the offer's terms, Buyer did not object to it, and it does not materially change the contract |
| Limitation on warranty | Part of contract as Buyer accepted Seller's counteroffer | Not part of contract as Buyer did not agree to it | Not part of contract as it materially changes the terms of the contract |

After the offeree commences performance, but prior to completion of performance, the offeror might try to revoke the offer. Because only complete performance would bind the offeror, the offeree needs protection against revocation midway through performance. The law affords that protection; when the offeree begins to perform, the offeror cannot revoke for a reasonable time in order to give the offeree a chance to complete the performance.

### Effective Date of Acceptance—The Mailbox Rule

The offeror is the master of the offer and can set any conditions on the acceptance. The offeror can expressly limit the means of communicating acceptance, for example, by specifying overnight delivery, and can expressly provide that acceptance will be effective only on receipt.

If the offeror does not restrict the method of acceptance, the offeree may use any reasonable means to accept. If the offeror does not specify otherwise, acceptance is effective on dispatch by the offeree. This principle is frequently called the **mailbox rule,** as a mailed acceptance is effective on its deposit in the mailbox. The rule protects the offeree from unknown revocations. Because revocation is effective on receipt, an offeree who has not received a revocation can dispatch an acceptance knowing that a contract has been formed.

## *Consideration*

**Consideration** refers to the requirement that a promise be part of a bargained for exchange in order for it to be enforceable. Offer and acceptance are the bargaining process. Consideration consists of two elements: (1) a legal detriment by the promisee that (2) is bargained for by the promisor. A legal detriment exists where the promisee does or promises to do something he or she was not previously obligated to do, or refrains from or promises not to do something he or she had a legal right to do. The detriment is bargained for if it is given in exchange for the promise. *See* Table 5-2 for an illustration of how consideration is present in a contract between Roofer and Owner to roof Owner's house for $2,500.

Past consideration is not bargained for and, therefore, cannot provide the consideration for a present promise. For example, assume that Employer says to Worker, "In consideration of your many years of service to this company, I promise to pay you a pension of $2,000 per month when you retire." Worker's past services were not given in exchange for the promise of a pension. Therefore, there is no consideration for the promise.

### The Preexisting Duty Rule

A promise to perform or the performance of a preexisting legal duty is not a detriment and, therefore, is not consideration. For example, if Professor says to Student, "I promise to pay you $50 if you don't cheat on the final exam," the promise is unenforceable because Student is already under a legal duty not to cheat.

**TABLE 5-2 Consideration**

| *Promise* | *Consideration* | *Detriment* | *Bargained for* |
|---|---|---|---|
| Owner's promise to pay $2,500 | Roofer's promise to roof the house | Roofer was under no prior obligation to do the job | Roofer's promise induced Owner's promise |
| Roofer's promise to roof the house | Owner's promise to pay $2,500 | Owner was under no prior obligation to pay Roofer | Owner's promise induced Roofer's promise |

The preexisting duty rule has made modifications of existing contracts unenforceable. For example, assume that Owner and Builder contract for the construction of a swimming pool at a price of $5,000, with payment due on completion. After Builder starts work, Builder finds that due to unanticipated soil conditions the pool will cost $7,000 to build. Owner promises to pay Builder an extra $2,000 and Builder completes the job. Under the preexisting duty rule, Owner's promise of an additional $2,000 is unenforceable because the only consideration given by Builder was completion of the pool, something Builder was obligated to do by the original contract. However, if Builder also promised that Owner could pay for the pool 30 days after completion, Builder has given new consideration—30 days' credit—which would satisfy that element of the contract.

Recently, a trend away from strict application of the preexisting duty rule has emerged. The *Restatement (Second) of Contracts* provides that for executory contracts, that is, those not fully performed on either side, a good faith modification in response to unanticipated conditions is enforceable without consideration.

Courts in a growing number of states are adopting this approach. UCC Section 2-209 provides that any good faith modification of a contract for the sale of goods is enforceable without consideration.

### Mutuality of Obligation

When the consideration for a promise is another promise, the parties must be under mutual duties to perform. If one party's promise is illusory, such as a promise to perform "if I feel like it," mutuality is lacking and the other party's promise is unenforceable. This problem can arise where one party retains discretion over whether, and to what extent, he or she will perform. Courts frequently infer duties to use reasonable efforts to perform or to exercise the discretion in good faith to avoid interpreting such promises as illusory.

The following case is an example of the necessity of consideration (the bargain element) for there to be an enforceable contract.

**FORBES *v.* SHOWMANN, INC. DBA THE WOODHOUSE DAY SPA**
Court of Appeals, Ohio First District
Appeal No. C-180325 (June 14, 2019)

Plaintiff-appellant Amanda Forbes appealed the trial court's judgment granting summary judgment in favor of defendant-appellee Showmann, Inc. dba. The Woodhouse Day Spa (Showmann) on Forbes's claim of breach of contract. The appellate court affirmed the trial court's judgment on Forbes's breach of contract claim. [The appellate court, however, reversed the trial court granting of summary judgment in favor of Showmann on another of Forbes's claims, not relevant here.]

## *Mock, Presiding Judge*

### Relevant Facts and Background

Forbes was hired as a nail technician by Showmann in 2011. On January 28, 2017, Forbes attended a work-related holiday party where Showmann distributed raffle tickets for employees to place in various containers in order to win certain prizes. It is undisputed that Forbes did not pay for her raffle ticket. One of the raffle prizes offered was a cruise package that included a $2000 Carnival Cruise gift card, a $500 Southwest Airlines gift card and a $200 Uber gift card ("the cruise package"). Only employees who had worked for Showmann for at least two years were eligible to enter the raffle for the cruise package. Forbes entered the raffle, and Chris Wood, the owner of Showmann, announced at the party that Forbes had won the cruise package. Forbes stated in her affidavit that she requested her prize the day after the raffle but she did not receive it. Showmann terminated Forbes's employment a few weeks after the holiday party. Wood testified in his deposition that Forbes was not given the cruise package because that specific raffle prize was conditioned on the recipient being an employee at the time the cruise was taken. Forbes testified in her affidavit that she was not told that the prize was conditioned upon being an employee at the time the trip was to be taken until after she was terminated.

Forbes sued Showmann for breach of contract.

**Breach of Contract**

A contract consists of an offer, an acceptance, and consideration. *See Tersigni v. Gen. Tire, Inc.*, . . .

> Without consideration, there can be no contract. Under Ohio law, consideration consists of either a benefit to the promisor or a detriment to the promisee. To constitute consideration, the benefit or detriment must be "bargained for." Something is bargained for if it is sought by the promisor in exchange for his promise and is given by the promisee in exchange for that promise.

(Citations omitted.) Whether there is consideration supporting a contract is a question of law.

Here, there is no evidence in the record of any benefit accruing to Showmann or any detriment suffered by Forbes by her accepting a complimentary raffle ticket for the cruise package that would constitute consideration for a contract. It is undisputed that Forbes did not pay for the ticket to enter the raffle. Forbes argues that the consideration she gave in exchange for the cruise package was working for Showmann for two years. But that was not consideration; it was merely a condition to being eligible to receive a complimentary raffle ticket for the cruise package.

Because Forbes did not bargain, i.e., pay, for the ticket used to enter the raffle for the cruise package, there was no consideration and, thus, no contract was formed. *See, e.g., Scott v. Sons of Am. Legion Agnew Shinabarger Post 307*, . . . (holding that a contract was formed where a raffle sponsor made an offer of a grand prize, plaintiff accepted the offer by paying $100 for a raffle ticket, and the raffle sponsor benefitted from that purchase because it had received money to put in its scholarship fund). Because no contract was formed, Forbes cannot sustain her breach-of-contract claim, and the trial court properly granted summary judgment to Showmann on that claim.

**Business Application:** This case shows the bargain theory in action. Consideration is the bargain element of a contract. It is the price paid for a promise. When someone makes a promise to you, what should you be thinking, if you want that promise to be one that a court will enforce as a contract?

# STATUTE OF FRAUDS

Generally, oral contracts are enforceable, although their existence may be difficult to prove. Certain types of contracts, however, are not enforceable unless they are evidenced by a writing. The **Statute of Frauds** requires written evidence for promises:

- Made in consideration of marriage.
- For sales of goods priced $500 or more.
- For transfers of real property other than a lease of less than one year's duration.
- That cannot, by their terms, be performed within one year.
- To answer for the debt of another.

The first three promises are self-explanatory. Promises that by their terms cannot be performed within one year refer only to those promises that expressly call for more than a year's commitment. If the promise can be performed within one year, it does not fall within the Statute of Frauds even if a longer duration is contemplated. For example, if Worker promises Company to work for the next two years, the contract must be evidenced by a writing because it cannot be performed within one year. But if Worker promises Company to work until retirement, the Statute of Frauds does not apply because Worker can retire at any time. A writing is not required, even if Worker is 25 years old and intends to work for 40 more years.

Promises to answer for the debt of another come within the Statute of Frauds only if they are made to the creditor. A promise made to the debtor does not require a writing. Even where the promise is made to the creditor, a writing is not required if the promisor is also the debtor. For example, if Jill telephones the Ace Department Store and says, "Jack is coming over. Sell him a new suit and send me the bill," no writing is required. Jack never becomes indebted to Ace. When Jack makes a purchase, Jill becomes a debtor; thus, she has promised to pay her own debt rather than Jack's.

A promise to answer for the debt of another does not require a writing if the main purpose of the promise is to benefit the promisor. For example, assume that Big Bank holds a mortgage on David Debtor's home. Bank promises an insurance company that if Debtor fails to pay the premium for fire insurance, Bank will pay. Bank's main purpose is to protect its interest in the property, as the mortgage would be of little value if the property was destroyed by fire and was not insured.

## *Compliance with the Statute of Frauds*

The Statute of Frauds does not require that the contract be in writing; it requires only that there be a written evidence of the contract signed by the party to be charged with enforcement of the contract. For example, a typical laundry ticket could be sufficient to satisfy the Statute of Frauds' requirement of a signed writing in a lawsuit against the laundry. Courts can also integrate several documents to arrive at the written evidence needed to satisfy the Statute of Frauds. Letters between parties or internal company memos may combine to show the existence of a contract.

The requirement of a signature is satisfied by any mark that is intended to authenticate a document. For example, a company's name on stationary letterhead would satisfy the signature requirement.

A federal statute known as E-Sign was enacted to encourage the use of electronic signatures, such as those used in online transactions, in interstate commerce. E-Sign states that a contract may not be denied legal effect, validity, or enforceability solely because an electronic signature or electronic record was used in its formation.

In goods transactions between merchants, UCC 2-201 permits a written confirmation of a contract to satisfy the requirement of a signed writing if the party who receives the confirmation has reason to know its contents and does not send written notice of objection to the sender of the confirmation within ten days after the confirmation is received. This allows the sender to enforce the contract against the recipient of the confirmation even though the recipient's signature is not on any writing. For example, if a merchant telephoned an order to a supplier for goods priced over $500, and the supplier sent an invoice to the buyer, who sees it and does not object to it within 10 days, the supplier can enforce the purchase agreement against the buyer even though the buyer did not sign anything. The written confirmation without written notice of objection substitutes for a signed writing in these circumstances.

**Decision Making in the Legal Environment**

This link instructs on what to look for in a business contract.

http://smallbusiness.findlaw.com/business-contracts-forms/how-to-write-a-business-contract.html

Even where no writing exists at all, courts may enforce an oral contract where the parties have performed part of their obligation, and the performance is referable to the contract. That is, if the performance can be explained only on the basis of the existence of a contract, the performance serves as a substitute for a signed writing.

## ALTERNATIVES TO THE BARGAIN THEORY OF CONTRACTS

Alternatives to the bargain theory of contracts exist for courts to provide remedies in cases not meeting classical contract law's requirement of a bargained-for exchange. These alternative theories stem from an area of law known as the *law of equity.* Courts have drawn upon equity law to apply doctrines to do equity in a given case. The three alternative theories are: promissory estoppel, the doctrine of moral obligation, and the doctrine of quasi contract.

### *Promissory Estoppel*

Under the doctrine of **promissory estoppel,** courts have enforced promises that lacked consideration and oral promises that would otherwise be unenforceable under the Statute of Frauds. Under the doctrine, a party is "estopped" to deny the existence of a promise. Three conditions must be met for the doctrine of promissory estoppel to apply:

1. There must be a *promise* from a promisor to a promisee.
2. There must be *reliance* by the promisee upon the promise.
3. The reliance must be to the promisee's *substantial economic detriment.*

The promise must be one that a reasonable promisor should foresee would induce reliance. The promisee's reliance must be reasonable. The requirement of substantial economic detriment means that an injustice can be avoided only by enforcing the promise.

Promissory estoppel has been traditionally used as a defense. For example, if a landlord told a tenant that the landlord would not enforce a provision in the lease that says that interest would be charged on late rental payments, the tenant could raise promissory estoppel as a defense to a claim by the landlord for interest in addition to the unpaid rent. The trend is for courts to permit promissory estoppel to be used as an affirmative claim to enforce promises that are not contracts under contact law because they lack the requirements of a contract (such as consideration).

### *Moral Obligation*

Generally, a moral obligation to keep a promise is not sufficient to make the promise legally enforceable. However, if a promise becomes unenforceable by operation of law, a subsequent promise to keep the original promise is enforceable without new consideration. For example, assume John owes Mary $500, but because the statute of limitations period for bringing suit has expired, John's debt is uncollectible. If John promises to pay the $500 anyway, the promise is enforced without new consideration.

### *Quasi Contract*

If a doctor finds a pedestrian unconscious on the street and treats the pedestrian, no contract has arisen between the two. An unconscious pedestrian cannot accept the doctor's offer.

However, where a party confers a benefit on another party with a reasonable expectation of payment, and the recipient of the benefit would be unjustly enriched if not required to pay for it, a court implies a contract as a matter of law. Under such a *quasi contract*, a doctor is able to recover the reasonable value of the services provided.

## POLICING THE BARGAIN

Courts generally do not get involved in reviewing the fairness of particular contracts. If an agreement has been reached, a court cannot protect a party from a bad deal. In certain cases, however, courts refuse to enforce a promise because of a party's status. Courts protect particularly vulnerable parties deemed to lack the capacity to contract. In other cases, courts may rescind or reform a contract if a party's conduct produces a defect in the bargaining process. Finally, courts may refuse to enforce all or part of a contract if its substantive provisions are illegal or unconscionable.

### *Capacity*

People so mentally infirm that they cannot understand the nature and consequences of their actions lack the capacity to contract. People who have not yet attained the age of majority—usually 18 but in some states 21—also lack contractual capacity. The overwhelming majority of capacity problems arise in contracts made by minors.

Minors have the right to disaffirm their contracts at any time prior to reaching the age of majority. On reaching the age of majority, a party may choose to disaffirm or ratify the contract. Ratification may be implied from the party's conduct or from the party's failure to disaffirm within a reasonable time after reaching the age of majority. An adult has no power to disaffirm. An adult is bound by a contract with a minor unless the minor disaffirms.

If a minor disaffirms, the law in most states only requires the minor to return to the adult any remaining consideration. It does not require the minor to make restitution. For example, assume that Minor buys a car on credit from Dealer. After making only one payment and with an outstanding balance of $8,000, Minor is involved in an accident that totally destroys the car. In most states, if Minor disaffirms, Minor need only return the remaining wreck to Dealer and need not make restitution for the damage or the value of the use of the car.

Minors are responsible for their contracts for necessities, such as food, clothing, shelter, and medical care. A minor who disaffirms such a contract is liable in quasi contract for the reasonable value of the benefit received.

## *Defects in the Bargaining Process*

Defects in the bargaining process may result in a court rescinding, or occasionally reforming, an agreement. A party's consent may have been obtained through misrepresentation or under duress or may be the result of a mistake.

### Misrepresentation

Where a misrepresentation of a material fact is made and a party justifiably relies on the misrepresentation, the deceived party may rescind the transaction and receive restitution for any benefits conferred on the deceptive party. Misrepresentations need not be fraudulent (i.e., intentional), or even negligent, as long as they are material. A misrepresentation is material if it would likely influence the conduct of a reasonable person.

Only misrepresentations of fact are actionable. Misrepresentations of opinion are not actionable unless the deceived party is relying on the deceiver's expertise. Statements that an item is the "best buy" or a "superb value" usually are dismissed as nonactionable opinion. Similarly, predictions of future events are usually considered to be nonactionable opinion.

In certain circumstances, nondisclosure may amount to actionable misrepresentation. Deliberate concealment is actionable, as is deceptive partial disclosure. There is a duty to disclose latent defects and to correct misconceptions caused by the nondisclosing party. A duty to disclose also arises if the parties are in a fiduciary or other special relationship.

Nondisclosure or misrepresentation is actionable only if justifiably relied on. Reliance is not justified if the deceived party knows the representation is false or could discover it through a reasonable investigation.

### Duress

Duress occurs when one party's wrongful act overcomes the free will of another party. If a party's agreement is obtained with threats of physical harm, the contract is void because of duress. The law considers the contract to have never been made. Duress can also result from economic pressure. Economic duress that results from a wrongful act renders a contract voidable. The victim of the duress may rescind the contract.

For example, assume that Repairer had a contract to repair a machine for Mechanic. Because the machine was indispensable to Mechanic's business, Repairer agreed to pick up the machine at the close of business on Friday and have it ready for Mechanic to pick up Monday morning. When Mechanic arrived on Monday, Repairer said that the machine was ready but would not be returned to Mechanic unless Mechanic promised to pay a debt that Mechanic's brother owed to Repairer and had refused to pay. Mechanic desperately needed the machine, so she promised to pay her brother's debt. Mechanic may rescind her promise because of duress.

### Mistake

The parties may allocate the risk of mistake in their contract. The allocation may be expressed, or it may be implied from what a reasonable person would expect under the circumstances. For example, assume that Jack finds a gemstone and sells it to Jill for $50. Neither party knows what type of gem it is, but both assume that, although it is pretty, it is not very valuable. Under these circumstances, it is reasonable to imply that Jill is assuming the risk that the gem is worthless and Jack is assuming the risk that it is valuable. If the gem turns out to be a diamond worth $5,000, the mistake is not grounds for Jack to rescind the contract.

If the parties have not allocated the risk, a mutual mistake in a basic assumption allows either party to rescind the contract. If only one party is mistaken, rescission is allowed under some circumstances. Many courts allow rescission if the nonmistaken party knew or should have known of the other party's mistake. More liberal courts allow rescission if enforcement would be oppressive to the mistaken party and rescission would not impose a hardship on the nonmistaken party.

Sometimes the parties reach an oral agreement but make a mistake in reducing it to writing. In such a case, a court reforms the writing to conform to the original agreement.

### Unconscionability

UCC Section 2-302 authorizes a court to deny or limit enforcement of a contract or part of a contract that it finds to be unconscionable. Unconscionability is determined as of the time the contract is made. Unconscionability exists where one party did not have a meaningful choice and where the terms are so one-sided as to be oppressive. Absence of meaningful choice has been found where there was a large disparity in bargaining power, the terms were hidden in fine print, or the term were presented on a take-it-or-leave-it basis.

Courts have analogized to the UCC and applied the concept of unconscionability to contracts that did not involve sales of goods. Unconscionability is most commonly found in consumer transactions.

**Law and Ethics in Business Policies**

This link supplements the discussion on unconscionable contracts.

http://www.legalmatch.com/law-library/article/what-is-an-unconscionable-contract.html

**Business Application/Ethical Issues**

You are the president of a large real estate rental company. Your standard residential lease has a clause that provides, "Tenant agrees that landlord shall not be liable for any personal injuries or property damage sustained by tenant on landlord's property or resulting from landlord's negligence." A recent decision from your state's supreme court held that a similar clause in another landlord's lease was unconscionable. The court refused to enforce the clause.

Several of your resident managers have advised you not to drop the clause from your leases. They reason that although a court would not enforce the clause, the tenants do not know that. In their experience, the clause deters tenants from pressing claims for minor injuries. As one resident manager explained, "If you take the clause out, every time someone slips and skins a knee, we'll see a claim." Your liability insurance company agrees and will raise your premiums if you do not retain the clause.

What are the ethical issues in this problem? What would you do? Explain.

## *Illegality*

A contract is illegal if its formation or performance is tortious, forbidden by statute, or contrary to public policy. For example, contracts to bribe public officials, to embezzle money, to gamble in a state that prohibits gambling, and to sell cocaine are illegal.

The concept of public policy is difficult to define with precision but it enables courts to deny enforcement to contracts which they believe injure the public interest. One such contract that has received considerable judicial attention is the covenant not to compete.

**Understanding the Private Law Sector**

This link supplements the discussion on non-compete agreements.

http://www.nolo.com/legal-encyclopedia/noncompete-agreements-how-create-agreement-29784.html

Covenants not to compete arise out of basically two situations: the sale of a business and an employment contract. In the sale of a business the buyer may push to include a provision within the sales contract that would prevent the seller from turning around, opening up a new business and competing against the new buyer's business. Likewise, an employer who trains an employee and imparts skills and knowledge of the business would be concerned about the employee, upon leaving the employ, using those skills and knowledge to compete against the former employer. This protection against that threat could be covered in an employee signing a covenant not to compete in such event.

Covenants not to compete come with a presumption that they are illegal because preventing someone from employment appears to be an unreasonable restraint of trade. Hence, courts scrutinize covenant not to compete provisions to determine if they are, in fact, reasonable, and thus enforceable.

First, in order to be enforceable a covenant not to compete must be reasonable as to the duration of the restriction. Restrictions that are five or ten years in duration are more suspect than those that are one or three years in duration. The final determination on reasonableness as to time turns on the length of time necessary to protect the business establishment against a new competitive threat by a former employee or the seller of a business.

Second, the restriction should be reasonable as to geographies. The territorial restriction should be no greater than the radius within which the business competes. To restrict an employee of a local hardware store from securing another such job any place within the United States is unreasonably broad and hence not enforceable.

Third, the covenant not to compete should be reasonable as to the scope of the restriction. The restriction should be confined to the relevant type of business or employment. Hence, it is unreasonable to restrict a seller of a grocery business to refrain from work in a plumbing business regardless of how short a period of time or how narrow the geographic restriction. The plumbing business is just too far afield from the grocery business.

If an agreement is illegal, usually a court will not enforce the agreement. There are several exceptions to this general rule. Courts enforce a contract that contravenes a statute if enforcement would be consistent with the purpose of the statute. For example, if a party does business without a required license and the license statute's purpose is a "tax" to raise money rather than protect customers and clients, courts would enforce the unlicensed party's contracts. If the license is required for protection, courts would enforce the contracts on request of the customers or clients but not on the request of the unlicensed party.

Courts considering illegal contracts often inquire into whether the illegality involves *moral turpitude*, that is, serious misconduct. If the illegality does not involve moral turpitude and the parties are not *in pari delicto*, that is, not equally blameworthy, courts allow the more innocent party to recover in quasi contract for benefits conferred on the other party. If the illegality does not involve moral turpitude, a party who renounces the bargain and prevents the illegal act from taking place may recover in quasi contract.

The following case is an example of treatment by courts of a covenant not to compete in an employment contract.

## H&R BLOCK EASTERN ENTERPRISES, INC. *v.* VICKI D. MORRIS

11th Circuit U.S. Court of Appeals
606 F.3d 1285 (2010)

Block prepares taxes and related services for individuals and companies nationwide. It employed Morris as a seasonal tax preparer in its College Park, Georgia 2000–2005 tax seasons. In 2004 Morris and Block entered into an agreement that included a non-competition covenant. The pertinent section contains a non-competition covenant that restricts Morris for a period of two years after the termination of the Agreement, resignation or termination as an employee from providing tax services to any of Block's clients with whom Morris had serviced, within Morris' district of employment or within a twenty-five (25) mile radius of the office to which Morris was assigned.

Block declined to re-hire Morris for the 2006 tax season. Morris started Dreams Tax Service. She prepared 47 returns for former Block clients whom she had serviced while at Block. Block sued seeking injunctive relief and damages.

The District Court found in favor of Morris reasoning that the covenant not to compete was unenforceable because it prevented Morris from accepting unsolicited business from former clients. Block appealed.

## *PER CURIAM*

A restrictive covenant in an employment contract . . . is considered to be in partial restraint of trade and will be enforced only if it (1) is reasonable, (2) is supported by consideration, (3) is reasonably necessary to protect the restraining party's interest, and does not unduly prejudice the interests of the public. Georgia courts apply strict scrutiny to restrictive covenants in employment contracts, and the reasonableness of the restraint is a question of law for determination by the court, "which considers the nature and extent of the trade or business, the situation of the parties, and all other circumstances." . . . "A three-element test of duration, territorial coverage, and scope of activity has evolved as a helpful tool in examining the reasonableness of the particular factual setting to which it is applied."

* * *

### *The Non-Competition Covenant*

The district court determined the non-competition covenant was unenforceable because it prevented Morris from accepting unsolicited business from her former Block clients. In reaching this decision, the district court applied rulings involving nonsolicitation covenants rather than non-competition covenants.

On appeal, Block argues the district court erroneously concluded the non-competition covenant was invalid. Block contends the non-competition covenant is enforceable when evaluated under the proper standard and considering the interplay of provisions in the Agreement. In response, Morris argues the provision is unreasonable in geographic scope because it has two geographic restrictions—a district restriction and a 25-mile radius restriction. Morris also asserts the non-competition covenant contravenes public policy by limiting the number of businesses providing tax preparation and filing services.

A non-competition covenant, "which is de-signed primarily to protect the employer's 'investment of time and money in developing the employee's skills.' prohibits the employee from performing competitive activities in a certain geographic area for a limited time." A non-competition covenant "may preclude the employee from accepting related business (whether solicited or not) from any clients (whether previously contacted by him or not) if the employee is officed in, or is to perform the restricted activities in, the forbidden territory." A restrictive covenant subject to strict scrutiny may apply to the territory in which the employee served. A non-competition covenant must also "contain a territorial limitation sufficient to 'give the employee notice of what constitutes a violation of the restrictive covenant [by] specify[ing] with particularity the territory in which the employee[s' conduct] is restricted.'" To determine whether a non-competition covenant satisfies this requirement, "a court must examine the 'interplay between the scope of the prohibited behavior and the territorial restriction.'" For example, "[a] broad territorial limitation may be reasonable if the scope of the prohibited behavior is sufficiently narrow."

Applying the three-element test of duration, territorial coverage, and scope, we conclude the Agreement's non-competition covenant is reasonable, considering the nature and extent of the business, the situation of the parties, and other relevant circumstances. With respect to duration, the two-year duration of the . . . clause is within the time frame permitted by law. . . .

With regard to territorial coverage, the non-competition covenant was geographically limited to (1) Morris's district of employment and (2) a 25-mile radius from the Block office where Morris worked. . . . The restricted geographic area was illustrated by a map accompanying the Agreement, and was thus identified and disclosed to Morris at the time she signed the contract. Although Morris contends the geographic restrictions are unreasonable, the district court found "Block . . . presented evidence showing that Morris serviced clients from communities in the extreme outer-edges of the twenty-five mile territor[y]." Moreover, the geographic restrictions are reasonable considering the "interplay" between the territorial restriction and the scope of prohibited behavior—the covenant applies only to clients served by Morris, and only covers territory in which she actually worked. Accordingly, in these circumstances, the noncompetition covenant's territorial limitation is reasonable.

Finally, the scope of prohibited activities is sufficiently narrow. A non-competition covenant "must balance an employee's right to earn a living without unreasonable restrictions, and an employer's right to protection from the former employee's possible unfair appropriation of contacts developed while working for the employer." Here, the non-competition covenant prohibited Morris from preparing tax returns or providing any other service Morris "provided or offered as an employee of the Company" to any of the Company's Clients. The Agreement limited Company Clients to those persons or entities "with whom [Morris] had contact" by providing services as an employee of the Company. This covenant does not prohibit Morris from preparing taxes or providing a related service to the general public, or Block clients generally. Morris is only prohibited from serving those clients she serviced while employed at Block during the 2005 tax season. The covenant appropriately balances Morris's right to earn a living with Block's right to protect its customer relationships and Block's investment in developing Morris's skills.

The non-competition covenant is limited to a specific geographic area, the types of activities performed by Morris at Block, the customers serviced by Morris at Block, and a two-year duration. After considering the nature of the tax preparation business, the situation of the parties, and after applying the three-element analysis, we conclude this non-competition covenant is reasonable under Georgia law.

* * *

REVERSED on the issue of the Covenant Not to Compete.

**Business Application:** How should you respond when your boss asks you to sign a covenant not to compete (otherwise known as a non-compete agreement)?

# CONTRACT INTERPRETATION

Frequently, contract disputes do not involve the existence or enforceability of a contract. Rather, they focus on what the contract's provisions mean. In interpreting contracts, courts inquire into how a reasonable person in the position of the parties would interpret the agreement. Often, courts look to the past practices of the industry. In written documents, ambiguities often are resolved against the drafter because that is the party responsible for the ambiguity.

## *The Parol Evidence Rule*

The **parol evidence rule** provides that if a contract is reduced to writing and the parties intend the writing to be the final and complete evidence of the agreement, prior or contemporaneous representations or agreements (i.e., parol evidence) may not be used to vary or contradict the writing. Parties often specify that their writings are intended to be the final expressions of their agreements to the exclusion of all prior representations. Such clauses are called *integration*, *merger*, or *zipper clauses.* Nonetheless parol evidence may establish reasons for rescinding the contract, such as fraud, duress, mistake, or lack of capacity. Parol evidence may also be used to explain the meaning of ambiguous terms contained in the writing. Finally, parol evidence may be used to establish modifications agreed to after the original written contract.

**Decision Making in the Legal Environment**

This link discusses the pros and cons of written employment contracts.

http://www.nolo.com/legal-encyclopedia/written-employment-contracts-pros-cons-30193.html

# PERFORMANCE AND BREACH

A breach of contract occurs if a party has a duty to perform and fails to do so. A party may not have a duty to perform if conditions precedent to that duty have not been fulfilled. A party's duty to perform may be discharged by unforeseen subsequent events.

## *Conditions*

The two types of conditions contained in contracts are express and constructive. **Express conditions** are those established by the parties themselves. For example, if George buys a $100,000 life insurance policy naming Sally as beneficiary, the insurance company has promised to pay Sally $100,000 if George dies. George's death is an express condition precedent to the insurance company's duty to pay Sally.

**Constructive conditions** are implied as a matter of law from the order of performance contemplated by the parties. If one party is to perform first, that party's performance is a constructive condition precedent to the other party's duty to perform. If both parties are to perform at the same time, each party's performance is a constructive condition concurrent to the other party's duty to perform.

Constructive conditions need only be substantially fulfilled for a party's duty to perform to arise. For example, assume that Owner contracts with Builder to build a house according to stated specifications, with Owner to pay for the house on completion. Although the specifications call for using a certain brand of pipe for the plumbing, Builder uses a different brand that is identical in quality to the pipe specified.

Builder's completion of the house as specified is a constructive condition precedent to Owner's duty to pay. The condition has not been literally fulfilled because of the deviation from the specified brand of pipe. However, because the construction condition precedent of completing the house has been substantially fulfilled, Owner must pay.

### *Excuses for Nonperformance*

The parties in their contract may expressly or impliedly allocate the risk of unforeseen changes in circumstances. Often, they fail to do so. Generally, if unforeseen events render performance impossible, the duty to perform is discharged. For example, if the subject matter of the contract is destroyed, the duty to perform is discharged. Similarly, supervening illegality discharges the duty to perform. Death of an individual who was to personally render services also discharges the duty to perform.

UCC Section 2-615 extends the doctrine of impossibility to cases of unforeseen impracticability. Courts in a few states have added this liberalization to their general law of contracts, but the majority of states have confined it to the sale of goods.

A related doctrine is the rule of frustration of purpose. It was first recognized in a 1903 English case.[2] The defendant agreed to pay the plaintiff £75 to use the plaintiff's apartment for two days to view the coronation of King Edward VII. The coronation was unexpectedly canceled due to the King's illness. Performance of the contract remained possible, but the purpose of the contract had been frustrated. Accordingly, the duty to perform was discharged.

### *Breach by Anticipatory Repudiation*

Most breaches of contract occur at the time for performance. Sometimes, a party may declare prior to the time for performance that he or she has no intention of ever performing. In such a case, the other party may treat the anticipatory repudiation as a current breach of contract and sue immediately for relief. For example, assume that Seller agrees to sell Buyer 100 widgets a month for six months. After two months, Seller tells Buyer that it will not sell any more widgets. Although the time for performance of the next four months' supply of widgets has not yet arisen, Buyer may treat Seller's repudiation as an immediate breach.

## REMEDIES

The basic remedy for breach of contract is an award of money damages. The basic measure of damages is lost expectation. Expectation damages are calculated to place the victim of the breach in the position he or she would have been in had the contract been performed. The two alternative measures of damages are reliance and restitution. Reliance damages are calculated to place the victim of the breach in the position he or she would have been in had the contract never been made. Restitution damages are designed to place the breaching party in the position he or she would have been in had the contract never been made.

---

2 Krell v. Henry, 2 K.B. 740 (1903).

To illustrate the differences among the three measures of damage, assume that Builder agreed to subdivide a lot and build two apartment buildings and Owner agreed to pay Builder $1 million. Builder completed the first building at a cost of $350,000. The building had a market value of $600,000. Before Builder started work on the second building, Owner repudiated the contract. It would cost Builder $300,000 to build the second building.

If the contract had been fully performed, Builder would have made a profit of $350,000. It will take $700,000 (the lost profit plus the $350,000 spent on the first building) to put Builder in the same position as if the contract had been fully performed. Thus, Builder's expectation damages are $700,000.

Builder spent $350,000 that it would not have spent if there had been no contract. It will take $350,000 to put Builder in the same position as if no contract had been made. Thus, Builder's reliance damages are $350,000.

Owner received a building worth $600,000 that Owner would not have had if there had been no contract. To place Owner in the same position as if no contract had been made, Owner must pay Builder $600,000. Thus, Builder's restitution damages are $600,000.

There are several limitations on the amount of damages. First, damages must be calculable with reasonable certainty. Uncertainty is frequently a problem when the damages requested include lost profits. A new business with no track record to use as a basis for calculating lost profits may be unable to recover them because they are too uncertain.

Second, damages must be reasonably foreseeable. This principle was established in an 1854 English case.[3] The plaintiff's mill was shut down because of a broken shaft. The defendant agreed to ship the shaft to a company that would make a new one. The defendant breached the contract by excessively delaying the shipment, thereby prolonging the period that the mill was closed. The plaintiff sought to recover the profit lost during the excessive closing, but the court denied recovery because the defendant had no way of knowing that the mill was shut down.

Third, the victim of the breach must make reasonable efforts to mitigate damages. For example, if a supplier breaches a contract to supply widgets to a manufacturer, the manufacturer must make a reasonable effort to obtain an alternate source of supply.

Sometimes the parties may specify the amount of damages in the contract. Such provisions are called **liquidated damages.** They are enforceable if they are intended as remedies rather than penalties, if actual damages would be difficult to calculate, and if they represent reasonable estimates of the damage done.

Sometimes a party wants a court to order the breaching party to actually perform the contract rather than pay damages. Orders of **specific performance** are available if money damages would not provide an adequate remedy. However, an award of specific performance is subject to the court's equitable discretion. A court would not order specific performance if the order would be difficult to enforce or overly harsh on one of the parties. The party requesting specific performance must have acted promptly in asserting his or her rights and must be free of wrongdoing or bad faith.

---

3 Hadley v. Baxendale, 156 Eng. Rep. 145 (1854).

# CHAPTER PROBLEMS

1. Define the following terms:
   *a.* Offer
   *b.* Acceptance
   *c.* Mailbox rule
   *d.* Consideration
   *e.* Statute of Frauds
   *f.* Promissory estoppel
   *g.* Parol evidence rule
   *h.* Express and constructive conditions
   *i.* Liquidated damages
   *j.* Specific performance

## *Business Application*

2. Sally Black sent an unsolicited recipe for fruit flavors to be used in making ice cream to General Foods Corporation, along with a letter asking General Foods to compensate her if the company should decide to use it. A vice president of General Foods replied with a letter thanking her for her suggestion, but added, "We shall be happy to examine your suggestion but only with understanding that our use of it and your compensation, if any, rest entirely at our discretion." Ms. Black did not reply to the letter. Six months later General Foods introduced a new product that followed Ms. Black's suggestion exactly. Is Ms. Black entitled to compensation? Explain.

3. First Colonial Bank ran an advertisement in a local newspaper which invited investors to "Deposit $14,000 for 3½ years and receive an RCA 20" color TV and $20,136.12 upon maturity. Rate shown is 8¾ percent. TV carries manufacturer's warranty; deposits are fully insured to $100,000 by FDIC. Substantial penalty for early withdrawal."

   The advertisement contained an error. To get $20,136.12, an investment of $14,000.00 earning 8¾ percent had to remain on deposit for four years. Pamphlets on display in the bank's lobby advised this.

   Sally Saver responded to the advertisement and deposited $14,000. She did not see the display. First Colonial gave her the advertised TV and a certificate of deposit (CD) redeemable in 3½ years with interest at a rate of 8¾ percent. No one advised her of the mistake in the ad. Three and one-half years later, Sally liquidated the CD. She received $18,823.93, representing three and one-half years' interest at 8¾ percent. Is the bank liable for the remaining $1,312.19? Explain.

4. Architectural Glass & Metal Co. (AGM), an Indiana company, telephoned Falconer Glass Industries, a New York company, and ordered a special type of glass manufactured by Falconer for use in a construction project in Indianapolis. Over the phone, the parties agreed on quantity, price, delivery, and payment terms. Falconer then mailed to AGM a form confirming the order. The form contained many preprinted terms, including one limiting Falconer's liability for defects in the product to replacement of the defective product or refund of the purchase price, and one requiring that any lawsuits arising out of the order be brought in New York. The product proved to be defective and the defects caused AGM $19,000 in damages. Is Falconer liable? If so, may AGM sue Falconer in Indiana, or must it sue in New York? Explain.
5. William Story made a promise to his nephew, William Story, 2d, that if he would refrain from drinking liquor, using tobacco, swearing, and playing cards or billiards for money until he became 21 years old, then he, William Story, would at that time pay William Story 2d, $5,000. William Story 2d fully performed his part of the agreement. William Story 2d had not been paid when William Story died. The executor of the estate of William Story would not allow the claim of William Story 2d for $5,000. Is William Story 2d's claim for the $5,000 enforceable? Explain.
6. Crabtree entered negotiations with Elizabeth Arden Sales Corp. concerning his employment as a sales manager. Ms. Arden, the corporation president, orally offered Crabtree a two-year contract starting at $40,000 per year, increasing to $45,000 after six months and $50,000 after one year, with an expense allowance of $5,000 per year. Crabtree replied, "Sounds interesting." Ms. Arden then had her secretary write a memo on a telephone order blank that happened to be at hand as follows:

| EMPLOYMENT AGREEMENT WITH CRABTREE | |
|---|---|
| Begin | $40,000 |
| 6 months | 45,000 |
| 6 months | 50,000 |
| $5,000 per year expense money (2 years to make good) | |

Two days later Crabtree telephoned his acceptance. On his first day at work, a payroll card was made up and signed by the company's general manager. It classified Crabtree as a sales manager and further stated:

| | |
|---|---|
| First six months of employment | $40,000 per annum |
| Next six months of employment | $45,000 per annum |
| After one year of employment | $50,000 per annum |

Crabtree received the first scheduled $5,000 pay raise but did not receive the second. When he inquired about it, Ms. Arden fired him. If Crabtree sues, will the contract be enforceable? Why or why not?

7. You own and operate a department store. For many years, you have rented space to Acme Furriers, Inc., to operate a fur concession in your store. Although Acme was a separate company, the appearance given the general public was that it was a department within your store. Unknown to you, Acme contracted with Fur Storage, Inc. (FSI) to provide cleaning and storage services to it. Acme accepted furs from customers in the spring and, for a fee, agreed to clean and store them until the late fall. Acme, in turn, paid FSI to clean and store the furs.

   Acme went bankrupt and closed. Acme's customers came to you to retrieve their furs. You approached Acme's president, who told you about FSI. You then asked FSI for the furs. FSI told you that Acme owed $1,500 for cleaning and storage of the furs. You offered to pay the $1,500, but FSI stated that Acme also owed it $4,500 for other services not involving your store. FSI demanded that you pay the entire $6,000 before it would release the furs. The customers are demanding their furs. The weather is getting colder by the day. What should you do? Explain.

8. Owner contracted with Red Roof Co. (RRC) for a new roof to be constructed on Owner's house for $3,000. The contract specified the type of shingles to be used and the color—asphalt gray. RRC completed the job, but ran out of asphalt gray shingles. It used three other colors—two other shades of gray and a dark blue. As a result, the roof is perfectly sound but Owner thinks it looks terrible. Must Owner pay RRC? Why or why not?

9. Gravel Contractors, Inc. (GCI) was the low bidder for a road construction contract and was awarded the contract by the state of Alaska. GCI's bid was so low because it owned a gravel pit near the site and intended to use gravel from that pit. After GCI's contract was announced, residents living near the gravel pit objected to GCI hauling gravel from it. The local zoning board ruled that GCI's proposed use of the pit violated local zoning laws. GCI now has to purchase and haul gravel from a site 25 miles away and will incur an additional $20,000 in costs. Instead of making a $10,000 profit on the job, GCI will lose $10,000. Must GCI perform under the contract? Explain.

10. Al's Restaurant leased a storefront from Jane's Realty for three years. The lease provided that Al would pay a monthly rent of $2,000, maintain the premises in good repair, arrange for trash collection, and hold the restaurant open for business at least five days per week. The lease further provided that for any breach, Al's would be liable for $4,000 liquidated damages. Is this provision enforceable? Explain.

CHAPTER 6

# THE LAW OF INJURIES (TORT LAW)

## CHAPTER OUTLINE



## LEARNING OBJECTIVES

After learning this chapter the student should be able to:

- Distinguish a tort from a breach of contract and a crime.
- Classify various torts under the appropriate headings: intentional, negligent, or strict liability.
- Recite the elements of a variety of torts, and apply them to factual situations involving business operations.

A **tort** is a civil wrong other than a breach of contract. The law recognizes the right of a victim of a tort to recover compensation in the form of money damages from the wrongdoer (tortfeasor).

A tort is not a crime, although many torts may also lead to criminal proceedings. In a tort action the victim sues to recover compensation from the tortfeasor for the injury that occurred. In contrast, in a criminal case the government brings charges seeking punishment (usually a fine or imprisonment) against the wrongdoer.

**TABLE 6-1 Classification of Torts**

| *Intentional Torts* | *Negligence* | *Strict liability* |
|---|---|---|
| Intentional wrongdoing | Unreasonable conduct | Vicious animals<br>Defective products<br>Abnormally dangerous activities |

A breach of contract is not a tort. Contract duties arise by agreement of the parties. Tort duties, however, arise by operation of law and exist whether or not a person agrees to them. Tort law reflects society's determination of which injuries should be compensated, which interests protected, and which conduct deterred. In this way the law establishes standards for actions and behavior of people and companies.

Tort law is important to business. Businesses harmed by the wrongful conduct of others may sue to recover damages. When businesses or their agents cause damage to others—whether they are customers, competitors, or strangers—liability may result. Insurance against possible damage awards is a necessary cost of doing business.

When an employee of a business commits a tort, the liability of the business is determined under the principle of vicarious liability or *respondeat superior* (let the master answer). Under this principle a business is liable for the torts of an employee who is acting within the scope of his or her employment. For example, if a pizza delivery driver causes an automobile accident while delivering a pizza, the driver's employer would be responsible for the damages inflicted on the other motorist.

The various types of torts can be divided into three categories: intentional torts, negligence, and strict liability torts (*see* Table 6-1).

## INTENTIONAL TORTS

Intentional torts are voluntary acts that invade a protected interest. In each of these torts, the tortfeasor intends to do the act that causes injury. The tortfeasor is liable for all reasonably foreseeable harm resulting from that intentional act.

### *Punitive Damages*

Because a high degree of culpability attaches to intentional torts, the victim is entitled to **punitive damages.** These are damages intended to punish the offender, and further compensate the victim for wounded sensibilities. They are damages awarded above and beyond the compensatory damages. Compensatory damages include those for medical expenses, loss of wages, disability and pain and suffering. The amount of punitive damages to be awarded is normally within the province of the jury. Over the years large punitive damage awards have grabbed public attention. In the O. J. Simpson civil case the jury awarded punitives amounting to $25,000,000. The McDonalds' coffee cup spill case was first reported with a punitive damage award of $4 million. However, The United States Supreme Court made it clear in *BMC v. Gore* that excessive punitive damage awards would be a denial of Due Process.

The following torts, although not exhaustive, are categorized as intentional torts. They include intentional torts against person, property, or both (*see* Table 6-2).

**Business and Government Interface**

This American Tort Reform Association link lists punitive damages reform, state-by-state.

http://www.atra.org/issues/punitive-damages-reform

## *Battery and Assault*

Battery is an unprivileged, unwanted touching of another. Any unwelcome contact, from a friendly slap on the back to a malicious slap in the face, constitutes a battery. Some possess a privilege to commit battery; for example, soldiers in war, and executioners lawfully charged by the sovereign with carrying out the death penalty.

To be liable for a battery, the tortfeasor must intend to touch the other person, an article of clothing that person is wearing, or something the victim is carrying. A flick of another's hat or grabbing at an umbrella the victim is carrying constitutes a battery, although the injury here would ordinarily be slight.

Assault is causing another person to be apprehensive about a battery. Threatening to strike someone or advancing toward another with intent to sexually violate that person is deemed an assault, while the actual touching is the battery.

**Understanding the Private Law Sector**

This link, from the Texas Trial Lawyer's Association, busts the myth of the McDonald's hot coffee spill case.

https://www.ttla.com/index.cfm?pg=McDonaldsCoffeeCaseFacts

## *Intentional Infliction of Emotional Distress*

The tort of intentional infliction of emotional distress provides a remedy for conduct intended to unjustifiably upset the victim. Simple insults and indignities do not give rise to this tort. For the tort to occur (1) the conduct must be outrageous, (2) the perpetrator must intend to cause emotional distress, and (3) the plaintiff must actually suffer severe mental distress.

**TABLE 6-2 Classification of Intentional Torts**

| *Against a Person* | *Against Property* | *Against Property and Person* |
|---|---|---|
| Battery | Disparagement | Wrongful discharge |
| Assault | Palming off | |
| Intentional infliction of emotional distress | Interference with contract | |
| False imprisonment | Trespass | |
| Defamation: libel and slander | Nuisance | |
| Deceit | | |
| Invasion of privacy | | |

## *False Imprisonment*

False imprisonment is interference with a victim's freedom of movement. A restraint that prevents a person from going where he or she pleases is considered false imprisonment, even if the restraint is accomplished nonviolently. It can take place on an open street or in a store. It is not necessary to actually harm the victim; the tort protects the victim's interest in freedom of movement. The victim of false imprisonment must be consciously aware of the restriction. Hence, an unconscious person or one who is sleeping may not be falsely imprisoned when in those states.

False imprisonment may arise when a merchant detains a suspected shoplifter. However, the law recognizes that merchants have a special interest in protecting against theft. If a merchant reasonably believes that a person has taken goods without paying for them, the merchant is privileged to restrain the person for a reasonable period of time and in a reasonable manner. Restraint beyond what is reasonable to investigate the merchant's suspicions and summon the police, if necessary, destroys the privilege and leaves the merchant vulnerable to a successful lawsuit.

## *Defamation: Libel and Slander*

The tort of defamation protects a person's interest in his or her reputation and good name. Libel is written or some other recorded defamation, while slander is oral defamation. A person who attacks another's reputation or causes another to be held up to hatred, contempt, or ridicule, or to be avoided or shunned, may be liable for the tort of defamation. The tort of defamation requires proof that:

- The tortfeasor made a defamatory statement.
- The defamatory statement identifies the victim to a reasonable reader or listener.
- The tortfeasor communicated the defamatory statement to a third party.
- The victim's reputation was damaged.

The advent and proliferation of social media has expanded defamatory actions and damages beyond the traditional print media, as the next case illustrates.

### NELSON *v.* THE SUPERIOR COURT OF LOS ANGELES COUNTY

Court of Appeals of California
(California 2nd App, Dist., 2018)

Jeff Nelson runs a media and publishing company with focus a on health, nutrition, and veganism. His company, VegSource, creates original content and documentaries for sale, cooking DVDs, and a variety of health products in the vegan sector. VegSource has a YouTube channel where Nelson and other speakers extol the vegan lifestyle. Advertisers pay to advertise on the YouTube channel.

Nelson invited Charles Marlowe, a YouTube personality to speak at the company sponsored Healthy Lifestyle Expo. Marlowe had a troubled past, including drug addiction, and credited veganism with helping get his life back on track. After the public announcement, someone using the pseudonym Chantelle Robin (and apparently others) began releasing a cache of videos on a phony YouTube account viciously attacking Nelson, apparently in response to Nelson's invitation to Marlowe.

Commenters posted on social media that Jeff Nelson practices "bestiality and paedophilia [sic] and incest," has "mouth sores," and sells food that causes "mouth herpes." Nelson and his company VegSource Interactive (collectively, Nelson) sued for defamation. He alleged that Robin posted a video on YouTube, titled "Vegan Cheetah has MOUTH SORES! The Shocking Truth of the Vegsource Diet!! Jeff Nelson Bite Size." The text on the screen of the video stated: "Due to the RESTRICTIVE Vegsource McDougall Diet . . . And close, *intimate* collaboration . . . The Vegsource Industry Has an outbreak of MOUTH SORES" and "Vegsource Jeff Nelson . . . [is] selling a MAGICAL DIET And it's causing MOUTH HERPES & uncontrollable lying." The video included photographs of Nelson and his wife that were "doctored to make it appear as if they had mouth herpes" and placed "next to stock photographs of persons with mouth herpes."

He suspected that the commenters were YouTuber competitors who are doing it not just out of spite but also for profit. To discover the identity of the commenters Nelson served subpoenas on Google, Tumblr, YouTube, and Twitter, requesting potentially identifying information, including the commenters' IP addresses. Before those companies responded to the subpoenas, however, they notified Robin, who filed a motion to quash the subpoenas. The trial court granted the motion to quash. Nelson appealed the ruling.

## *Segal, J.*

* * *

. . . [In quashing Robin's motion] [t]he [lower] court stated: "Robin does not represent herself as 'unbiased' and 'having specialized knowledge,' nor does she characterize her videos or comments as 'Research Reports' or 'bulletins' or 'alerts', and the social media used was not like Yelp . . . in which statements could reasonably be understood as conveying facts." . . .

* * *

"Defamation is a 'false and unprivileged publication that exposes the plaintiff "to hatred, contempt, ridicule, or obloquy, or which causes him to be shunned or avoided, or which has a tendency to injure him in his occupation."'" "The elements of a defamation claim are (1) a publication that is (2) false, (3) defamatory, (4) unprivileged, and (5) has a natural tendency to injure or causes special damage." . . . "Libel is a false and unprivileged publication by writing, printing, picture, effigy, or other fixed representation to the eye, which exposes any person to hatred, contempt, ridicule, or obloquy, or which causes him to be shunned or avoided, or which has a tendency to injure him in his occupation. A corporation can be libeled by statements which injure its business reputation. . . ."

. . . "The question is 'whether a reasonable fact finder could conclude the published statement declares or implies a provably false assertion of fact.'" "To determine whether a statement is reasonably susceptible of a defamatory interpretation, 'courts use a totality of the circumstances test.'" "[A] court must put itself in the place of an average reader and determine the natural and probable effect of the statement . . ." "Use of 'hyperbolic,' 'informal', 'crude', [or] 'ungrammatical' language, satirical tone, [or] vituperative, 'juvenile name-calling' provide support for the conclusion that offensive comments were nonactionable opinion. Similarly, overly vague statements, and 'generalized' comments . . . 'lack[ing] any specificity as to the time or place of' alleged conduct may be a 'further signal to the reader there is no factual basis for the accusations.'" "On the other hand, if a statement is 'factually specific,' 'earnest', or 'serious' in tone, or the speaker 'represents himself as "unbiased," "having specialized" or "first-hand experience," or "hav[ing] personally witnessed . . . abhorrent behavior"' this may signal the opposite, rendering the statement actionable. . . ."

"As Internet technology has evolved over the past two decades, computer users have encountered a proliferation of chat rooms and websites that allow them to share their views 'anonymously,' by using 'screen names' traceable only through the hosts of the sites or their [ISPs]." "The Constitution protects anonymous speech, including speech on the Internet, but '[w]hen vigorous criticism descends into defamation . . . constitutional protection is no longer available.'" . . .

* * *

. . . "First Amendment protection for anonymous speech requires a libel plaintiff seeking to discover an anonymous libel defendant's identity to make a prima facie showing of all elements of defamation". . . .

. . ."The dispositive question . . . is whether a reasonable trier of fact could conclude that the published statements imply a provably false factual assertion." . . . "To meet this standard in seeking compulsory disclosure of an anonymous Internet speaker's identity . . . '[a] plaintiff need produce evidence of only those material facts that are accessible to [it],' for example, evidence of the allegedly libelous statement, its falsity, and its effect on the plaintiff.". . .

We begin (and end) our analysis with the "mouth herpes video," what Nelson calls one of the "worst of Robin's statements," . . . Although even facially neutral words may be defamatory, these statements are not facially neutral. They are libelous per se because "a listener could understand the defamatory meaning without the necessity of knowing extrinsic explanatory matter.". . .

Robin argues the video alleging the VegSource diet causes mouth herpes and the doctored photographs of Nelson and his family were "pure satire." Robin stated he or she posted the video "in response" to a video Marlowe had posted "wherein [Marlowe] indicated that the type of vegan diet practiced by the subject of his video . . . is so restrictive as to give her mouth sores." According to Robin, Marlowe's video claims there is a "vegan mouth sore epidemic" and shows the subject of the video "touching her mouth, and depicts altered or photo-shopped pictures of the cracks on her mouth."

* * *

Moreover, even if the two videos had been posted on the same webpage and views of Robin's video had already seen Marlowe's video, Robin's argument that the average viewer would have understood Robin's video was satire is unpersuasive.

* * *

. . . .Because Nelson made a prima facie showing that Robin defamed him, the trial court erred in granting Robin's motion to quash.

[The court ordered that the lower court set aside its order to quash.]

**Business Application:** What steps can a business owner who operates through social media take to protect it against competitors who are out to defame and harm the business through anonymous internet attack?

Because the First Amendment of the U.S. Constitution protects the right of free speech, defamation is more difficult to prove when the target of the statement is a public figure. In such cases, the public figure must prove that the tortfeasor knew the statement was false or made the statement in reckless disregard of the truth. In contrast, when the target of the statement is a private person, liability may exist where the tortfeasor simply negligently publishes a defamatory statement.

Another limitation on recovery for defamation in most states is the requirement that a victim of slander establish actual damage to his or her reputation. However, some statements that are clearly defamatory are presumed to cause damage. These statements are referred to as *slander per se.* The following statements fall under this category:

- A statement adversely reflecting on a person's business, trade, or profession.
- A statement that a person is afflicted with a communicable disease, usually a sexually transmitted one.
- A statement that a person has committed a crime that is morally reprehensible.
- A statement imputing sexual misconduct to a person.

Slanderous statements falling outside the per se category require proof that the statements caused actual damage to reputation, such as loss of business or a contract. Many states afford a presumption of damages for libel.

In some situations, an individual is privileged to make an otherwise defamatory statement. This occurs when the communication serves an important public interest. For example, a former or current employer is privileged to tell a prospective employer about a job applicant's qualifications. However, the privilege can be lost if the statement is made in bad faith. To avoid the danger of running the risk of committing defamation, many employers simply adopt a policy of providing only a neutral recommendation that states the date of hire, the position(s) held and the date of discharge.

Truth is an absolute defense to the tort of defamation. The burden, however, is on the defendant to prove that the alleged defamatory statements were in fact true.

## *Deceit*

Deceit is a knowing and intentional misrepresentation of a material fact. To recover damages, the following elements must be established:

- A knowingly false representation of a material fact.
- An intent to induce the listener to rely on the representation.
- Justifiable reliance on the representation by the listener.
- Damages to the duped party resulting from such reliance.

Clearly, the range of what can be considered fraud or misrepresentation is great; as the morals of the marketplace change, so does the definition of deceit. For example, in the distant past, negotiations between buyers and sellers were characterized by the notion of *caveat emptor*, or "let the buyer beware." This attitude gave way to an obligation on the part of a seller to inform a buyer of hidden defects. This is particularly true when vendors deal with consumers. This expansion of vendors' obligation of fuller disclosure is an example of law intersecting with high moral values. In commercial transactions between parties on relatively equal bargaining levels, for example, a manufacturer and supplier, the obligation to disclose is not as strict. These parties can generally be expected to investigate and protect their own interests.

## *Invasion of Privacy*

Most people assume that they have a right to privacy, but very few can describe the dimensions of this right. Tort law recognizes four distinct causes of action for interfering with privacy rights: (1) intrusion, (2) public disclosure of private facts, (3) false light in the public eye, and (4) appropriation.

**Law and Ethics in Business Policies**

This Privacy Rights Clearinghouse link delves into the issues of workplace privacy and employee monitoring.

https://www.privacyrights.org/workplace-privacy-and-employee-monitoring

### Intrusion into Seclusion

The more traditional notion of what the right of privacy protects is represented by an intrusion. Tortious intrusions include unauthorized physical entry into another's premises or snooping into someone's home or other private premises, eavesdropping, repeated or unwanted telephone calls, or unauthorized prying or gaining access into someone's bank account or other personal affairs. Liability may occur if the nature of the intrusion is such that it would be objectionable or offensive to a reasonable person.

### Public Disclosure of Private Facts

Another type of invasion of privacy, public disclosure of private facts, involves disclosing to the public the intimate facts of one's life. Information revealed to the public must not have been publicly known, and the disclosure must be offensive to a person of ordinary sensibility. Private facts that the courts have protected include the public disclosure of an unpaid debt, medical pictures of one's anatomy, and details of one's sexual relations.

### False Light

The third form of interference with privacy involves placing someone in a false light in the public eye. A person has the right to be free from having false information publicly disseminated. Although similar to defamation, it is broader and includes acts that would be objectionable to a reasonable person even though they are not necessarily defamatory. Examples of the tort are publicizing that a person is dead when he is in fact not, or that a person heroically rescued people from a burning building when this is untrue.

### Appropriation

Tort law prohibits the appropriation or use of the plaintiff's name or likeness for financial benefit without consent. This was the earliest form of privacy protection recognized by the courts. The most common example is the use of the name or picture of a celebrity for business purposes without the celebrity's consent. However, private, unknown people are also protected.

## *Disparagement*

False statements that injure a person's interest in property, as opposed to one's reputation, amount to disparagement. Assume that a patron accuses a butcher of selling spoiled meat. Because this statement tends to injure the butcher's reputation, it would be defamatory. Assume, however, that the patron falsely informs potential customers that the butcher went out of business. This does not directly injure the butcher's reputation; however, it injures the business by keeping potential buyers away from the butcher's business. This statement may constitute disparagement.

Disparagement is harder to prove than defamation. Plaintiffs must prove that the statements were false and malicious and that they resulted in actual monetary loss by, for example, causing certain customers to avoid dealing with the business.

## *Palming Off*

When an advertiser represents its goods in a way that deceives the average buyer into believing them to be the goods of a competitor, the advertiser is liable to that competitor for palming off. The misrepresentation may involve imitating the trademark, labels, containers, appearance of business, or any other distinctive characteristic of the competitor. Assume a local company that sells cheap wrist watches stamps the name Rolex (a watch of high quality) on the face of its watches and advertises them as such. This would amount to unlawful palming off—a practice that would injure Rolex in two ways. First, it would take away customers who would purchase the watches mistakenly thinking that they were made by Rolex. Second, it would injure Rolex's image by associating the inferior watch with its name. Here, Rolex could obtain both an injunction restraining the company from misrepresenting its goods and damages for loss of business.

Palming off is not the only type of false advertising that injures competitors. Most often, false advertisements misrepresent the quality, price, or nature of the advertised goods. Some states, and a federal statute, give competitors an action against competitors who falsely advertise in this manner. These false advertisements harm competitors by taking customers away from them.

## *Interference with Contract*

The intentional and wrongful interference with a contract is a tort. The origin of this tort can be traced to *Lumley v. Guy*, an English case decided in 1853.[1] In that case, an opera singer was obligated, pursuant to a contract, to sing at a theater. A competitor of the theater, aware of the contractual relationship, nevertheless persuaded the singer to break her contract. Liability was imposed against the competitor for interference with contract.

Tortious interference of contractual rights is not confined to existing contracts; it extends to potential contracts as well. Hence, it is a tort to prevent a person from obtaining employment, or to impede a business from contracting with customers, or to dissuade a publisher from contracting with an author.

---

1 118 Eng. Reprint 749.

## *Trespass*

The tort of trespass is really two distinct torts: trespass to personal property (movables, such as merchandise), and trespass to real property (land).

A trespass to personal property is committed by interfering with someone's right to possess his or her personal property by, for example, taking merchandise for a short time, or harming the goods. The tortfeasor is liable for damages if the victim can prove:

- Interference with the owner's right of possession.
- Intent by the tortfeasor to do the act that constituted the interference.
- Interference caused damage to the owner's personal property.

When the interference with personal property is so great that it deprives the owner of its value, courts find that the tortfeasor converted the property and order the tortfeasor to pay the fair market value of the property to the owner. This constitutes another related tort, known as *conversion.* Common acts constituting conversion are the destruction of property, theft, receipt of stolen goods, and wrongful transfer or retention of property. The owner has the option of demanding the property back or receiving the fair market dollar value at the time of conversion.

Trespass to real property is an unlawful interference with another's land. This tort action protects a landholder's interest in the exclusive possession of his or her properties. A person who physically intrudes on another's property commits a trespass. However, the intruder need not physically set foot on the property to be liable; he or she may be held liable for setting events in motion that cause the intrusion. For example, someone on his or her land who sets a fire to a neighbor's land commits a trespass to real property. A trespass may be committed by a single act or by a continuing presence on another's land.

## *Nuisance*

A nuisance is a substantial and unreasonable interference with the use and enjoyment of an interest in land. A cause of action for nuisance thus protects landholders' interests in the use and enjoyment of their properties. In environmental litigation, nuisance includes interferences in the form of smoke, odor, noise, and vibration.

Trespass and nuisance are distinguishable. A trespass is an invasion of the right to exclusive possession of land, as by entry on it. A nuisance is an interference with the interest in the private use and enjoyment of land and does not require direct interference with possession. For example, the flooding of another's land constitutes a trespass because it interferes with the landholder's interest in possession. In contrast, a noxious odor spewing from a nearby factory smokestack might constitute a nuisance to the neighboring owners' use and enjoyment of their properties. Some courts do not differentiate between such subtleties; the label is not as important as the wrongful action and injury.

When determining whether a nuisance exists, the courts balance various factors—a practice referred to as *balancing the equities.* All landholders' rights to use and enjoyment of their properties are necessarily subject to the rights of other landholders to do the same. Consequently, the courts weigh the utility of the conduct of one landholder against the gravity of the harm caused to another. Generally, if the harm outweighs utility, the courts deem the conduct a nuisance. Other relevant considerations are the existence of practical means to avoid causing the harm and the location of the properties.

## *Wrongful Discharge*

Employment relationships are based on contracts. Employees agree to perform services for their employers, who agree to compensate their employees. Most employees are hired for an indefinite period of time. Frequently nothing is said about when, how, or under what circumstances the contract may be terminated.

The traditional rule is that an employment contract of indefinite duration is terminable at the will of either party. If nothing is said about the length of employment, the employee is free to quit, and the employer is free to fire the employee, at any time, for any reason, or for no reason at all.

This traditional employment-at-will doctrine has eroded over the years. Courts in most states still agree that an employer has the power to discharge an at-will employee for any reason. However, most states have decided that when an employer fires an employee in a manner that contravenes public policy, however, the employee may recover for the tort of abusive or wrongful discharge. These courts disagree over what constitutes public policy. However, most of the courts that recognize the tort of wrongful discharge require that the public policy be expressed by a constitutional provision or a statute. For example, in one case it was deemed a wrongful discharge for an employer to fire an employee when the employee refused to pump water out of the deck of a boat into the waterway because there was a statute that prohibited such pumping.[2] Some courts allow the public policy to be expressed in a state's common law. Recognition of wrongful discharge based upon employer actions that are contrary to public policy is an example of society's concept of morality influencing the law.

The next case presents a majority and a minority opinion for the common law recognition and extension of a public policy exception to the employee-at-will doctrine.

### DUKOWITZ *v.* HANNON SECURITY SERVICES

Supreme Court of Minnesota
841 N.W. 2d 147 (2014)

Hannon Security Services (Hannon) hired Jane Dukowitz as a security officer. In early December her supervisor told her that her position would not be open past the end of the month. Dukowitz applied for unemployment benefits. Hannon terminated Dukowitz, and her position became open two days after she applied for the benefits.

Dukowitz sued Hannon for wrongful discharge alleging that Hannon violated the public policy when it terminated her employment in retaliation for her seeking unemployment benefits. The trial court found in favor of Hannon and the court of appeals affirmed. The Supreme Court of Minnesota affirmed the court of appeal decision. There was a strong dissenting opinion.

---

2 Sabine Pilot Services v. Hauck, 687 S.W. 2d 734 (Tex. 1985).

### *Justice Stras*

The . . . question presented in this case is whether the public-policy exception to the employment-at-will rule applies to a termination resulting from an employee's application for unemployment benefits. . . .

* * *

In Minnesota, the employer-employee relationship is generally at-will, which means that an employer may discharge an employee for "any reason or no reason" and that an employee is "under no obligation to remain on the job." In *Phipps*, we . . . limited the cause of action . . . to discharges resulting from an employee's good-faith refusal to violate the law.

* * *

*Nelson*, the other case relied upon by Dukowitz, was similarly limited in scope. In *Nelson*, we considered the effect of Minnesota's Whistleblower Act . . . on the cause of action we had recognized in *Phipps*. Although we acknowledged some possible overlap between the two, we held that the common-law cause of action that we had recognized in *Phipps* survived the enactment of the Whistleblower Act.

* * *

*Phipps and Nelson*, therefore, recognize a common-law cause of action for wrongful discharge only in those circumstances in which a termination is the result of an employee's refusal to do an act that the employee, in good faith, believes to be illegal. Neither case recognizes a broader cause of action that arises every time an employee's termination results from an employer's violation of a clear mandate of public policy. . . .

* * *

. . . [N]either Dukowitz nor the dissent can delineate the contours of the tort that they urge us to adopt, which presumably would make an employer liable whenever a court can identify a clear statement of public policy that the employer has violated by discharging an employee. . . .

Indeed, given the difficulties of defining a clear statement of public policy, it is not surprising that even those states that have adopted a public-policy exception to at-will employment have disagreed on the parameters of the cause of action . . .

Second, we decline to expand the public-policy exception to the employment-at-will rule when the Legislature has already delineated the consequences for an employer that interferes with an . . . application for unemployment benefits. . . .

* * *

Affirmed.

### *Justice Wright, dissenting*

* * *

The majority first expresses a "general reluctance" to recognize a new cause of action unless "the Legislature intends for us to do so." Indeed, the Legislature plays a significant—even the most significant—role in formulating the public policy of the state. But the Legislature's role is not exclusive. As a common-law court, we have "the power to recognize and abolish common law doctrines."

We have explained that the common law "is not composed of firmly fixed rules" and "[a]s society changes over time, the common law must also evolve." . . . When applied here, the majority's view—that any extension of public policy is better left to the Legislature—presents an overly narrow view of the common law and abdicates this court's responsibility for developing it.

* * *

. . . The majority contends that the public-policy exception is inappropriate because "the Legislature has already provided other remedies to vindicate the public policy of the state." In my view, the mere existence of another remedy is not sufficient to crowd out this common-law wrongful-discharge claim. Indeed, [in Nelson] we have specifically held that the existence of a statutory remedy does not preclude common-law wrongful-discharge claims. . . .

. . . Generally, when developing our common law, we look to the common law of other states. Here, the overwhelming majority of jurisdictions recognize the public-policy exception to the employment-at-will rule. . . .

With the foregoing principles in mind, I now turn to the question that the majority avoids—whether an employer's retaliation against an employee who files for unemployment benefits violates a clear mandate of public policy.

* * *

. . . [W]e have recognized that the extension of unemployment benefits to those who are eligible is "the declared public policy of our state. . . ." To ensure that benefits are available to under-and unemployed workers, the Legislature has forbidden employers from obstructing or impeding an application for unemployment benefits. Indeed, that the Legislature has deemed such conduct criminal underscores the strong public policy at stake and allays any concerns about the judiciary's ability to discern "what employers" decisions contravene a clear mandate of public policy. . . ."

. . . Permitting employers to discharge employees who seek unemployment benefits deters eligible, economically vulnerable individuals—including part-time workers, seasonal workers, or workers who have their hours reduced—from seeking unemployment benefits to which they are statutorily entitled. Moreover, permitting such terminations exacerbates the very problem that unemployment insurance is designed to remedy—economic insecurity.

* * *

Because I conclude for the foregoing reasons that Dukowitz has a cognizable cause of action for wrongful discharge under the public-policy exception to the employment-at-will rule, I respectfully dissent.

**Business Application:** What internal policies and standards should a business adapt when it comes to discharging an employee for cause?

## *Defenses to Intentional Torts*

Consent and privilege are two common defenses in intentional tort cases. A defendant can avoid liability by proving either that the plaintiff consented to the defendant's conduct or that the defendant was privileged to do what would otherwise be an intentional tort.

Whether a plaintiff has consented to the defendant's conduct is determined by the plaintiff's behavior under the circumstances, not by the plaintiff's actual feelings. Consent may be expressed. For example, it is common for hospitals to require patients to sign a consent form before undergoing medical procedures. Consent may also be implied by conduct, as, for example, where an employee voluntarily shows up for an employer's drug test without verbalizing consent. Courts inquire into the reasonableness of the consent, and will declare consent ineffective if it violates law or public policy.

Conduct that would otherwise be an intentional tort may nevertheless be privileged. For example, someone acting in self-defense can avoid liability for what would otherwise be a battery. When creating privileges, courts are deciding that the importance of certain conduct outweighs the risks of harm. A privilege is lost if the defendant acts in bad faith.

## NEGLIGENCE

Often damage is caused by unintentional or careless conduct. Under certain circumstances, the injured party can recover damages for the tort of **negligence.** Negligence is unintentional conduct that falls below the standard of care that is necessary to protect others against exposure to an unreasonable risk of a foreseeable injury.

### *Elements of Negligence*

Negligence is conduct that is unreasonable under the circumstances. A plaintiff must prove the following elements to recover against a defendant for the tort of negligence:

- The existence of a duty to exercise the degree of care that a reasonable and prudent person would exercise under similar circumstances.
- A breach of that duty by a failure to adhere to the standard of reasonable conduct.
- The unreasonable conduct was the actual and proximate cause of the plaintiff's injury.
- Actual injury to the plaintiff.

#### Duty

Before liability for negligence is imposed, a court must first determine that the defendant was under a duty to protect the plaintiff from the injury that occurred. For example, assume a passenger in the front seat of a van is injured when the van collides with a telephone pole. Could the passenger successfully sue the manufacturer of the van for negligence, claiming that the manufacturer had a duty to design the vehicle so that in collisions under 40 mph the passenger would not come into contact with the interior compartment of the van? Should the manufacturer be under a duty to design a crashworthy vehicle? In determining the existence of a duty, a court would weigh the nature and foreseeability of the risk of harm (here, the risk of collisions) against the social utility of the defendant's conduct (here, the social utility of a van) and the costs of taking precautions (here, the cost of redesigning the van).

In the example involving the van, a federal appellate court considered the foreseeability of automobile collisions, but found that it was outweighed by the burden of imposing precautions on the manufacturer, a burden that would require redesigning a van to the extent that it would no longer be useful for its intended purpose as a cargo carrier. The court also noted that imposing such a duty on the manufacturer would drastically increase the price of vans. In the court's opinion, this would have the effect of depriving society of a reasonably priced light-cargo carrier.[3] Thus, when determining the existence of a duty, courts balance as a matter of policy the social value of the parties' interests.

### Breach of Duty

In the absence of a statute, the question of whether the defendant breached the duty of care is one that the jury determines (or the judge, if sitting without a jury). A standard of conduct, known as the *reasonable person standard,* is applied. Whether the defendant has breached a duty of care is determined by comparing the defendant's conduct to that of a reasonable and prudent person under the same or similar circumstances. When the defendant is a person with special training, such as a doctor, lawyer, or accountant, the standard takes into consideration the defendant's training. Thus, an accountant is held to the standard of a reasonably informed accountant; a certified public accountant would be held to the standard of a reasonably informed certified public accountant.

### Actual and Proximate Cause

The plaintiff must also prove that the defendant's conduct was the actual and proximate cause of the injury. Determination of the existence of actual and proximate cause is ordinarily a matter for the jury to decide (or the judge, if sitting without a jury).

Actual cause refers to the direct causal connection between the defendant's conduct and the plaintiff's injury. The simplest way to determine whether an injury resulted from the defendant's conduct is to ascertain whether the plaintiff would have been injured *but for* the defendant's action. For example, a landlord's negligent failure to provide a fire escape could cause the death of someone who is thereby prevented from fleeing a fire. However, the absence of a fire escape would not cause the death of someone who suffocated in bed during the fire. When there are several causes of an injury or damage, each defendant whose conduct contributed to the injury can be held responsible for the damage if his or her conduct was a substantial factor causing the injury.

In addition to being the actual cause of the plaintiff's injury, the defendant's conduct must also be the **proximate cause**. A defendant is liable only for those injuries that are proximate, as opposed to injuries that are remote. Proximate cause, thus, has to do with the likelihood (foreseeability) of the injury. If the plaintiff's injury could not be reasonably foreseen by the defendant at the time of the defendant's act or omission, the defendant's conduct will not be considered the proximate cause of the injury. The element of proximate cause requires the plaintiff's injury to be the natural, probable, and foreseeable result of the defendant's conduct.

### Injury

Generally, injury includes damage to property or person. A plaintiff who sustains physical injury is entitled to recover for damage, including medical expenses, loss of wages, and even pain and suffering. It may also include injury for loss of consortium, that is the loss of services, society and sex. The establishment of damages for physical or mental injury usually requires the testimony of medical experts. The defendant often has its own medical experts to rebut the plaintiff's medical experts. This "battle of the experts" generally requires the trier of the fact to determine whose expert opinion to believe.

---

3 Dreisonstok v. Volkswagen of America, 489 F. 2d 1066 (4th Cir. 1974).

## Procedural Doctrines

Two procedural doctrines help plaintiffs prove their case of negligence. The first one, the doctrine of *negligence per se*, employs a statute to establish negligence; the second, the doctrine of *res ipsa loquitur*, employs reason to establish a presumption of negligence.

### Negligence Per Se

Negligence may arise as a result of a violation of a statute or regulation. When enacting statutes or regulations, legislatures and agencies sometimes weigh the risk of harm resulting from certain conduct and the conduct's social utility. In many states the violation of such a statute or regulation in certain circumstances is considered **negligence per se,** which means that the violation, by itself, is considered unreasonable. For violation of a statute or regulation to qualify as negligence per se (1) the injured person must be within the class of persons the statute or regulation was designed to protect, and (2) the injury must be of a type that the statute or regulation was designed to prevent. Assume, for example, that a statute prohibits the mislabeling of any drug. From his local pharmacy Jack Plaintiff purchases a drug labeled aspirin; in reality it is a poisonous substance. If Plaintiff becomes ill or dies as a result of ingesting the mislabeled drug, the manufacturer would be negligent per se. Plaintiff is a consumer, a person within the class the statute was designed to protect, and the statute is designed to prevent the very type of injury that occurred.

However, assume that a local health ordinance requires a restaurant to have smooth flooring for drainage and cleaning. One Star Restaurant violates the statute by having corrugated flooring. Jill Patron trips and injures herself when her high heel lodges within a riveted portion of the floor. Here, the violation of the statute would not constitute negligence per se. The statute is for sanitation purposes and is not designed to protect patrons against the injury that befell Jill.

### Res Ipsa Loquitur

In some accidents it is not easy for the plaintiff to discover which act or omission led to the injury suffered; the plaintiff can find no direct evidence of negligence. For example, if a pedestrian is suddenly and unexpectedly struck by a falling brick while passing a construction site, the plaintiff may have difficulty knowing how or why the brick fell. To help deserving plaintiffs, courts have developed a rule of evidence referred to as **res ipsa loquitur** (the thing speaks for itself). Application of the doctrine of res ispa loquitur creates a presumption of negligence. The rule is applicable when the accident would not ordinarily occur without negligence. In addition, other causes—including conduct by the plaintiff—must be sufficiently eliminated by the evidence. As well, the instrumentality causing the injury must be within the defendant's control. Because of this rule, many plaintiffs are able to establish their cases without direct evidence of negligence.

## Defenses to Negligence

Even when the plaintiff can successfully prove the elements constituting negligence, defenses may be raised to defeat recovery. Contributory negligence, comparative negligence and assumption of the risk are the more common defenses.

### Contributory Negligence

In a few states the plaintiff's contribution to the injury, however slight, will bar plaintiff's recovery. Like negligence, the contributory negligence must be proximate, a contributing foreseeable cause of the injury. In a few other states, for the bar to occur, the contribution must be substantial. The doctrine of contributory negligence has given way in the vast majority of the states to the doctrine of comparative negligence.

### Comparative Negligence

Almost all states have adopted **comparative negligence** as a defense. Under this principle, recovery is reduced by the percentage that the negligence contributed to his or her injury. Assume, for example, that the defendant company negligently designed a refuse bin so that it was unstable. The plaintiff purchased the bin and negligently placed it on an irregular and inclined surface. The plaintiff was injured when the bin overturned in a windstorm. If the jury determines that the plaintiff's damages are $40,000, that the defendant was 75 percent at fault, and that the plaintiff was 25 percent at fault, plaintiff's recovery would be reduced by 25 percent to $30,000. In many states the plaintiff would be barred from any recovery if his or her percentage of contribution was greater than or equal to the defendant's percentage of contribution.

### Assumption of the Risk

**Assumption of the risk** prevents a plaintiff from recovering against a negligent defendant, because the plaintiff is held to have assumed the risk of his or her injury. Assumption of the risk consists of a voluntary exposure to a known risk. It differs from comparative or contributory negligence in that contributory or comparative negligence is based on carelessness, whereas assumption of the risk is based on voluntariness—willful exposure to a known risk. A plaintiff who continues to drive an automobile with full knowledge that it has defective brakes is deemed to have assumed the risk of injury that is likely to result. If the plaintiff does not know about the defective brakes but really should, then he or she is guilty of comparative or contributory negligence. Some states have collapsed the doctrine of assumption of the risk into the doctrine of comparative negligence on the basis that one who voluntarily assumes an unreasonable risk is, infact, negligent.

## STRICT LIABILITY

By emphasizing the factors of intent and reasonable conduct, the areas of intentional torts and negligence use a fault standard to determine liability. The third area of tort law, **strict liability,** does not emphasize fault. Liability is strictly imposed in certain situations even if the actor does not intend to do the act or exercises all reasonable care.

The areas in which strict liability apply are where injuries (1) are caused by a defective product that is unreasonably dangerous because of its defect, (2) result from harboring dangerous or vicious animals, or (3) result from abnormally dangerous activities, such as blasting operations.

### *Abnormally Dangerous Activities*

Individuals or companies engaged in hazardous activities, such as oil drilling, are strictly liable for any injuries arising from those activities. It does not matter that the offender did not intend to cause injury or was exercising all reasonable care; nor does it matter that the victim may have failed to take reasonable precautions for his or her own protection. Fault does not matter; liability is strictly imposed. It is based upon economics and a policy of risk-spending over society for hazardous activities.

**Understanding the Private Law Sector**

This link expands on, "What is an Ultrahazardous Activity?"

http://www.legalmatch.com law-library/article/ultrahazardous-activity-liability.html

The theory of strict liability serves to reimburse victims harmed by abnormally dangerous activities carried on voluntarily. It treats the risk of injury as a cost of engaging in the activity. Under strict liability, those engaged in abnormally dangerous activities must pay for the damage they cause. Under negligence, the victim would not be compensated if reasonable care were undertaken in the performance of such dangerous activity. Negligence theory provides no recovery to the victims of dangerous yet reasonable activity; strict liability does.

Abnormally dangerous activities involve a serious risk of harm to people, land, or property. The risk is usually one that cannot be eliminated even if the actor exercises great care. Businesses engaged in abnormally dangerous activities bear responsibility for the injuries they cause despite any precautions taken to prevent them.

**Understanding the Private Law Sector**

This link discusses insuring against tort liability.

http://tort.laws.com/liability-insurance

Activities are usually abnormally dangerous when they are out of place in their locality. Blasting operations and storage of large quantities of explosives or flammable gases are abnormally dangerous when conducted in cities. Such activities pose serious threats to human life and the integrity of property.

**Business Application/Ethical Issues**

Early one December morning, methyl isocyanate (a lethal gas) leaked from a fertilizer production plant in Bhopal, India. The plant was owned by Union Carbide of India, a subsidiary of Union Carbide, a U.S.-based corporation. The leakage resulted in the worst industrial disaster in history—more than 3,500 people were killed and more than 200,000 people were injured. Union Carbide had insurance of $200 million to cover such a disaster. Because the disaster occurred in India, for practical and legal reasons, the survivors and decedents' representatives are forced to sue in India.

India does not provide for jury trials. Its discovery rules are more restrictive than those in the United States. Judgments are generally significantly less than they are in the United States, and the court system is much slower.

Union Carbide had a similar plant with the same design in West Virginia, and is consequently exposed to a potential disaster and liability through suits in the Unites States.

What are the ethical issues? What should Union Carbide do?

# CHAPTER PROBLEMS

1. Define the following terms:
   *a.* Tort
   *b.* Punitive damages
   *c.* Palming off
   *d.* Wrongful Discharge
   *e.* Negligence
   *f.* Proximate cause
   *g.* Negligence per se
   *h.* Res ipsa loquitor
   *i.* Comparative negligence
   *j.* Strict liability

## *Business Application*

2. Luella Davis was indebted to Public Finance Corporation. She informed Public Finance that she was no longer employed, was on public aid, and was unable to make payments on the indebtedness. Over an eight-month period, in attempts to collect the debt, employees of Public Finance called Mrs. Davis several times a week, sometimes more than once a day, and frequented her home weekly. On one occasion an agent of Public Finance telephoned Mrs. Davis at the hospital where she was visiting her sick daughter. On another occasion an employee of Public Finance persuaded Mrs. Davis to write a check on the promise that the check would not be cashed. The employee then informed an acquaintance of Mrs. Davis that she was writing bad checks. On still another occasion a Public Finance employee went to Mrs. Davis's home and took an inventory of her household furnishings, refusing to leave until Mrs. Davis's son entered the room. Public Finance was aware that Mrs. Davis suffered from hypertension and a nervous condition. Both of these ailments were aggravated as a result of Public Finance's conduct. Does Davis have any recourse against Public Finance? Explain.
3. Paul Luedtke and his brother Clarence were employed on Nabors Alaska Drilling, Inc.'s (Nabors) oil rigs. Paul supervised an oil rig crew. Nabors required him to undergo urinalysis as part of a physical exam conducted while off duty. He tested positive for use of marijuana. Consequently, he was suspended and told that he would have to pass two additional tests at monthly intervals to be reinstated. He refused and was fired. Clarence Luedtke, Paul's brother, was fired when he refused to submit to the drug testing. Do Paul and Clarence Luedtke have any recourse against Nabors? Explain.
4. Continental Telephone Company of Vermont (Contel) ran a series of advertisements in Vermont Newspapers featuring certain of its employees. Cynthia Staruski, a sales and service representative at Contel's office in Springfield, Vermont, was featured in one such ad. The ad included a photograph of Mrs. Staruski smiling broadly. In large letters beside her

photograph were the words "Hi, I'm Cindy Staruski." Accompanying this was text, attributed with quotation marks to Staruski, describing her job responsibilities and saying that "it has been exciting and reassuring to know that Continental continues to expand its equipment and services to meet its obligations to serve you." Upset by Contel's publication of her name and likeness in this manner, Staruski sued in tort for invasion of privacy. What should be the result and why?

5. Geary was employed as a salesperson for U.S. Steel Corporation. He discovered that one of U.S. Steel's products was defective. He complained to his supervisor, who told him to mind his own business. He then contacted the vice president in charge of marketing for the product, who investigated. The investigation led to the removal of the product from the market and a reprimand to Geary's supervisor. The supervisor fired Geary "for making me look bad." What cause of action, if any, does Geary have? Explain. What policy should U.S. Steel adopt to handle situations of this nature?

6. Hidell Corporation has offices in an isolated area with an unusually high crime rate. On several occasions, employees have been victims of robbery and other violent attacks. In December, Paul Peters was robbed and severely beaten in an unlit employee parking lot when getting in his car to go to an executive meeting scheduled for 7 p.m. The attacker, an unemployed drifter, was found. What causes of action would Paul Peters have and against whom? Explain. What if anything can Hidell do to reduce potential liability for such episodes?

7. Hearn ran a classified advertisement in *Soldier of Fortune* magazine (SOF) that read "EX-MARINE—67–69 'NAM VET, EX-DI, weapons specialist—jungle warfare, pilot, M.E., high risk assignments, U.S. or overseas (404) 991-2684." After seeing the ad, Black called Hearn and proposed that Hearn kill Black's wife. Hearn did so. Black's mother-in-law and daughter sued SOF on the theory that SOF negligently published Hearn's classified ad. Analyze the suit under each of the elements of the tort of negligence. What is the result?

8. Hank Gathers played basketball in Los Angeles for Loyola Marymount University, which had an NCAA Division I basketball team. Gathers had a serious heart disorder and was under medication to normalize his heart rhythm. His doctor and coach knew of his medical condition. Nonetheless, Gathers insisted on playing. Because of Gathers's condition, the coach had a special medical device to revive him in the event he fell unconscious. On one occasion, Gathers passed out at the foul line during a game and was revived. During his final game, Gathers fell unconscious after a slam dunk. Efforts to revive him were of no avail and he died. Who is legally responsible for Gathers's death, if anyone? Explain. What should a college do under such circumstances?

9. Kathy Anderson sued Service Merchandise and Sylvania Lighting Services Corporation under the doctrine of res ipsa loquitur for injuries she suffered when an overhead light fixture fell and struck her as she stood in the checkout line of a Service Merchandise store. Service Merchandise has a maintenance contract with Sylvania, which had previously performed maintenance work on the lighting system. Notwithstanding this contract, Service Merchandise employees had occasionally changed light fixtures when they burned out.

The trial court granted summary judgment for Service Merchandise and Sylvania. The trial judge ruled that the lighting system was not under the exclusive control of each defendant and therefore the doctrine of res ipsa loquitur did not apply. No other information indicated any specific negligence by Service Merchandise or Sylvania. For that reason, the trial court dismissed Anderson's action. Anderson appealed. What should be the result?

10. On December 3, 1971, a dam burst at a phosphate mine operated by Cities Service Company in Polk County, Florida. Approximately 1 billion gallons of phosphate slime retained in a settling pond escaped into Whidden Creek. The slime reached the Peace River, killing countless fish and inflicting other damage. What recourse do affected property owners have against Cities Service? Explain.

# PART III

# THE LEGAL AND ETHICAL ENVIRONMENT OF BUSINESS ORGANIZATIONS

CHAPTER 7

# THE LAW OF BUSINESS ORGANIZATIONS

## CHAPTER OUTLINE



## LEARNING OBJECTIVES

After learning this chapter the student should be able to:

- Compare and contrast the relationships among principals, agents, and third parties.
- Identify the advantages and disadvantages of the major types of business organizations.
- Compare and contrast the partnership and the corporation in the areas of creation, operation, and termination.
- Compare the dissolution and winding-up process for partnerships and the dissolution process for corporations.

- Define the corporate structure and the interrelationship of the corporation's directors, officers, and shareholders.

Businesses are organized under a variety of legal structures. The dilemma faced by a new business is what organizational structure to embrace. The three most common organizational forms are the sole proprietorship, the partnership, and the corporation, although there are variants of these forms. Types of business organizations are compared in Table 7-1.

The sole proprietorship is the simplest form of business organization. It involves one person who owns and operates a business. Although this structure is discussed briefly, the chapter's main focus is on more complex business organizations—the partnership and the corporation. Both of these business forms are examined in terms of creation, operation, and termination.

These organizations—the partnership and the corporation—engage in a variety of activities to carry on business. To do this, they involve agents who act on behalf of the enterprises. Hence, before the discussion of partnerships and corporations begins, it is necessary to examine the law of agency.

# AGENCY

An agent acts on behalf of another. The party for whom an agent acts is the **principal.** Every business organization, whether it be a sole proprietorship, partnership, or corporation, employs agents. Agents ordinarily have authority to bind their principals, and may enter into contracts on behalf of their principals. As well, principals are liable to third parties for some tortious acts committed by agents within the scope of their agency. The agent is liable to the principal for entering into unauthorized contracts and for the agent's torts.

**TABLE 7-1 Business Organizations Compared**

| *Organization* | *Ownership* | *Management Control* | *Liability Exposure* | *Duration* | *Tax-Paying Entity* |
|---|---|---|---|---|---|
| Sole proprietorship | Self | Self | Unlimited | Limited | Yes |
| Joint venture | Venturers | Venturers | Unlimited | Limited | No |
| Partnership | Partners | Partners | Unlimited | Limited | No |
| Limited partnership | Limited partners | General partners | Limited for limited partners | Limited | No |
| Corporation | Shareholders | Board of directors | Limited | Perpetual | Yes |
| Subchapter S corporation | Shareholders | Board of directors | Limited | Year to year | No |
| Limited liability company | Partners | Partners | Limited | Perpetual | No |

## *Creation of Agency Relationship*

Agency relationships usually arise by mutual consent. For example, a national tire manufacturer may contract with a distributor of wholesale tires to be its exclusive agent within a local geographical area. This creates an agency relationship by contractual agreement.

Not every agency, however, is created so formally. All that is really necessary is assent to an agency relationship. Assume, for example, that Fred asks a neighbor to buy some baseball cards the next time he is at the baseball card store. The neighbor consents. No contract results because the agreement lacks consideration. Nonetheless, the neighbor is Fred's agent by consent.

An agent's authority is derived from the principal. That authority may be express, implied, apparent, or result from a ratification.

### Express Authority

Many agencies are created by express direction. For example, a power of attorney is a written instrument that expressly authorizes another to act as one's agent (*see* Form 7-1).

Many agency agreements are created orally, and they are just as effective as written agency agreements. One of the more common agencies created orally is the employer-employee relationship. Here, the employee acts as an agent of the employer.

### FORM 7-1 Power of Attorney

I, Henry Hansome, of sound mind, and over the age of eighteen years, do hereby invest in my attorney in fact, Elma Nichol, the following powers:

1. To deposit and withdraw funds from my savings and checking accounts and to sign all checks, deposit slips, and any other instruments necessary to perform such.
2. To sell securities that I presently own and deposit the proceeds from such into my savings account, and to sign all instruments to accomplish such.
3. To manage my real estate; pay taxes, insurance, and mortgage payments; and sign all instruments to accomplish such.
4. To make all medical decisions on my behalf and in my stead, should I become incompetent to do so, including a decision that no extraordinary medical procedures be used to prolong my life when there is no reasonable prognosis for recovery from a comatose or vegetative state.

Witness signatures

Henry Hansome

Witness signatures

On February 12, 2020, Henry Hansome appeared before me and acknowledged his signature.

Notary Public

### Implied Authority

Agency relationships may arise by implication. Usually agency authority by implication arises as a natural addition to express authority. For example, assume that an agent is hired to manage a swimming pool. This express authorization gives rise to the agent's implied authority to do all things reasonable and necessary to perform the managerial tasks. The agent could enter into contracts for the supply of chemicals to purify the water, repair the filtration system, and replace unsafe diving boards. This implied authority is derived from the express authorization.

### Apparent Authority

In certain cases, a principal is estopped (prevented) from denying that he or she authorized an agent's act. This occurs when the principal clothes an agent with **apparent authority,** thereby giving third parties the impression that the agent is empowered to act.

Assume for example that HVAC Corporation employs service repair persons to repair air conditioning and heating units and to install new ones. Frank Delitch had been having trouble with his air conditioning unit for several winters. He called Delitch to repair his unit. Henry Gable, a long time service repairman for the company was dispatched. His truck was emboldened with the name of the company and writing that said "HVAC, All Brands, Best Prices in Town." Gable's uniform also reflected the same writing. Gable discovered that Frank's unit was not repairable. He wrote up a contract to sell him a new unit. Although Gable did not have the actual authority to negotiate the price of a new air conditioning unit, he in fact, negotiated a price that was actually below his employer's cost. Frank signed the contract. Gable signed on behalf of HVAC. Since HVAC Corp had clothed Gable in the appearance of authority by the lettering on the truck and on Gable's service uniform, HVAC must honor the below cost price.

In the following case a finding of apparent authority resulted in a victory against the car dealership who clothed its agent with authority.

**DRESSELY *v.* CAL PROPERTIES**
Minnesota Court of Appeals
Minn. Ct. of App. No. A1-81902 (2019)

Cheryl Lang, owner of CAL Properties, began operating a car dealership known as Inver Grove Auto. CAL Properties employed Ferrozzo as its general manager to engage in its operations and to manage its flooring arrangements. The parties use the term "flooring arrangements" to mean obtaining funds from investors to purchase vehicles at auction for sale at the dealership. The investor would receive their initial investment on the vehicles when it sold and an additional profit from the sale. Ferrozzo, on behalf of CAL Properties, entered into a flooring arrangement with Dressely; but Ferrozzo used the funds for his own benefit rather than to purchase vehicles for the dealership's benefit. Even after Lang informed Ferrozzo of certain limitations on his authority, as a result, Ferrozzo continued to operate beyond the authority communicated to him. Thereafter, Lang fired Ferrozzo after discovering he created a checking account in the name of Inver Grove Auto LLC. Lang refused to pay Dressely the outstanding amounts owed on the flooring arrangements. Dressely sued CAL Properties for the amounts due on the flooring arrangements. The district court entered judgment against CAL Properties on apparent agency and awarded Dressely the outstanding amounts. CAL Properties appealed, maintaining that Ferrozzo did not have the authority to enter into the relationship with Dressely. CAL Properties appealed.

## *Slieter, Judge*

* * *

"Whether an agent is clothed with apparent authority is a question of fact. Even though an agency relationship is a legal determination, it hinges on "the factual arrangement between the parties."

"Agency is the fiduciary relationship that results from the manifestation of consent by one person to another that the other shall act on his [or her] behalf and subject to his [or her] control, and consent by the other so to act." The principal, generally, is bound by the actual authority provided to the agent and the apparent authority delegated to the agent. "Apparent authority is that authority which a principal holds an agent out as possessing, or knowingly permits an agent to assume. The doctrine is based on the conduct of the principal, not the conduct of the agent."

The Supreme Court explained these requirements to establish apparent authority:

> The principal must have held the agent out as having authority, or must have knowingly permitted the agent to act on its behalf; furthermore, the party dealing with the agent must have actual knowledge that the agent was held out by the principal as having such authority or had been permitted by the principal to act on its behalf; and the proof of the agent's authority must be found in the conduct of the principal, not the agent.

And

> [I]f a principal acts or conducts his [or her] business, either intentionally or through negligence, or fails to disapprove of the agent's acts or course of action so as to lead the public to believe that his [or her] agent possesses authority to act or contract in the name of the principal, the principal is bound by the acts of the agent within the scope of his [or her] apparent authority as to persons who have reasonable grounds to believe that the agent has such authority and in good faith deal with him [or her].

* * *

The district court found Ferrozzo acted with apparent authority as an agent of CAL Properties when entering into the . . . flooring arrangements with Dressely. "In determining whether apparent authority exists, the [district] court may consider any statements, conduct, lack of ordinary care, or manifestations of the principal's consent, such that a third party might be justified in concluding that the agent acted with apparent authority." The district court, in reaching its conclusion, considered evidence that CAL Properties held Ferrozzo out as "the 'face' of the dealership such that persons dealing with him regarding the dealership's affairs could reasonably believe they were dealing with the corporation." Lang hired Ferrozzo as the general manager to run the daily operation with duties that included entering into flooring arrangements with investors. Although Lang limited Ferrozzo's ability to enter into flooring arrangements after learning about the first flooring arrangement with Dressely, she never communicated this limitation to Dressely. Even when Lang first met Dressely, she failed to clarify that Ferrozzo acted improperly by entering into the flooring arrangement with him on behalf of CAL Properties. Lang allowed Ferrozzo to represent to Dressely—in her presence—that [Lang] was merely [Ferrozzo's] bookkeeper. . . . The district court found that the evidence before it "strongly indicate[d] that, at all relevant times, CAL Properties knew that Mr. Ferrozzo was holding himself out as the owner of the dealership and that . . . CAL Properties acquiesced in and consented to the misrepresentation."

The district court's findings of fact are supported by the record and justify the determination that CAL Properties held Ferrozzo out as having authority to bind it.

[The district court decision is AFFIRMED.]

**Business Application:** How can a business minimize the risk of an agent binding the principal by apparent authority?

### Ratification

A principal may ratify, or approve, unauthorized action taken by an agent. When ratification occurs, the principal is fully responsible for the agent's action. For ratification to be effective, the principal must have full knowledge of the transaction; the fact of the existence of a principal must have been disclosed to the third party at the time of the unauthorized act.

Assume, for example, that Doakes's auto breaks down and she leaves it at Main Standard gas station, where she is known by the owner. The owner of the gas station mistakenly, without authorization, acts as agent for Doakes and contracts to sell Doakes's auto for $400 to an interested customer. When Doakes learns of the mistake she is at first upset, but thereafter accepts payment. The acceptance of payment is an act ratifying the transaction. Her ratification creates an enforceable contract.

## *Principal and Agent Relationship*

Once an agency relationship exists, the law imposes certain duties and obligations on the parties to that relationship. The agent has certain responsibilities to the principal, and the principal, in turn, owes certain duties to the agent.

### Duties of Agent to Principal

Agents are characterized as fiduciaries. A fiduciary holds a position of trust and is held to the highest standard in the law. As fiduciaries, such persons owe to their principals the duties of obedience, care, loyalty, and accounting. An agent who breaches any of these duties is liable for damages to the principal and forfeits any compensation.

**Obedience.** An agent owes a duty to obey the principal's instructions. For example, an agent may not bid higher on an item at an auction than the principal's instructions dictate. Or, if the principal instructs the agent not to purchase a particular brand of goods, the agent must comply.

Blind obedience, however, is not required. The agent is under no obligation to act contrary to law. Additionally, where a change of circumstances occurs that would jeopardize the principal's interest, the agent may deviate from the principal's instruction. For example, an agent is not required to comply with a principal's direction to store bales of hay at a particular location when circumstances render that location a fire hazard.

**Care.** The agent must exercise proper skill and care in carrying out agency responsibilities. Anything less than reasonable care subjects the agent to liability for negligence. As is explained later in the chapter, the principal may also be liable to third parties for injury negligently caused by the agent.

**Loyalty.** The agent owes a duty of loyalty to the principal. The agent may not act against the principal's interest, or in any way engage in self-dealing. A real estate agent may not, for example, secretly purchase the very property he or she is selling for a principal. Moreover, the agent may not represent both parties to a transaction—the buyer and seller—without fully disclosing this representation to each party. Neither may agents take advantage of a business opportunity without sharing that advantage with the principal.

**Accounting.** Agents owe a duty to the principal to account for all monies generated by the agency. This should be done by accounting statements at agreed-on intervals.

Agents must not commingle their personal funds with those of their principals. Professionals, such as lawyers, accountants, brokers, and others, seriously jeopardize their licenses if they do. Separate trust accounts must be maintained.

### Duties of Principal to Agent

The principal owes certain duties to the agent. They include the duty to comply with the contract and to reimburse the agent for expenses and losses incurred as a result of the agency.

**Contract Compliance.** A principal has the power to breach a contract, but does not have the right to do so. Any breach results in liability to the agent. Assume, for example, that Bright-Lite Company lists its property for sale with Discount Realty under an exclusive listing. This means that Bright-Lite agrees to authorize only its agent to sell the property and collect a commission. Discount Realty would be in breach of the exclusive agency contract by selling the property through another agent. If this occurred, Discount Realty would still be entitled to the commission.

**Reimbursement.** The agent is entitled to reimbursement (or indemnification) for all expenses incurred as a result of duties performed within the scope of agency authority. Hence, a pilot hired to fly corporate passengers from New York to Atlanta would be entitled to reimbursement for fuel for the trip.

The agent is also entitled to indemnification for any losses incurred while operating within the scope of the agency. For example, assume that an agent is hired to dump a company's wastes at a particular site. The agent is then fined by the city for dumping without a license. The company is required to compensate the agent for the amount of the fine.

## *Principal and Third-Party Relationship*

An agent acts on behalf of a principal. The principal is normally responsible for the acts of his or her agent. Acts engaged in by agents may involve (1) contracts, (2) torts, and (3) crimes. This section examines the principal's legal liability for each of these agency acts.

### Contracts

Normally, a principal is liable for contracts entered into by his or her agent. This is true as long as the agent has authority—express, implied, or apparent—to enter into the contract. If, however, the third party is on notice or should reasonably know that the agent lacks authority, the principal would not be bound.

Assume that Dax, on behalf of his employer, Pixie Fish Market, enters into a contract with Fisher whereby Fisher is to sell, and Pixie is to buy, all the salmon Fisher catches. Pixie and Fisher are bound by contract. Assume, however, that before Dax entered into the contract Pixie informed Fisher that Dax was no longer authorized to enter into contracts for Pixie. Any contract after this notification would not bind Pixie.

### Torts

The principal is normally liable for the tortious negligent acts committed by the agent within the scope of the agency. In the employer-employee context, this doctrine is known as *respondeat superior* (let the master respond).

Questions often arise as to whether the employee was operating within the scope of employment when the tort was committed. Assume that Hank, a truck driver, is to make a delivery for his employer. Instead of making the delivery, Hank deviates from the course, drives to a bar, and crashes the truck into the bar's plate glass window. Hank's employer would not be liable for the damages because it occurred outside of the scope of his employment, while Hank was on a frolic of his own.

Principals are not ordinarily liable for the acts of independent contractors. An **independent contractor,** a type of agent, must be distinguished from an employee. The employer possesses control over the physical conduct of the employee, and may dictate the means and method by which the employee accomplishes the employer's work. This is not the case with an independent contractor. Here, the principal may not dictate the means and methods of performance, but only the result. For example, assume that Frank hires Louise, a taxicab driver, to take him downtown. Louise is an independent contractor because Frank does not have the authority to control the specifics of the travel, such as the speed and route. Ordinarily, Frank could only dictate the destination. Consequently, Frank, the passenger-principal, would not be liable to a pedestrian whom Louise negligently injured.

### Crimes

Generally, the principal is not liable for the crimes of an agent. Of course, a principal who directs the agent to perform an illegal act, or who is aware that the agent is acting criminally but does not act to stop the crime, is criminally liable. And if the agent's criminal act is committed in the scope of an illegal business, the principal is liable.

Some states impose criminal liability on business owners for violating certain laws designed to protect the health and safety of the public. For example, in those states a grocery store owner may be held criminally liable should an employee sell adulterated meat, even without the owner's knowledge.

## *Agent and Third-Party Relationship*

The general rule is that an agent is not a party to a contract entered into with a third party on behalf of a principal. This general rule holds true, however, only if the specific identity of the principal is disclosed to the third party. If the principal is only partially disclosed, the agent also becomes a party to the contract. A partially disclosed agency occurs when the fact that the agent is acting for a principal is disclosed, but the identity of the principal is not (*see* Table 7-2).

**TABLE 7-2 Liability of Principals and Agents for Contracts**

| | *Disclosed* | *Partially Disclosed* | *Undisclosed* |
|---|---|---|---|
| Agent liability | | X | X |
| Principal liability | X | X | X |

### Liability of Principals and Agents for Contracts

Agents who enter into written contracts must clearly designate their authority to avoid liability. The designation, "H. B. Corporation, by J. Adams, agent," for example, is sufficient to inform the third party that J. Adams is acting only as an agent for an identified principal.

Agents are liable to third parties for their torts. Under the doctrine of respondeat superior, the principal is liable for the negligent torts of the agent committed within the scope of the agency. Hence, both the agent and the principal may be liable to a third party for the agent's wrongs. Their liability is termed *joint and several.* This means that the third party may collect an entire judgment against either the principal or the agent, or a share of the judgment against each.

## *Termination of the Agency Relationship*

A principal-agency relationship may terminate in any number of ways. For example, it may terminate under the terms of the agency contract. Clauses stating, "This agency shall terminate in two years," or "This agency shall end when the sale of the building is complete," specify the moment of termination. Even absent a specific provision for termination in the contract, the parties may always terminate the agency relationship by mutual consent.

At times, a change in circumstances can cause an agency to end. Changes in circumstances resulting in termination of the agency include death of the principal or agent, impossibility of performance, and destruction of the subject matter of the agency.

The agency relationship may also terminate on the unilateral action of either party. Either party has the power to terminate the relationship, even if he or she does not have the right. Simply stated, the law does not force a party to continue in a personal service relationship against his or her will. Unilateral termination, however, may constitute a breach of contract, in which case the nonbreaching party may have an action for damages.

The principal has a duty to notify third parties of the termination of the agency relationship. Actual notice must be given to those who have extended credit or contracted with the principal through the agent. Absent such notice, the agent may still possess apparent authority and continue to bind the principal. Constructive notice of the termination should be given to all other third parties. Constructive notice may be accomplished by publishing the fact of termination in a newspaper that is designed to reach third parties with whom the agent has had contact. Notice is not required when the termination is due to death, insanity, or bankruptcy, as these are already on the public record.

## SOLE PROPRIETORSHIP

A sole proprietorship is owned by a single person. This organization is normally a small business, such as the corner grocery or the local computer repair shop.

The principal advantage of the sole proprietorship is that the owner has exclusive control over its operations. The proprietor may make managerial decisions without accounting to board members, partners, or stockholders. Sole proprietors may hire employees to act as agents for the proprietorship. This relationship is governed by the law of agency just discussed.

This form of business also has disadvantages. First, the owner is exposed to unlimited liability. That means the owner is personally liable for all debts of the business. These debts may be incurred as a result of a contract obligation or tort liability. Second, the sole proprietorship is normally not in the best position to raise large sums of money. This is true because its ability to repay loans is limited by the assets of the individual proprietor.

## PARTNERSHIP

The partnership form of organization involves two or more persons and, as such, is more complex than the sole proprietorship. In all states but Louisiana, partnership law is governed by the Uniform Partnership Act (UPA).[1] Partnership law employs the principles of agency law previously discussed.

### *Definition of Partnership*

**Decision Making in the Legal Environment**

This link provides help so you may think through the process for forming a partnership.

https://www.huffpost.com/entry/7-things-every-partnership-agreement-needs-to-address_b_58ebed0be4b0ea028d568bf5

The UPA defines a partnership as "an association of two or more persons to carry on as co-owners a business for profit." To determine whether a partnership exists, each of the elements of the definition must carefully be examined.

An association implies voluntariness. Two or more persons may associate to form a partnership. Thus, a partnership is consensual and ordinarily formed by a contract.

The partnership is treated as a distinct entity for some purposes and as an aggregate of persons for others. For example, under the UPA the partnership may own, buy, and sell property in its own name. The partnership files a federal income tax return for information purposes. Each partner is an agent of the partnership. These characteristics make the partnership look like a distinct entity.

On the other hand, the partnership does not pay income taxes; rather, the individual partners pay taxes on respective portions of what the partnership earns. Also, a

1 The UPA was originally proposed and adopted in 1914 by the National Conference of Commissioners on Uniform State Law.

partnership dissolves on the death or departure of a partner. These characteristics make the partnership appear to be composed of an aggregate of persons.

The UPA requires that a partnership consist of "two or more persons." *Person* is defined broadly to include individuals, partnerships, corporations, and other associations.

A fundamental element of a partnership is that the persons must "carry on as co-owners." Evidence of co-ownership of the business includes sharing profits and jointly owning property, contributing capital, and jointly participating in managerial decision making.

Finally, the UPA specifies that the business must be for profit. This would exclude ventures formed for religious, charitable, or fraternal purposes.

## *Formation of Partnership*

Under most circumstances, the creation of a partnership does not require a formal written agreement. Partnerships may be formed informally, by handshake, or may arise by implication, as when, for example, the parties share profits and co-manage the business.

Nonetheless, it is desirable to have an agreement in writing, referred to as *articles of partnership.* The existence of such an agreement often helps to avoid conflict by clarifying the rights and responsibilities of the parties. The normal partnership writing covers the matters found in Table 7-3.

In the absence of an agreement, the UPA controls. For example, the UPA states that absent an agreement, partners shall share profits and losses equally.

## *Rights of Partners*

The partnership agreement should be consulted to determine the rights of partners as to each other. In the absence of an agreement covering the specific issue in question, the UPA governs. Rights concerning partnership property, profit sharing, and management participation are discussed next.

### Partnership Property

Each partner has a right to possess partnership property in furtherance of the partnership business. The partners have an equal right to use or possess the property for this purpose. Hence, each partners' right in partnership property is indivisible: each has a full right to the whole.

Ordinarily, the initial contributions made by the partners, referred to as *capital contributions,* constitute partnership property. Any additional property acquired by the partnership is also deemed partnership property. Of course, the intent of the parties controls whether an item is owned by a partner personally or by the partnership. Offering some help in this area, the UPA states: "Unless the contrary intention appears, property acquired with partnership funds is partnership property."

**TABLE 7-3 Matters Covered in a Typical Partnership Agreement**

| |
|---|
| Names of the partners |
| Name of the partnership |
| Location of the partnership |
| Purposes of the partnership |
| Duration of the partnership |
| Allocation of profits and losses among partners |
| Capital contributions by partners |
| Partners' rights and responsibilities |
| Dissolution procedures |
| Buyout provisions for death or withdrawal |

### Profit Sharing

The UPA provides that the partners share profits and losses equally. This may be altered by agreement. For example, partners may agree to share profits in proportion to their capital contributions. Assume that X contributed $20,000, Y contributed $30,000, and Z contributed $50,000. Under such an agreement, X would receive 20 percent ($20,000/$100,000) of the profits; Y would receive 30 percent ($30,000/$100,000); and Z would receive 50 percent ($50,000/$100,000). The parties similarly could designate the same or a different ratio for loss sharing. Failure to do so would result in the same ratio of loss distribution as that specified for the profit sharing.

Partners are not entitled to salaries, absent an agreement to the contrary. This is true even if one partner does the bulk of the work, or even all of the work. A partner is, however, entitled to reasonable compensation for services rendered for winding up the partnership affairs (as discussed later in this chapter).

### Management Participation

Each partner has an equal right to participate in the management of the partnership. As with profit sharing, this may be altered by agreement.

On ordinary decisions, the vote of the majority controls unless the partnership agreement specifies otherwise. Any decision on extraordinary matters, however, requires unanimous consent. Extraordinary matters include a change of the partnership purpose, admission of a new partner, or a decision to relocate the business.

Additional rights enjoyed by partners include reimbursement, inspection, accounting, and assignment. Partners are entitled to *reimbursement* for payments made in connection with the ordinary conduct of the business. This includes, for example, the purchase of office supplies or the payment of taxes on partnership property. Partners are also entitled to be indemnified for personal liability resulting from conducting the partnership business.

Every partner has the right to *inspect* and copy any part of the partnership books. The books contain financial information, minutes of meetings, and other information germane to the conduct of the business.

The UPA grants a partner the right to an accounting. An accounting is a detailed statement of the financial affairs and condition of the business. Partners may desire and demand an accounting when, for example, they believe they have been wrongfully excluded from the partnership business.

Finally, any partner has the right to assign (sell or give away) his or her monetary interest in the partnership. This may be accomplished without the other partners' consent. However, the assignee (the one to whom the property is assigned) does not become a partner unless all partners consent. Hence, the assignee does not obtain any nonfinancial rights in the partnership, such as, for example, the right to management participation. The assignee is entitled only to the respective share of the profits and any other financial rights assigned.

## *Obligations of Partners*

Each partner stands in a fiduciary relationship to each other partner. (This relationship was discussed in the section on agency.) The partner, as fiduciary, owes certain obligations to the partnership, among which is the duty of loyalty. This duty exists between partners. This duty existed within the common law and was expressed well in the words of Justice Benjamin Cardozo in *Meinhard v. Salmon*:

> Joint adventurers . . . owe to one another, while the enterprise continues the duty of the finest loyalty. Many forms of conduct permissible in a workaday world for those acting at arm's length are forbidden to those bound by fiduciary ties. A trustee is held to something stricter than the morals of the marketplace. Not honesty alone, but the punctilio of an honor the most sensitive, is then the standard of behavior. As to this there has developed a tradition that is unbending and inveterate. Uncompromising rigidity has been the attitude of courts of equity when petitioned to undermine the rule of undivided loyalty by the disintegrating erosion of particular exceptions. Only thus has the level of the conduct for fiduciaries been kept at a level higher than that trodden by the crowd. It will not consciously be lowered by any judgment of this court.

The fiduciary duty of loyalty means that one partner may not exclude other partners from the benefits of the partnership property. For example, one partner may not rent out partnership property without sharing the information and the rental income with all partners. Moreover, when partnership opportunities arise out of a relationship to the partnership business, a partner must afford all partners the right to participate. For example, assume that the partnership is in a relationship with a condominium agency from which it purchases condo units in hotels. When a "deal" is offered by that condo agency to one of the partners, that partner owes a duty of loyalty to the other partners. The partner may not appropriate a partnership opportunity that has arisen through business relations of the partnership. Only after offering the opportunity to the partners, and the partners decline, may the partner "go it alone." The partner must make full disclosure to the other partners of the details of the proposed transaction and not present it in a way so as to discourage other partners. The rule here is the duty of highest loyalty and good faith.

The UPA adopts this "high road" of fiduciary duties. Although the UPA does not expressly adopt the partnership duty of loyalty, the duty has nonetheless been deeply rooted in case law since Justice

Cardozo's pronouncement in *Meinhard v. Salmon.* This foundational concept came under attack with the Revised Uniform Partnership Act (RUPA), which declares that "[a] partner does not violate a duty or obligation under the [Act] or under the partnership agreement merely because the partner's conduct furthers the partner's own interest." The RUPA has been adopted by most states and the District of Columbia. The RUPA further states that a partnership agreement may not "eliminate the duty of loyalty . . . but . . . may identify specific types or categories of activities that do not violate the duty of loyalty, if not manifestly unreasonable." The battle lines between "freedom to contract" and fiduciary notions of loyalty are drawn. The battle continues to rage between the state legislatures who have adopted the RUPA and the courts that generally disdain the overthrow of the fiduciary duty of loyalty. It remains to be seen if Justice Cardozo's words were prophetic when he declared that the fiduciary duty of loyalty "will not consciously be lowered by any judgment" of a court.

## *Relationship to Third Parties*

A partnership creates a principal-agent relationship. The partnership is the principal. Partners are agents of the partnership. As such, the previously discussed agency principles are applicable.

Partners are jointly liable on the contracts of the partnership. Joint liability requires that all partners be sued on the contract obligation. The individual partners, however, would not be held liable unless all the partnership assets were first used up to satisfy the indebtedness.

Unlike contractual liability, partners are jointly and severally liable for torts. That means that all partners need not be sued at once. For example, one partner may be sued for the whole amount. Additionally, the release of one partner does not release other partners from liability. As well, partnership assets do not have to be used up first to satisfy the judgment; the partners are personally liable. Any partner, however, who is required to pay on the judgment and who did not personally commit the tort, may recover against the partner(s) who committed the tort.

In some cases, partner and partnership liability to third parties may arise by estoppel, or **apparent partnership.** This may occur under two circumstances. First, a person (apparent partner) may represent that he or she is a partner when in fact this is not true, and the partnership has no knowledge of the representation. If a third party, in reliance on this representation, extends credit to the partnership, the apparent partner would be liable for any injury the third party sustains.

Second, a partner may have knowledge that a nonpartner is misrepresenting himself or herself as a partner. Any partner with such knowledge who consents to the misrepresentation is liable to third parties who sustain injury as a result of reliance on the representation.

## *Termination of Partnership*

Termination of a partnership is a legal process that involves two stages: dissolution and winding up.

### Dissolution

The UPA defines dissolution as a "change in the relation of the partners caused by any partner ceasing to be associated in the carrying on . . . of the business." Some dissolutions are merely technical.

They occur, for example, when a partner dies or retires. These events result in a dissolution because there is a change in the relation of the partners. However, in most of these cases, the surviving partners wish to continue the business; the dissolution is only a bookkeeping entry whereby a new partnership is formed. In the absence of agreement, the UPA provides that a retiring partner or the estate of a deceased partner is entitled to the value of his or her share in the partnership plus interest or, in lieu of interest, profits.

The partnership agreement may designate a date for termination, or the partners may at any time mutually agree to dissolve the partnership. In either case, dissolution occurs and the liquidation process begins.

A partner may seek to dissolve the partnership by obtaining a court decree. A court issues the decree if a partner is judicially declared to be insane or is otherwise incapable of performing the partnership duties; a partner is guilty of impairing the ability of the business to continue; or where it is impractical to continue the business, as when the partners are constantly unable to cooperate and make decisions.

When a partnership dissolves for any reason other than death of a partner, illegality or bankruptcy, notice must be given to third parties. Specific notice must be given to those creditors with whom the business has dealt. Constructive notice, by publication in a newspaper distributed in the area of the business, must be given to all other third parties. Failure to give proper notice may result in liability for unauthorized contracts and debts.

### Winding Up

The winding-up process involves the liquidation of assets and distribution of its proceeds. The UPA establishes the rules for distribution of assets in the following order: (1) to creditors other than partners; (2) to partners who are creditors; (3) to partners to repay capital contributions; and (4) to partners for profits. In the event of insufficient partnership assets to pay creditors, the partners must contribute the amount necessary to satisfy the liabilities.

Difficulties may arise when assets are insufficient to satisfy partnership debts and when the partners are indebted to personal creditors. The general rule is that partnership creditors have first priority on partnership property and personal creditors have first priority on partners' property.

## *Limited Partnership*

The basic disadvantage of the general partnership is that it subjects all partners to unlimited personal liability. However, all states except Louisiana have adopted legislation affording an alternative to the general partnership limiting the liability of some partners. This alternative is called **limited partnership** and is governed in these states by the Uniform Limited Partnership Act (ULPA).[2] Under this uniform act, the partnership consists of general and limited partners. General partners manage and control the partnership and they are liable without limit. Limited partners enjoy limited liability, as

2 Since its adoption by the National Conference of Commissioners on Uniform Laws in 1976 ULPA has undergone amendment in 1985 and 2001.

long as they do not participate in the management or control of the partnership and as long as they comply with state law.

Limited partnerships may be formed only by compliance with the state statute. This requires the filing of a certificate of limited partnership with a state agency, often the secretary of state. The certificate contains the name of the partnership, its purpose, and its location; the names of partners; and other information.

Limited partnerships are usually formed for investment purposes. The limited partners are passive investors who are like shareholders in a corporation. The partnership may be formed for the purpose of, for example, erecting an outlet mall or drilling for oil. As members of a partnership, the partners enjoy tax advantages.

## CORPORATIONS

The corporate form of business has existed in some form as far back as the days of the Code of Hammurabi (about 1750 B.C.). Its early usage, however, was restricted to the government and the church. Later, the sovereign, through special legislation, chartered private corporations to perform trade. In the United States, corporations were introduced in the 18th century and since then have been growing in numbers and popularity. Today, corporations are a dominant institution in our economy, accounting for about 90 percent of the gross national income.

### *Characteristics of Corporations*

Corporations are distinct from sole proprietorships and general partnerships in several respects (*see* Table 7-1). First, a corporation is a separate legal entity for all purposes. It is an artificial being created by legislation. As such, a corporation can purchase, hold, and sell property in its own name. It enters into contracts in its own name. It can be sued and can sue in its own name. It is a tax-paying entity.

Second, a corporation is not mortal; theoretically, it has a perpetual existence. A partnership certainly terminates at the death of the last partner. A corporation, in contrast, is not dependent on the life of particular individuals for existence. Corporations continue until dissolved, merged, or otherwise terminated.

A third distinct characteristic of the corporation is that the owners of the corporation, called *shareholders*, enjoy limited liability. This is a prime feature of the corporation that makes it attractive to investors. Unlike general partners, a shareholder can lose only what he or she invests. Creditors cannot, under ordinary circumstances, reach the personal assets of the shareholder to satisfy debt. In this respect, shareholders resemble limited partners.

A fourth important characteristic of the corporation is the ease of transferring ownership interests. Sale of a partnership normally involves a detailed process of valuation and an interruption of the affairs of the partnership. A corporation's ownership, represented by shares of stock, may be bought and sold freely without business interruption.

A fifth characteristic of the corporate form is the separation of ownership from management. Shareholders always own the corporation but often do not manage it.

## Business Application/Ethical Issues

As a successful tire salesperson for Swift Wholesale Tire, Inc., Louis Rosenmund called on Warren Hubbard, manager of the King Tire Store. On one visit, Rosenmund told Hubbard that the owner of the Tough Tire Store in Westerville wanted to sell his store due to a lack of business. Hubbard replied: "Louis, with your sales ability and my business judgment, we could turn that business around. I'll put up the money to buy the business, if you will manage the daily operations. You can take a monthly salary of $3,500, and the rest of the profits will be ploughed back into the business. We can split the profits later. Since we'll have to act quickly, I'll go ahead and buy the property. The incorporation papers will be filed as soon as possible after the purchase."

Rosenmund quit his $40,000-per-year position with Swift and started working at the Tough Tire Store. Hubbard purchased the store and named himself owner on the title. Rosenmund had business cards and newspaper advertising printed that included both his name and Hubbard's under the name of the business. Three months later, the Tough Tire Store was a success.

Whenever Hubbard visited the store, Rosenmund asked about the corporation papers. Hubbard's response was vague. Finally, Hubbard told Rosenmund to meet him at the office of Richard Stone, an attorney, who opined that Rosenmund was an employee and that Hubbard had no additional obligation to him.

When Rosenmund arrived, Stone introduced himself as Hubbard's attorney. He told Rosenmund that his services as an employee of Tough Tire were no longer required.

What are the ethical issues? What should Rosenmund have done to protect himself legally.

Sixth, and perhaps an undesirable aspect of the corporation, is that it pays taxes on its earnings. Then, when it distributes dividends to its stockholders, they pay taxes on those earnings. This results in double taxation, which has led many small corporations to elect the form of subchapter S status.

A subchapter S corporation is a creation of the tax laws. It is treated as a partnership for purposes of taxation. Hence, only the shareholders are taxed on earnings, not the corporation. This type of election is available only to corporations that have 100 or fewer shareholders, and all shareholders must elect the subchapter S status. To qualify for favorable subchapter S treatment, a corporation must strictly adhere to IRS filing guidelines.

Finally, the corporate form requires compliance with an array of formalized procedures. Incorporation can be very costly as a result. Also, government more closely supervises corporations than partnerships or sole proprietorships. Each state has detailed statutes covering the regulation of corporations.[3]

**Business and Government Interface**

This link helps determine in which state to incorporate your business.

https://www.incorporate.com/choosing_a_state.html

3 About one-half the states have adopted the Model Business Corporation Act (MBCA) as approved by the National Conference of Commissioners on Uniform State Law (NCCUSL) and the House of Delegates of the American Bar Association (ABA), or a revision of that act, in whole or in part.

## *Creation of Corporations*

The formation of a corporation is controlled by state statutory law. Normally, promoters come together to form a corporation. They handle the plans for financing the corporation and draw up the corporate charter, referred to in many states as the *certificate*, or *articles, of incorporation* (*see* Form 7-2).

Promoters involve themselves in the sale of stock subscriptions and in contracting for loans, goods, and supplies. The promoters are normally personally liable for these contracts because the corporation is not in existence during this state of formation. After the corporation forms, however, it may adopt the promoters' actions and agree to indemnify them.

The next step is to file the articles of incorporation with the designated state office, usually with the secretary of state. This is accomplished by incorporators who may be the same persons as the promoters. Articles of incorporation normally include the name of the corporation, principal place of business of the corporation, purpose of the corporation, powers of the corporation, names of incorporators, amount and types of authorized stock, and designation of an agent of the corporation who is to receive all official papers.

After the state receives the filing and issues a charter, the first shareholders' meeting occurs. At that meeting shareholders (1) verify the issuance and values of the shares of stock, (2) elect a board of directors of the corporation, and (3) adopt a set of bylaws to govern the operation of the corporation. The next meeting is that of the newly elected board of directors. The board elects officers and covers any other matters necessary to begin business.

After all of the procedures for formation of the corporation have been completed, a *de jure* corporation exists. Neither the state nor other parties may challenge its existence. At times, although the incorporators make a good-faith attempt to comply with the statute, they fail. In these cases, a court may find that a *de facto* corporation exists, that is, even though there has not been full compliance, nonetheless it is treated as a corporation. This may occur if, for example, the incorporators failed to pay the filing fee.

To exist, a *de facto* corporation must act as a corporation. A *de facto* corporation may not be challenged by any parties except the state. Shareholders in a *de facto* corporation enjoy limited liability.

When an organization substantially deviates from the statutory mandated procedure, it is neither a *de jure* nor a *de facto* corporation. Many states require the filing of articles of incorporation before a corporation comes into being. Even here, however, it is still possible for a court to treat a business which has not filed its articles as a corporation under estoppel principles. For example, a business that holds itself out as a corporation and incurs debts as a corporation but is not a corporation is not allowed to deny its corporate existence for purposes of avoiding repayment of the debt.

Sometimes a corporation is used for the exclusive purpose of hiding the assets of shareholders, and thereby shielding them from personal liability. Often, these organizations do not act like corporations but are only such in name. They are merely the alter ego of the shareholders. For example, in one case, the owners of a taxicab company incorporated the operation of each taxicab. They did not have board of directors' meetings, keep any minutes of the "corporations," or even keep separate financial books for each "corporation." The scheme was a sham to protect the assets of the taxicab company from creditors. In such cases, creditors are able to **pierce the corporate veil** and hold shareholders personally liable for the business's debt.

### FORM 7-2 Certificate of Incorporation

The undersigned, desiring to form a corporation for profit, do hereby certify:

First. The name of the corporation shall be TransAir Mobile, Inc.

Second. The principal place of business will be in City, State.

Third. The purposes for which said corporation is formed are

1. Manufacturing air mobiles for use as public transportation within cities.
2. Marketing the concept of air mobiles as a more efficient form of public transportation.
3. Lobbying cities, counties, and other governmental agencies in attempts to influence them to adopt air mobiles as a major form of city transportation.
4. Doing all things necessary and lawful to accomplish these purposes.

Fourth. The following persons shall serve as interim directors until the first meeting called to elect a board of directors:

Dr. Angela Moore

Laura Williams

Nelson Odis

Fifth. The corporation shall be authorized to issue 1 million shares of no par value common stock.

In witness whereof, we, the incorporators, subscribe our names this 5th day of January, 2020.

Ruth Anne Hills

Constance Rivers

Howard Randal

## *Types of Corporations*

Corporations may be classified in a number of ways (*see* Table 7-4). Some corporations are domestic. A corporation is considered domestic within the state in which it is incorporated. It is considered foreign when transacting business in any other state. Transacting business does not include merely maintaining bank accounts, holding directors' or shareholders' meetings, or borrowing money. Each state regulates foreign corporations doing business within the state. States usually require that the corporation register in the state and obtain a certificate of authority from the secretary of state.

Failure to do so may result in criminal penalties and limitations on the corporation's right to enforce its contracts.

Public corporations are established by the government. For example, a local municipality may incorporate. The U.S. Postal Service is an example of a federal public corporation.

Quasi-public corporations are public service companies, such as public utilities. Although they are private, the high degree of government regulation and protection makes them public in nature. An example would be a public utilities corporation, e.g., a gas and electric company that services the public.

**Private corporations** are those established for private interests and include the bulk of existing corporations. Private corporations may further be divided between nonprofit and profit. Nonprofit corporations are formed for charitable or religious purposes. Profit corporations are usually formed to carry out business for profit.

Private corporations for profit may be further subdivided into closely held corporations and publicly held corporations. A corporation owned by one or a few shareholders (who normally have family or other close ties and also manage the business) is termed a *closely held corporation.* These corporations do not publicly offer their stock. Ninety percent of all private-profit corporations fall in this category. The *publicly held corporation*, in contrast, has a number of unrelated shareholders who are passive investors; they do not actively manage the company. The shares of stock are traded freely on stock exchanges.

The professional corporation has been legalized by every state. Until the 1960s, lawyers, doctors, accountants, and other professionals could not incorporate. They could not take advantage of certain corporate tax breaks and pension benefits. Professional corporation statutes now allow them to do so; however, these professionals are still personally liable for their wrongful acts.

**TABLE 7-4 Types of Corporations**

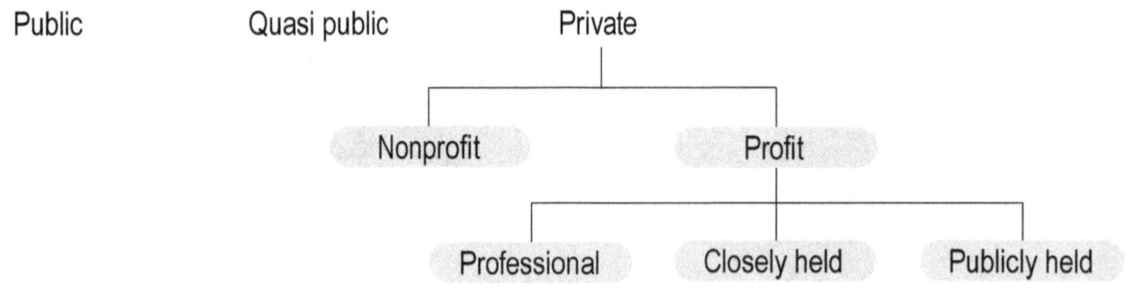


## *Corporate Management*

Shareholders elect a board of directors to manage the corporation. The board, in turn, delegates the day-to-day operations to officers. The directors and the officers comprise the management of the corporation.

### Directors

The articles of incorporation normally list the initial board of directors that serves until the first shareholders' meeting. At that meeting, shareholders elect a new board or, as often is the case, reelect the same board.

State statutes, the articles of incorporation, and bylaws may establish eligibility requirements for board membership. For example, the corporation's bylaws may require that a board member own stock in the company or be a resident of the state of incorporation. In the absence of such restrictions, anyone is eligible to be elected to the board of directors.

**Decision Making in the Legal Environment**

Business and government interface: This link explains various board governance and management styles.

https://leadtogether.org/governance-models-an-essay-by-nathan-garber-with-reflections-by-michael-soule.

Ordinarily, board members serve one-year terms. This, however, is also governed by the bylaws. Although boards normally consist of at least three members, some states permit as few as one board member.

Directors must meet regularly. Some boards meet only once a year, others monthly, and still others more frequently. A quorum of board members must be present to hold a meeting. The number necessary for the quorum—normally a majority—is designated in the bylaws. Bylaw provisions may permit the board to make decisions by telephone, email, video-conferencing, or through the mail.

The board of directors establishes the policy of the company and is responsible for guiding the company in a manner consistent with that policy. Other decisions made by the board include declaring dividends, proposing amendments to articles of incorporation and bylaws, proposing candidates for the board, removing officers, and establishing the salary of the chief executive officer and other high echelon management employees.

Commonly, some boards delegate some of their powers to executive committees. Executive committees may be composed of board members, officers, and others. They normally relieve the boards of detail work by studying alternatives and making suggestions. For example, the board may decide to implement a pension/profit-sharing plan and ask the executive committee to research alternatives and come up with a proposal.

Directors stand in a fiduciary relationship to the corporation. They must act with loyalty and due care in their actions and decision making. They may not act in their own self-interest; in all business relationships with the corporation they must make full and fair disclosure. Where a conflict of interest arises, a director may not vote on the issue that is the subject of conflict.

Board members are protected in their decision making by the **business judgment rule.** The business judgment rule, when applicable, affords board members great latitude in their decision making. This rule is designed to encourage board members to make difficult decisions, freed from the fear of liability, even should those decisions, in hindsight, turn out to be harmful to the corporation. In effect, courts recognize their limitations in reviewing business decisions and defer to the corporate directors who are presumed to act in the best interests of the company. For the business judgment rule to be applicable, the board must have made an informed and rational decision, free from conflicts of interests.

### Officers

Officers of the corporation are appointed by the board of directors pursuant to the bylaws. They are responsible for implementing the policies of the board and for the oversight of the day-to-day operations of the business. Officers include a president, vice president, secretary, and treasurer. Large corporations may have a number of vice presidents, including such specialized officers as vice president—marketing, comptroller, and financial secretary.

Officers are agents of the corporation, and, as such, may bind the corporation. Like directors, officers owe fiduciary duties to the corporation.

## *Shareholders*

**Decision Making in the Legal Environment**

This article from an International Journal of Leadership Studies link explains the leadership role of the Board chairperson through a team approach.

https://www.regent.edu/acad/global/publications/ijls/new/vol3iss1/gabrielsson/GabrielssonHuseMinichill_IJLS_V3Is1.pdf

The publicly held corporation is usually financed by issuing securities to investors, known as *shareholders.* Of the various classifications of shareholders, the most common distinction is between common stockholders and preferred stockholders. A primary difference between the two is that, ordinarily, preferred stockholders are entitled to receive their dividends before common stockholders and, on dissolution, preferred stockholders are entitled to distributions of assets before common stockholders.

### Voting

Some stockholders have voting rights. Other stockholders may lack those rights or only be entitled to vote on extraordinary matters.

At the annual shareholders' meeting, the voting members elect directors and vote on other matters of corporate concern. There are two principal methods for voting for directors: straight and cumulative.

Under the straight method, each shareholder is entitled to one vote per share per director's position. Each vacant director's position is voted on at a time. The second method, cumulative, affords each shareholder one vote times the number of shares owned times the number of directors' vacancies to be filled. The election for all board members takes place at one time. For example, assume five vacant board positions must be filled. Harriet owns 1,000 shares of stock. She has 5,000 votes (1 × 1,000 × 5). She may vote the entire 5,000 shares for one candidate, or she may split her votes in any combination among several candidates. Cumulative voting gives minority shareholders the chance to elect some members(s) to the board.

### Dividends

Dividends are portions of corporate earnings distributed to shareholders. They are declared by the board of directors. A board maintains almost absolute discretion to declare or not declare dividends. It may not, however, declare dividends if the corporation is insolvent, or if the declaration would push the corporation into insolvency. In contrast, it may not refuse to declare dividends in bad faith—for example, to squeeze out minority shareholders.

Dividends may be in the form of cash or stock. Cash dividends are the most common type of dividend. They increase the wealth of the stockholder and are taxable to the receiver. Stock dividends may be declared by the board of directors. For example, a 10 percent increase in stock may be declared and distributed. In such a case, a shareholder who owns 100 shares would receive 10 additional shares. This does not change shareholders' percentages of ownership of the company; although a stockholder's net worth may be increased, there is no immediate realized gain that is taxable.

The stock split is sometimes confused with a stock dividend. In a stock split, the existing shares are divided, for example, two for one. A shareholder receives two shares for every one he or she owns. Again, this does not give the shareholder any additional interest or even theoretically increase net worth. If the stock is selling for $100 a share, in a two-for-one split the value of a share is theoretically reduced in half to $50 a share (although in reality the market value is usually a little higher). The prime reason for issuing a stock split is to make the stock more affordable to more people, thereby stimulating a flow of capital into the corporation.

### Preemption

Shareholders may be granted **preemptive rights** by the articles of incorporation. Preemptive rights ensure that existing shareholders may maintain their proportionate interest in the company. They require the corporation to offer new shares to existing shareholders before offering them to the public. Assume that Phil owns 100,000 shares in a corporation that has 1 million shares outstanding. Phil owns 10 percent of the company. Now assume that the company desires to raise more capital and does so by issuing 1 million new shares. If Phil does not have a first right to buy a proportional number of shares, his interest in the company could be diluted to 5 percent. If, however, Phil has preemptive rights, he would be entitled to purchase 100,000 shares and thus preserve his percentage of the relative ownership interest (10 percent). Of course, preemptive rights do not help Phil if he cannot afford to purchase the shares.

### Inspection

Stockholders have the right to inspect the books and records of the corporation; this includes the shareholders list, the minutes of meetings, and financial records. The one qualification on this right is that the shareholder must show a proper purpose. The purpose must be related to the status of a shareholder. It would not be a proper purpose if the shareholders list is to be used to buttress the mailing list for one shareholder's personal business. It would be proper, however, if the shareholder's purpose is to gain control of the company by soliciting proxies.

### Suits

Shareholders may sue the corporation individually or on behalf of the corporation. A shareholder who has been injured by wrongful corporate acts may sue the corporation. These acts may include a refusal to permit inspection of the shareholders list and illegal inside trading.

Derivative actions to recover monies on behalf of the corporation may be filed by individual shareholders when the board of directors refuses to act. Assume one of the directors has illegally absconded with company monies. Should the majority of the board refuse to sue to recover, any shareholder would have the right to sue on behalf of the corporation. Any recovery would directly inure to the benefit of the corporation.

As the next case illustrates, the business judgment rule does not always shield directors from liability.

**FEDERAL DEPOSIT INSURANCE CORPORATION *v.* LOUDERMILK**

Supreme Court of Georgia

No. 514Q0454 (July 11, 2014)

The Federal Deposit Insurance Corporation (FDIC) sued nine former officers and directors of the bank, alleging that they were negligent with respect to the making of loans, which led the bank to sustain nearly $22 million in losses. The defendants moved to dismiss the lawsuit, arguing that the business judgment rule relieves officers and directors of any liability for ordinary negligence. The FDIC responded that such a business judgment rule is not part of the common law in Georgia, and even if it were, it does not apply to bank officers and directors, insofar as the statutory law in Georgia explicitly requires bank officers and directors to exercise ordinary diligence and care. The United States District Court for the Northern District of Georgia certified the following question to the Supreme Court of Georgia:

Does the business judgment rule in Georgia preclude as a matter of law a claim for ordinary negligence against the officers and directors of a bank in a lawsuit brought by the FDIC as receiver for the bank?

### *Justice Blackwell*

. . .The business judgment rule is a fixture in American law, and it is a settled part of the common law in many of our sister states. But defining the rule is "no easy task," insofar as the particulars of the rule may vary a bit from one jurisdiction to another. Nevertheless, we find a classic statement of the rule in [a New York case]:

> Mistakes in the exercise of honest business judgment do not subject the directors to liability for negligence in the discharge of their fiduciary duties. . . . The directors are entrusted with the management of the affairs of the [corporation]. If in the course of management they arrive at a decision for which there is a reasonable basis, and they act in good faith, as the result of their independent judgment, and uninfluenced by any consideration other than what they honestly believe to be for the best interests of the [corporation], it is not the function of the court to say that it would have acted differently and to charge the directors for any loss or expenditures incurred.

* * *

. . . If an officer or director has honestly exercised "judgment" with respect to a business matter—that is, if her decision was made in a deliberative way, was reasonably informed by due diligence, and was made in good faith—the wisdom of the judgment cannot ordinarily be questioned in court. . . . So understood, the rule reflects the principle that managing the affairs of a corporation is a matter committed by law to the discretion of the directors, the reality that the making of profits involves the taking of some risks, and the recognition that businesspeople generally are more competent than judges to exercise business judgment.

* * *

From our precedents, we conclude that the business judgment rule is a settled part of our common law in Georgia, and it generally precludes claims against officers and directors for their business decisions that sound in ordinary negligence, except to the extent that those decisions are shown to have been made without deliberation, without the requisite diligence to ascertain and assess the facts and circumstances upon which the decisions are based, or in bad faith. Put another way, the business judgment rule at common law forecloses claims against officers and directors that sound in ordinary negligence when the alleged negligence concerns only the wisdom of their judgment, but it does not absolutely foreclose such claims to the extent that a business decision did not involve "judgment" because it was made in a way that did not comport with the duty to exercise good faith and ordinary care. We note as well that the business judgment rule applies equally at common law to corporate officers and directors generally and to bank officers and directors. Having concluded that such a business judgment rule is a part of our common law, we must consider whether the General Assembly has modified or abrogated the business judgment rule by statute. . . .

* * *

Our examination of the statutory law starts with OCGA § 7-1-490 (a), which concerns the care with which bank officers and directors are to perform their duties . . .

* * *

In the light of this statutory history, we conclude that OCGA § 7-1-490 (a) is perfectly consistent with the business judgment rule acknowledged at common law in the decisions of this Court. To be sure, subsection (a) provides that an officer or director who acts "in good faith and with that diligence, care, and skill which ordinarily prudent men would exercise under similar circumstances in like positions" "shall have no liability by reason of being or having been a director or officer of the bank or trust company." And no doubt, these provisions imply strongly that, if an officer or director *fails* to act in good faith or with such ordinary care, he is subject to liability. But taken in its legal context, the statutory reference to ordinary "diligence, care, and skill" is most reasonably understood to refer to the care required with respect to the process by which a decision is made, most notably the diligence due to ascertain the relevant facts. So understood, the implication of liability means only that an officer or director who acts in bad faith or fails to exercise such ordinary care with respect to the process for making a decision is liable.

**Business and Government Interface**

This U.S. Small Business Administration link answers the question, "How and Why Choose an LLC?" as a form of business organization.

http://www.sba.gov/content/limited-liability-company-llc

* * *

Both at common law and by statute, the standard of ordinary care for bank officers and directors is less demanding than the standard of "ordinary diligence" with which most ordinary negligence claims are concerned.

* * *

Finally, the business judgment rule makes clear that, when a business decision is alleged to have been made negligently, the wisdom of the decision is ordinarily insulated from judicial review, and as for the process by which the decision was made, the officers and directors are presumed to have acted in good faith and to have exercised ordinary care. Although this presumption may be rebutted, the plaintiff bears the burden of putting forward proof sufficient to rebut it. All together, the limited standard of care, the conclusive presumptions as to reasonable reliance, and the rebuttable presumptions of good faith and ordinary care offer meaningful protection, we think, to officers and directors who serve in good faith and with due care. The business judgment rule does not insulate "mere dummies or figureheads" from liability, of course, but it never was meant to do so. . . .

As described above, the business judgment rule precludes some, but not all claims, against bank officers and directors that sound in ordinary negligence. With that qualification, we answer the certified question in the negative.

**Business Application:** Construct facts that would lead to the result that the bank officers would not be protected by the business judgment rule.

### *Dissolution*

In theory, a corporation can live forever, although it can and does expire under various circumstances. The termination of corporate existence is referred to as *dissolution.* Dissolution may occur voluntarily or involuntarily.

**Decision Making in the Legal Environment**

This Internal Revenue Service link provides a practical checklist for closing a business.

http://www.irs.gov/Businesses/Small-Businesses-&-Self-Employed/Closing-a-Business-Checklist

Voluntary dissolution occurs when the corporation files a certificate of dissolution with the secretary of state. This normally requires both board of directors' and shareholders' approval. The main reason for voluntary dissolution is unprofitability of the company. Some profitable corporations, however, voluntarily dissolve to fend off hostile takeovers.

Involuntary corporate dissolutions are accomplished by administrative or judicial process. A corporation's failure to comply with certain administrative requirements, such as filing of forms, payment of taxes, and maintaining a statutory agent, may result in an action by the state attorney general to dissolve the corporation. Additionally, shareholders may file suit seeking dissolution of the corporation under circumstances where, for example, there is gross mismanagement or unfair treatment of shareholders.

On dissolution, the board of directors, or in some cases a court-appointed trustee, must wind up the affairs of the corporation. This entails liquidating the corporate assets and distributing the proceeds, first to creditors, and then to the shareholders.

## LIMITED LIABILITY COMPANY

One of the more attractive types of business organizations is the **limited liability company (LLC).** All states have adopted the LLC form of business organization, with variations. The LLC is a hybrid of the partnership and the subchapter S corporation, selecting the best characteristics of each. Like the subchapter S corporation, its owners enjoy limited liability, without, however, the restriction of number of owners and the necessity of electing the status annually. Like the partnership, the LLC avoids double taxation, and unlike the limited partnership there is no restriction on control and management of the business.

There are, however, some practical limitations. First, some states place restrictions on the transfer of interests, requiring unanimous agreement for the transferee to have management input. Additionally, jurisdictions that do not have LLC statutes may not recognize the limited liability aspects of an LLC transacting business in that jurisdiction.

# CHAPTER PROBLEMS

1. Define the following concepts and terms:
   *a.* Principal
   *b.* Apparent authority
   *c.* Independent contractors
   *d.* Apparent partnership
   *e.* Limited partnership
   *f.* Pierce the corporate veil
   *g.* Private corporations
   *h.* Business judgment rule
   *i.* Preemptive rights
   *j.* Limited liability company (LLC)

### *Business Application*

2. Wheeler spoke with Stewart, an agent of Stewart Insurance, an independent insurance agency, about obtaining insurance for his mobile home. Wheeler filled out an application for insurance on a Puritan Insurance Company form and made partial payment. Stewart informed Wheeler, "As quick as I write this receipt out and accept your money, you will be covered by Puritan." Stewart failed to send Wheeler's application to Puritan and to obtain insurance protection for Wheeler.

   Stewart did not have any express authorization from Puritan to bind the company. Puritan considered each application on arrival. Fire destroyed Wheeler's mobile home. Stewart informed Wheeler that the loss was not covered by Puritan. Do you agree? Explain. Would Wheeler have any other alternatives to recovery? Explain.
3. Loehr's is a used car dealer. One of its salespeople misrepresented the mileage of a used car in a sale to a customer. Under agency principles, is Loehr's liable for the damages due to the misrepresentation? What additional information, if any, do you need to answer the question? Explain. What can the owners of car dealerships do to minimize the risk of such misrepresentation occurring?

4. Lancaster was a mechanic in the locomotive shop at Norfolk and Western Railway Co. Lachrone, a hot-tempered foreman, lost his temper and approached Lancaster with a broom in a menacing manner. Lancaster developed a severe mental disorder as a result. Is Norfolk and Western Railway Co. liable for Lancaster's injury under agency principles? Explain.
5. Harris and Zajac worked together in a salvage operation business. They bought wrecked cars and rebuilt them or sold them for salvage. Zajac had a controlling voice in the management of the business. There was no written partnership agreement; neither did the business file a partnership tax return. Harris used his own money to buy cars, as did Zajac. The parties split the profits on the sales from time to time. Zajac withheld federal withholding and social security taxes on Harris's share of the profit. Is this a partnership? Why or why not?
6. Able, Baker, and Carter formed ABC Partnership. Able contributed \$5,000, Baker \$10,000, and Carter \$15,000. During the term of the partnership, Baker loaned ABC \$5,000 and Able loaned ABC \$6,000. The partnership is winding up its affairs after a voluntary dissolution. It owes creditors \$100,000. Assume ABC has assets in the amount of \$150,000 to distribute. How will Able, Baker, and Carter divide the profits or losses? What if ABC had \$132,000 to distribute?
7. Dr. Bennet signed articles of incorporation for Aero-Fabb Co. Because these articles were not in accord with the state statutes, the secretary of state did not issue a certificate of incorporation. Timberline leased equipment to Aero-Fabb Co. Aero-Fabb refused to pay. May Timberline enforce payment against Aero-Fabb? Explain.
8. Gries Sports Enterprises, Inc. (GSE) and Gries own 43 percent of the outstanding stock of the Cleveland Browns Football Co., Inc. (Browns), a Delaware corporation. Gries is a director and officer of the Browns. Modell owns 53 percent of the stock in the Browns and is a director, president, and chief executive officer of the Browns. Other board members include Modell's wife; Bailey, general counsel of the Browns; Berick, outside legal counsel; Wallack, a full-time employee; and Cole.

   Modell formed Cleveland Stadium Corporation (CSC). CSC leased the Cleveland Municipal Stadium from the city and subleased it to the Browns. Modell owned 80 percent of the stock in CSC. Berick, Bailey, Cole, Wallack, and Gries also owned stock in CSC.

   Modell had an outstanding personal indebtedness of \$4 million. In an effort to retire that debt, he set about to sell CSC to the Browns for \$6 million. Since he owned 80 percent of the shares in CSC, that would net him sufficient funds to pay off his \$4 million debt. A brokerage and investment firm rendered an opinion that CSC would be worth from \$6.2 million to \$6.9 million if acquired by the Browns.

   At the Browns meeting of the directors, Gries objected to the acquisition. By a four-to-one vote the board approved the acquisition. The Modells abstained.

   Gries and GSE filed suit seeking to set aside the transaction, contending that the transaction was "intrinsically unfair." The Browns defended by contending that the board's decision was protected by the business judgment rule. What additional information would you want to present to support the Browns' contention?

9. Mesa Petroleum owned 13 percent of Unocal's stock. It attempted to gain control of Unocal's stock by a cash offer for outstanding shares. It offered to purchase 64 million shares for $54 per share. It then intended to eliminate the remaining shares by exchanging Mesa stock for Unocal stock. Unocal's board is unanimously against accepting and recommending to its shareholders Mesa's offer. Assuming that Mesa's offer is fair and that the offering price is above the market price, what are some alternatives for the board to consider?
10. Home Owners Warranty Corp. (HOW) administers a homeowner's program for the benefit of member-builders. Two shareholders demand to inspect the books, records, and membership lists of HOW and its subsidiaries. Under which circumstances, and for what purpose, would HOW shareholders be entitled to such inspection?

PART IV

# THE LEGAL AND ETHICAL ENVIRONMENT OF BUSINESS AND ITS EMPLOYEES

CHAPTER 8

# EQUAL EMPLOYMENT OPPORTUNITY

## CHAPTER OUTLINE



## LEARNING OBJECTIVES

After learning this chapter the student should be able to:

- Recognize employment decisions having a high risk of disparate treatment liability.
- Determine the likelihood that an employment practice would result in disparate impact liability.
- Apply the bona fide seniority system, bona fide occupational qualification, and bona fide employee benefit plan exceptions to different problems.
- Evaluate the likelihood that an affirmative action plan is lawful.
- Determine when harassment amounts to illegal discrimination.
- Determine when to accommodate an employee's religious practices or physical or mental disability.

**The Business and Government Interface**

The following link is to the website for the Equal Employment Opportunity Commission, the federal agency that administers the EEO laws discussed in this chapter:

http://www.eeoc.gov/

Notice that the website contains links for employees & applicants as well as for the employers. Clicking the link "About EEOC" gets you to the laws and regulations, statistics, and publications, among other topics.

During the Reconstruction period, Congress passed several civil rights acts to protect the newly freed slaves. These acts were soon ignored, as segregation and discrimination became widespread within America's social institutions. Although many Americans worked against segregation in the late nineteenth and early twentieth centuries, it was not until the 1950s that the civil rights movement began to gain momentum. The movement achieved its most significant legislative victory with the passage of the Civil Rights Act of 1964, a comprehensive assault on discriminatory practices in America. Title VII of the Civil Rights Act prohibits discrimination in employment on the basis of race, color, religion, national origin, or sex. It is the broadest federal statute regulating employment practices. Today, it is one of several major sources of federal equal employment regulation.

These regulations weave a tangled legal web that can snare today's employers. They establish the following categories of illegal discrimination: race, sex, sexual orientation and gender identity, religion, national origin, age, veteran status, genetic information, and disability. Each of these categories is known as a *protected class.* The federal equal employment opportunity laws contain different provisions concerning coverage of protected classes, defenses, and enforcement. They are summarized in Table 8-1.

## THE CONCEPT OF DISCRIMINATION

**Law and Ethics in Business Policies**

The following link is to the Exelon Corporation Code of Business Conduct:

http://www.exeloncorp.com/assets/people-culture/docs/bro_codeofconduct.pdf

*See*, "Fair Treatment, Diversity and Inclusion" at page 12. In what ways does the policy reflect federal regulatory law? In what ways does it go beyond federal regulation?

Regardless of which protected class or statute is involved, the concept of discrimination is basically the same. Discrimination in any employment decision is illegal. This includes hiring, firing, promotion, job assignments, training programs, compensation, and similar decisions. The law does not require an employer to hire, promote, or retain anyone; it simply prohibits an employer from using membership in a protected class as a basis for an employment decision. The two types of illegal discrimination are:

- Disparate treatment of a member of a protected class.
- Disparate impact of an employment practice on a protected class.

The disparate treatment and disparate impact approaches were first developed by the courts in cases interpreting Title VII. They have also been applied in cases involving other federal equal employment opportunity laws.

### *Disparate Treatment*

**Disparate treatment** results when an employer, union, or employment agency treats one employee less favorably than another because of race, sex, religion, national origin, age, or disability. Thus, disparate treatment is intentional discrimination. In a disparate treatment case, the focus is on the defendant's motive.

## TABLE 8-1 Federal EEO Laws

| *Law* | *Coverage* | *Protected Class(es)* | *Defenses* | *Enforcement* |
|---|---|---|---|---|
| Title VII, 1964 Civil Rights Act | Employers with at least 15 employees; unions; employment agencies | Race, sex, religion, national origin | Seniority systems, ability tests, bona fide occupational qualifications (except race) | EEOC or private lawsuit after using EEOC remedies |
| Equal Pay Act | Similar to FLSA coverage | Sex (equal pay for equal work) | Seniority system, factors other than sex, quantity or quality of output | EEOC or private lawsuit |
| Age Discrimination in Employment Act | Employers with at least 20 employees; unions; employment agencies | Age (40 or older) | Seniority system, bona fide occupational qualification, reasonable factors other than age, employee benefit plan | EEOC or private lawsuit after using EEOC remedies |
| Americans with Disabilities Act | Employers with 15 or more employees | Disability, including a duty to accommodate | Undue hardship | Same as Title VII |
| §§ 503, 504, Rehabilitation Act of 1973 | Federal contractors and recipients of federal financial assistance | Handicap, including a duty to accommodate | | Private lawsuit, debarment from federal contracts |
| 1866 Civil Rights Act | Employers; unions | Race, national origin | | Private lawsuit |
| Executive Orders | Federal contractors | Affirmative action re race, color, national origin, sex, sexual orientation, gender identity | | Debarment from federal contracts |
| Genetic Information Nondiscrimination Act | Employers with at least 15 employees; unions; employment agencies | Genetic information | Inadvertent acquisitions and those through: wellness program, Family and Medical Leave Act certification, commercially or publicly available sources, biological monitoring for workplace toxic substance exposure, limited law enforcement purposes | EEOC or private lawsuit after using EEOC remedies |
| Vietnam-era Veteran's Readjustment Act of 1974 | Federal contractors and subcontractors | Qualified Vietnam-era veterans, recently separated veterans, special disabled veterans, and veterans who served on active duty during a war or campaign on an expedition for which a campaign badge has been authorized | | Veterans' Employment and Training Service (VETS) |

A plaintiff may prove disparate treatment with direct evidence of discriminatory motive. For example, an employer may have sent a rejection letter to a female applicant stating, "You are certainly well qualified, but this is a man's job."

Usually, direct evidence of discriminatory motive is not available. Motive, therefore, must be inferred from a defendant's conduct in view of the surrounding circumstances. A plaintiff may raise an inference of discrimination by showing that he or she (1) belonged to a protected class, (2) applied and was qualified for a job for which the employer was seeking applicants, and (3) was rejected, after which the position remained open and the employer continued seeking applicants with similar qualifications. A plaintiff who accomplishes this is said to have established a prima facie case of disparate treatment, or intentional discrimination. This approach may be adapted to establish a prima facie case of disparate treatment with regard to matters other than initial hire.

When a prima facie case of disparate treatment has been established, the defendant must provide a legitimate, nondiscriminatory explanation for the employment decision. The defendant is not required to prove that it did not discriminate, nor must it prove the factual validity of its explanation. However, a demonstration that an employment practice is required by business necessity may not be used as a defense against a claim of intentional discrimination.

Once the defendant provides an explanation, the plaintiff must prove that the explanation is really a pretext for discrimination. To do so, the plaintiff may attempt to show that the defendant's rationale lacks credibility, that the rationale was not uniformly applied, or that statistics indicate a general practice of discrimination by the defendant. The ultimate issue is a factual one: is the defendant's apparently valid reason really a cover-up for intentional discrimination?

Strong circumstantial evidence of intentional discrimination is provided by a statistical comparison between the percentage of minorities in the employer's workforce and the percentage of minorities in the relevant labor market. Employers are not required to hire a specified percentage of minorities, but the minority composition of the employer's workforce may suggest that the employer has discriminated. For example, assume that an employer has 1,000 qualified applicants for 100 openings, and that 500 applicants are black and 500 are white. If the employer hires randomly, one would expect 50 blacks and 50 whites to be hired. Fifty is said to be the "expected value." If the employer hires 47 blacks, it is still very likely that the selection is random and that the deviation from the expected value occurred by chance rather than by design. If only 10 blacks were hired, one may suspect discrimination. If no blacks are hired, it is almost certain that the employer discriminated. One cannot be absolutely certain, because it is possible to randomly select 100 whites. Nevertheless, the greater the deviation from the expected value, the less likely it is that the result occurred by chance.

If the frequency of all possible random outcomes is plotted on a graph, the result is a bell curve, as illustrated in Figure 8-1. A statistical measure, known as **standard deviation,** is derived from the bell curve. It measures the probability that a given result occurred by chance. On the curve below, point A is the expected value. Points B and C are equal distances away from point A. We expect to find 68 percent of all results between points B and C; and 34 percent between A and C. Points D and E are equidistant from points B and C, respectively. Between points D and E, we expect to find 96 percent of all results. The distance between each point and its closest neighboring point is one standard deviation. Thus, when the minority or sexual composition of an employer's workforce is two to three standard deviations less than the expected value, we are 96 percent to 98.8 percent sure that the hiring did not occur randomly. Under these circumstances, a court infers that the employer has committed intentional discrimination.

**FIGURE 8-1 Bell Curve**

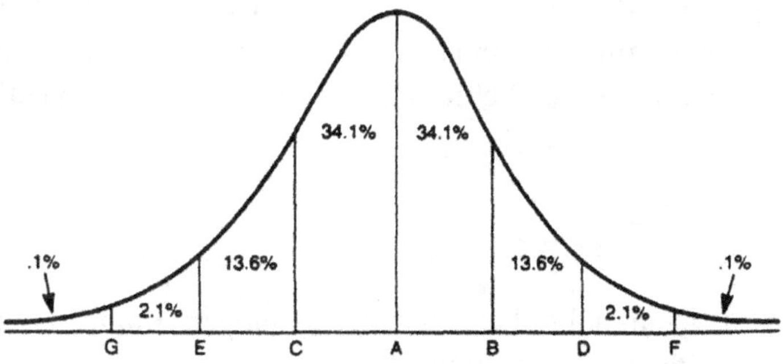


An employer faced with statistical proof of intentional discrimination may attempt to rebut the inference in several ways. The employer may argue that the statistical comparison is not valid because the plaintiff failed to select the appropriate relevant labor market. The appropriate relevant labor market depends on the skill required for the job. If the job requires little specialized skill, general population figures would provide an appropriate basis of comparison. If the job is highly specialized, the relevant labor market must be restricted to those who are qualified. For example, the workforce of an employer charged with discrimination in hiring messengers may be compared to the general population, whereas the workforce of an employer charged with discriminating in hiring certified public accountants must be compared to CPAs generally.

The employer's location may also influence the composition of the relevant labor market. Commuting patterns in a given metropolitan area may be significant in determining the relevant market of an employer located in the central city or in a suburb.

Besides attacking the validity of the statistical comparison, the defendant may also attack its probative value. For example, the employer might show that its workforce has experienced little turnover and little expansion since the effective date of Title VII. The employer might also offer nondiscriminatory explanations for statistical disparities.

In some cases, the evidence may show that both discriminatory and legitimate reasons contributed to the defendant's actions. These cases are called **mixed motive cases.** The defendant may claim that it would have taken the same action even if the plaintiff had not been a member of a protected class. As long as the plaintiff proves that membership in a protected class was a motivating factor in the decision, the defendant is liable, even though other factors also motivated the practice. The defendant may avoid the remedies of damages, reinstatement, hiring, promotion, and back pay, however, by proving that it would have reached the same decision without considering the plaintiff's protected class status. The available remedies would be only declarative relief, certain types of injunctive relief, attorney fees and costs.

Disparate treatment can take many forms. For example, an employer that segregates its workforce for fringe benefits purposes engages in illegal disparate treatment. Thus, an employer may not offer male employees lower life insurance benefits or higher pension benefits than similarly situated female employees even though women, as a group, live longer than men.

Another type of disparate treatment occurs when an employer uses a double standard for members of a protected class. This conduct is illegal, even if the employer does not otherwise discriminate. For example, an employer whose workforce is predominantly female acts illegally if it refuses to hire women with preschool children but hires men with preschool children. Such a policy is often called *sex plus discrimination.*

### *Disparate Impact*

Employers often impose requirements for particular jobs. For example, employers might require security guards to be at least six feet tall. On its face this requirement does not appear to disqualify any job applicant because of sex or national origin. However, if scrutinized, it may prove to disqualify a larger percentage of women, Latinos, and Asians than nonminority males. Because, on average, they are shorter than white males, these groups may be systematically excluded from consideration for the security guard jobs. The employment discrimination laws do not prohibit the use of such facially neutral criteria. When the criteria systematically exclude members of a protected class from job opportunities, the employer must justify their use or it will be liable for **disparate impact.**

In a disparate impact case, the plaintiff must prove that the challenged practice disqualifies a protected class at a significantly greater rate than the majority class. The defendant may avoid liability by proving that the practice is job related and consistent with business necessity. The defendant may still be liable if the plaintiff can prove that there was a less discriminatory practice available to meet the defendant's needs.

## EXCEPTIONS

The federal laws contain a variety of exceptions to their prohibitions against discrimination. The three most common exceptions are:

- Bona fide occupational qualifications.
- Professionally developed ability tests.
- Bona fide seniority systems.

### *The Bona Fide Occupational Qualification*

The **bona fide occupational qualification** (BFOQ) is a statutory exception to employment practices that might otherwise violate Title VII or the Age Discrimination in Employment Act. This exception allows an employer to discriminate in its hiring where religion, national origin, sex, or age is a bona fide occupational qualification reasonably necessary to the normal operation of the business.

The exception does not apply to racial discrimination. To establish a BFOQ, the employer must show that employees of a given sex, religion, national origin, or age are a business necessity because any other groups would undermine the essence of the business operation. This may be done by showing that certain qualifications possessed by persons of a given sex, religion, national origin, or age are essential to the employer's business and that it is impracticable to find members of the excluded class who possess these qualifications.

The BFOQ is interpreted narrowly, and the employer bears a heavy burden of proof. The employer must prove that the discrimination is necessary, not merely convenient.

## *Professionally Developed Ability Tests*

Title VII permits the use of any professionally developed ability test, provided that the test is not designed or used to discriminate. The EEOC has issued guidelines detailing the **validation** processes it approves for establishing the job relatedness of any selection procedure that has an adverse impact on a protected group. Under the guidelines, a test is considered discriminatory if it results in a selection rate for one race, sex, religion, or national origin that is less than four fifths of the selection rate for another. The burden then shifts to the user of the test to validate the test by one of three methods: criterion validity, content validity, or construct validity.

Criterion validity establishes a statistical relationship between performance on the test and an objective indicator of job performance. Criterion validity is established by a study comparing test scores to the specified measure of performance. For example, if a study showed that a statistically significant correlation existed between GMAT scores and grades in an MBA program, the GMAT exam would be criterion valid.

Content validity establishes that the test representatively samples a function of the job. A word processing test for a word processor is content valid.

Construct validity establishes that the test indicates a psychological trait required for the job. A test indicating leadership ability is construct valid for a police commander.

## *Seniority Systems*

Title VII, the ADEA, and the Equal Pay Act permit employers to apply different standards of employment pursuant to **bona fide seniority systems** that are not the result of an intention to discriminate. In *Teamsters v. United States*, the Supreme Court held that a seniority system can be bona fide even though it perpetuates the effects of pre-act discrimination.[1] The Court further held that a seniority system is bona fide where it applies equally to all employees regardless of membership in a protected class, was not established or maintained for the purpose of discriminating, and operates rationally in accord with practices in the industry.

---

1 431 U.S. 324 (1977).

# SPECIAL TOPICS IN EQUAL EMPLOYMENT OPPORTUNITY

In addition to the basic types of discrimination, employers face special problems when dealing with affirmative action and workplace harassment. Employers also must handle issues that are peculiar to sex, sexual orientation and gender identity, religion, national origin, age, disability, and genetic information discrimination.

## *Affirmative Action*

Affirmative action issues arise in two settings. First, employers might voluntarily adopt affirmative action plans that give preference to minority employees. Second, after finding that an employer has discriminated against minorities, a court might require the employer to take affirmative action. In either case, whites or males may argue that the voluntary plan or the court order illegally discriminates against them.

**Law and Ethics in Business Policies**

The following link is to GE's Code of Conduct:

http://www.ge.com/files_citizenship/pdf/theSpirit&TheLetter.pdf

Pages 39–41 discuss equal employment opportunity. Notice at page 41 the company explicitly addresses affirmative action.

Employers adopt voluntary affirmative action plans for a variety of reasons. One reason an employer might do so is to be eligible for contracts with the federal government. Executive Order 11246, administered by the Office of Federal Contract Compliance Programs (OFCCP), requires that government contractors take affirmative action to ensure that their employees are hired and promoted on a nondiscriminatory basis.

All federal contractors and subcontractors who do more than $10,000 in business with the federal government in one year must, according to the Executive Order, not discriminate in employment on the basis of race, color religion, sex, sexual orientation, gender identity, or national origin. In addition, the Executive Order requires federal government contractors to take affirmative action to ensure that equal opportunity is provided in employment.

The federal government program requires that an acceptable affirmative action plan with realistic goals and timetables be prepared by each contractor or subcontractor. The employer must first perform a utilization analysis, including evaluation of the size of the minority and female population and labor force in the area, the requisite skills among minorities and women in the area, and the available training programs and facilities. Having completed this analysis, the employer must identify the deficiencies in its workforce, and must then establish attainable goals for correcting and eliminating those deficiencies, along with timetables and methods for achieving the goals. An employer is not in violation of its plan if it fails to meet its goals provided that the employer has made good-faith efforts to do so. This is the principal difference between goals and quotas: if a contractor is required by law to meet the goals, they become quotas.

## *Harassment*

Harassment does not per se violate Title VII. Harassment that is discriminatory can violate Title VII. For example, an employee who is required to have sexual relations with a supervisor to secure, maintain, or advance in employment is subjected to conditions that are not imposed on employees of the opposite sex. An employee who is promoted as a reward for having sexual relations with a supervisor is given an opportunity that employees of the opposite sex do not have.

Sexual harassment is unwelcome sexual conduct that is a term or condition of employment. There are two types of sexual harassment: (1) quid pro quo harassment and (2) hostile environment harassment. Quid pro quo harassment is where job benefits are exchanged for sexual favors. ("Date me or lose your job.") Hostile environment harassment is where unwelcome sexual conduct creates an intimidating, hostile, or offensive environment.

**Employer Liability.** An employer's liability for harassment (called *respondeat superior liability* or *vicarious liability*) depends on the status of the harasser. If the harasser is a co-worker, the employer is liable only if it was negligent in controlling the working conditions. This same negligence standard applies to nonemployee harassers, like customers or independent contractors, that the employer has control over (such as when they are on the employer's premises).

However, if the harasser is a supervisor, the employer is strictly, or automatically, liable if the harassment results in a tangible negative employment action, such as a lack of a raise or promotion, or termination of employment. But, if no negative action is taken, the employer may avoid liability by establishing as an affirmative defense that (1) the employer exercised reasonable care to try to prevent and correct any harassing behavior, and (2) that the employee unreasonably failed to take advantage of the preventive or corrective opportunities provided by the employer.

In *Vance v. Ball State University*[2] the U.S. Supreme Court held that an employee is a "supervisor for purposes of vicarious liability" only if he or she is empowered by the employer to take tangible employment actions against the victim, like the power to hire, fire, demote, promote, transfer, or discipline.

The following case illustrates the application of Title VII harassment law.

**MANDEL *v.* M & Q PACKAGING CORP.**
Third Circuit U.S. Court of Appeals
706 F.3d 157 (2013)

Shannon J. Mandel (Mandel) sued M & Q Packaging Corp. (M & Q) alleging sexual harassment in violation of Title VII of the Civil Rights Act, and other claims not relevant here. The district court ordered summary judgment in favor of M & Q. Mandel appealed to the United States Court of Appeals for the Third Circuit, which reversed the district court's order regarding Mandel's sexual harassment claim. What follows is the Court of Appeals opinion.

---

2 133 S. Ct. 2434 (2013).

### *Roth, Circuit Judge:*

On October 25, 1996, Shannon J. Mandel was hired as an Inside Sales and Customer Relations Coordinator by M & Q Packaging Corporation (M & Q), which manufactures and sells packaging film. Mandel claimed that, throughout her employment from October 25, 1996, to May 23, 2007, she was sexually harassed and discriminated against by male managers, supervisors, and owners in alleged incidents such as being referred to as "woman," "darling," "the woman," "fluffy," "missy," "hon," and "toots"; having her body, clothing, and physical appearance commented on; being told that she was "foolish not to use [her] assets"; being told by Systems Manager David Benetz, when she asked for directions to a meeting at corporate headquarters, that "[f]or you . . . the meeting will start at my house tonight and we will conclude our part of it tomorrow morning"; being told by Quality Manager Harold Brenneman that he fantasized about her while he was having sex with his wife; being told in a review by Managing Director (and later President & COO) Michael Schmal that she was "too female" and "too emotional"; being solicited for dates by Vice President of Sales Curt Rubenstein even after she told him she was not interested; being told to clean the bathroom and make coffee when male employees were not asked to perform such tasks; and being paid less and given less vacation time than a male manager.

On April 6, 2007, during a meeting regarding sample orders, Bachert became angry, repeatedly called Mandel a "bitch," and screamed "shut the fuck up." Bachert had previously referred to Mandel as a "bitch," both in and out of her presence. As a result of the meeting, Mandel resigned on May 23, 2007, by submitting a letter with two weeks' notice to Schmal.

In her resignation letter, Mandel did not complain of harassment or discrimination, apparently because she was concerned she would be denied her vacation time. She did, however, refer to the Employee Handbook. The Employee Handbook included an Equal Employment Opportunity Policy, which informed employees that they should contact the personnel manager—in this case, Conway—if they felt they were being discriminated against. The Employee Handbook also included an Open Door policy, which directed employees to discuss any issues first with their supervisor and then with the personnel manager. Mandel testified in her deposition that she understood the policies in the Employee Handbook but felt uncomfortable going to Conway or Schmal with her complaints. Conway testified in his deposition that other than giving each employee a copy of the Employee Handbook, there was no training regarding discrimination or sexual harassment.

Although Mandel complained to Schmidt about being told to make coffee, she did not complain to her supervisors about other alleged incidents of harassment or discrimination. Mandel occasionally used profanity and sent emails containing sexual humor. Mandel also called Bachert "gay" on a few occasions, apparently as a joke in reference to jealous husbands who claimed Bachert made advances to their wives. Mandel was never disciplined during her employment with M & Q.

Title VII prohibits sexual harassment that is "sufficiently severe or pervasive to alter the conditions of [the plaintiff's] employment and create an abusive working environment." *Meritor Sav. Bank, FSB v. Vinson*, 477 U.S. 57, (1986). To succeed on a hostile work environment claim, the plaintiff must establish that 1) the employee suffered intentional discrimination because of his/her sex, 2) the discrimination was severe or pervasive, 3) the discrimination detrimentally affected the plaintiff, 4) the discrimination would detrimentally affect a reasonable person in like circumstances, and 5) the existence of *respondeat superior* liability. The first four elements establish a hostile work environment, and the fifth element determines employer liability.

We note that the parties do not dispute the District Court's finding that Mandel satisfied the first element because she had presented "sufficient evidence from which a reasonable jury could infer that the alleged harassment was based on her sex."

**ii. " Severe or Pervasive"**

To determine whether an environment is hostile, a court must consider the totality of the circumstances, including "the frequency of the discriminatory conduct; its severity; whether it is physically threatening or humiliating, or a mere offensive utterance; and whether it unreasonably interferes with an employee's work performance." *Harris v. Forklift Sys., Inc.*, 510 U.S. 17 (1993). The District Court summarized the alleged incidents and concluded that "none of the alleged incidents is sufficiently severe to establish a hostile work environment." The District Court's reasoning suggests that it improperly parsed out each event and viewed them separately, rather than as a whole. On remand, the District Court must consider the totality of the circumstances, rather than parse out the individual incidents, to determine whether the acts that collectively form the continuing violation are severe or pervasive.

**iii. "Detrimentally Affected"**

We agree with the District Court that an objectively reasonable person in Mandel's place might be offended by the alleged incidents. We are troubled, however, by the District Court's conclusion that Mandel failed to show that she was detrimentally affected by the alleged incidents:

> Here, Mandel only complained about one of the alleged incidents (Bachert's name calling), and she complained to a friend at work and not a supervisor. Further, she has presented no evidence that she had any psychological distress or that her ability to perform her job was impaired. Finally, the record contains evidence that Mandel actively participated in creating a work environment in which vulgarity and sexual innuendo were commonplace. Mandel's use of explicit language and her e-mails involving ongoing sexual jokes demonstrate a casual ease with this type of workplace behavior. The use of sexual humor does not on its own demonstrate that Mandel is incapable of being offended by degrading comments, but when combined with a lack of evidence of any subjective distress, a reasonable jury could not find that Mandel has proven that the harassment had a detrimental effect on her.

Although Mandel engaged in certain unprofessional conduct, the comments and conduct to which she was subject were often worse and apparently uninvited. Mandel complained about being told to make coffee, and although she did not complain to her supervisors about the other alleged incidents, there is some evidence that she complained to other employees. She also resigned shortly after Bachert called her a "bitch" during a meeting and alleged in her sworn EEOC Charge and questionnaires that she was detrimentally affected. A jury could reasonably conclude that Mandel did not invite these comments or conduct and that, despite her own conduct, was offended by them. Because the inherently subjective question of whether particular conduct was unwelcome presents difficult problems of proof and turns on credibility determinations, the District Court erred in granting summary judgment.

**iv. *Respondeat Superior* Liability**

The basis of an employer's liability for a hostile work environment claim depends on whether the harasser is the victim's supervisor or coworker. Because the District Court concluded that Mandel failed to establish a hostile work environment, it did not reach the question of employer liability. There is an inadequate record before us on appeal from which to determine whether *respondeat superior* liability exists. Because we reverse and remand for further proceedings on the hostile work environment claim, we leave the issue to the District Court to determine on remand.

**Business Application:** How should an employer investigate an employee's sexual harassment complaint? What policies should an employer have in place to reduce the risk of liability for sexual harassment violations of Title VII? (Or for other forms of harassment—racial, for example.) If you are the victim of harassment, what should you do to (a) try to stop it and (b) establish evidence to prove a claim of violation of law?

## *Sex*

Sexual discrimination in employment is not a new phenomenon. The concepts of men's work and women's work have been ingrained in society since civilization began. Today, sex roles in our society are changing, yet the notion of gender-based jobs remains a threat to the freedom to work, regardless of sex.

### Business Application/Ethical Issues

Frieda Rosenmund is a financial analyst for Stevedore Pants Company. Her supervisor is Gus Goyert. As the company's controller, Goyert hires the secretaries in the controller's office. Applications for secretarial positions are screened by Goyert. Selected applicants are then interviewed by Goyert and all the other employees in the controller's office. After conferring with the other employees, Goyert decides whom to hire.

Several applications have been sent to Goyert for an open secretarial position. Among the applicants is a male. Goyert looks over the man's application in Rosenmund's presence and announces with an air of finality, "Don't interview this one. I'm not going to hire any man as my secretary. He's probably gay, and I don't want any AIDS epidemic at Stevedore Pants."

What are the ethical issues? What would you do?

### Pregnancy

Only women can become pregnant, but not all women choose to do so. Title VII, as amended by the Pregnancy Discrimination Act of 1978 (PDA), equates discrimination on the basis of pregnancy, childbirth, or related medical conditions with sex discrimination.

An employer must treat pregnancy in the same manner as any other medical condition. It may not exclude pregnancy coverage from the medical insurance it provides for employees' spouses. To do so discriminates against male employees. The PDA, however, does not prohibit an employer from providing special pregnancy benefits, such as special maternity leave, that it does not provide to employees generally.

### Compensation

Sex discrimination in compensation violates Title VII. It may also violate the Equal Pay Act of 1963 (EPA).

The EPA prohibits differences in pay between the sexes for employees who are performing work that requires "equal skill, effort, and responsibility" and is "performed under similar working conditions." If even one worker is paid at a higher rate than members of the opposite sex who are doing equal work, a violation of the act may be found.

The term *equal* does not require that the work of men and women employees be identical, but only that it be substantially equal, to justify equal pay. Thus, small differences in job description do not make jobs so unequal as to justify a higher pay scale for one sex.

In writing the EPA, Congress referred to equality of "skill," "effort," and "responsibility" exercised "under similar working conditions" because these are criteria by which industry evaluates jobs for classification purposes. For example, in *Corning Glass v. Brennan*, the Supreme Court considered whether the differences between the day and night shifts were sufficient to justify paying male night-shift employees more than female day-shift employees.[3] The Court rejected the employer's argument that different shifts constituted different working conditions, noting that in the glass industry working conditions did not usually refer to the time of day during which work was performed.

Several exceptions to the equal work-equal pay standard are:

- Bona fide seniority and merit systems.
- Earnings based on quantity or quality of output.
- Factors other than sex.

Pay differentials based on seniority or on performance evaluations are justified, provided that the policy is uniformly applied. Systems in which employees are paid according to an individual production piece rate are immunized from liability by the quantity or quality of output exception.

Exceptions for factors other than sex immunize other legitimate bases for wage disparities. For example, although a shift differential results in unequal pay for equal work under similar conditions, the inequity may be justified because it arises from a factor other than sex.

An EPA violation does not exist where a wage disparity arises out of a bona fide management training program that rotates employees of one sex through all departments, thereby requiring them to work temporarily with members of the opposite sex who receive a lower rate than the trainees. However, courts scrutinize training programs that involve employees of only one sex to determine whether they are, in fact, bona fide exceptions. If the programs are informal, do not regularly result

---

3 417 U.S. 188 (1974).

in promotion to the position being trained for, and appear to be geared more to the employer's needs than to actual training, they are not likely to survive scrutiny.

Title VII has been interpreted to implicitly incorporate the EPA's affirmative defenses in compensation discrimination cases. However, intentional sexual discrimination in pay violates Title VII even though the employees do not perform equal work. Thus, an employer who pays truck drivers more than secretaries because the truck drivers are male and the secretaries are female does not violate the EPA but may violate Title VII.

### Sexual Orientation and Gender Identity

The legal status of employment discrimination on the basis of sexual orientation and gender identity is in a state of flux. The answer to the question, "Can an employer discriminate on the basis of sexual orientation and gender identity?" is, "It depends."

At the federal level, there is no federal statute forbidding sexual orientation and gender identity discrimination in employment. Title VII does not explicitly forbid it. The EEOC's enforcement policy is that discrimination against a transgender individual is discrimination on the basis of sex.

Since 1994, a bill has been reintroduced in every Congress that would forbid employment discrimination based on sexual orientation and gender identity. The bill is entitled the Employment Nondiscrimination Act (ENDA), but it has yet to be enacted by Congress.

In 2014, President Barack Obama signed an executive order forbidding federal contractors from discriminating on the basis of sexual orientation and gender identity. The executive order applies to one part of the economy, those businesses that do business with the federal government.

At the state level, the answer to the question of whether employment discrimination on the basis of sexual orientation and gender identity is unlawful is similarly complicated. Some states forbid both discrimination on the basis of sexual orientation and gender identity (an individual's appearance, mannerisms, characteristics), some forbid sexual orientation discrimination in employment only; and some, like federal law, do not have legislation forbidding either type of discrimination, but have governor-signed executive orders. A majority of states have no law banning this form of discrimination. The legal landscape is in a state of change.

## *Religion*

The term *religion* encompasses such traditional religions as Judaism, Catholicism, Protestantism, and Islam, but is far broader. It includes all moral or ethical beliefs that are sincerely held with the strength of traditional religious views. Atheism and agnosticism are considered religions for Title VII purposes.

### The Duty to Accommodate Religion

Title VII requires an employer to make reasonable accommodations to employees' religious beliefs and practices unless accommodation would work an undue hardship on the business. The most frequent charges of religious discrimination dealt with by the courts and the EEOC involve not raw prejudice, but instances in which an employer's work rule, innocent in intent, conflicts with an employee's religious belief. Such conditions trigger the employer's duty to accommodate the employee's religious beliefs.

An employer need not accommodate an employee's religious beliefs if to do so would impose more than a *de minimis* cost. For example, an employer need not give an employee the day off for his or her religious Sabbath if this would require the employer to pay another employee at an overtime rate to fill in.

An employer fulfills its duty under Title VII when it offers a reasonable accommodation to the employee. The employer is not obligated to agree to the accommodation requested by the employee even if it would cost the employer nothing.

## *National Origin*

Title VII forbids employment discrimination based on national origin against applicants or employees. National origin refers to the country from which an individual or the individual's ancestors came. It also includes persons with characteristics generally identified with particular national groups. Unlawful national origin discrimination includes discrimination directed at individuals because they are married or associated with persons or groups of a national origin.

Title VII prohibits treating people differently because of national origin. This includes harassment on the basis of national origin. Name calling would be an example of national origin harassment.

English-only language rules tend to have a disparate impact on national origin. The EEOC guidelines state that when an employer requires English to be spoken at all times, the agency will presume that such a rule violates Title VII and will closely scrutinize it.

Selection procedures that have an adverse impact on the basis of national origin and are not job-related and required by business necessity violate Title VII. For example, height or weight requirements tend to have an adverse impact based on national origin.

The Immigration Reform and Control Act (IRCA) prohibits employers from hiring illegal aliens. The IRCA also requires employers to verify the residence or citizenship status of every employee. However, the IRCA makes it illegal for an employer to discriminate in employment against someone who is not an illegal alien on the basis of that individual's citizenship or immigration status.

## *Age*

The Age Discrimination in Employment Act covers employers with 20 or more employees, employment agencies, and unions with 25 or more members or who operate hiring halls. The ADEA prohibits age discrimination against persons age 40 or older.

The ADEA contains BFOQ and bona fide seniority system exceptions. It also excepts employment decisions based on reasonable factors other than age and discharges for cause. These two exceptions are essentially denials of, rather than justifications for, age discrimination. They have been interpreted as codifying the employer's burden of rebutting a prima facie case of disparate treatment with legitimate, nondiscriminatory reasons for its actions.

The ADEA excepts **bona fide employee benefit plans** that are not subterfuges to avoid the act. This exception applies only where employers reduce benefits to older workers to offset the increased costs of those benefits as employees age. For example, employers may reduce life insurance benefits based on age. Often it may be difficult to distinguish between age and other characteristics correlated with age.

Employers should be particularly sensitive to ADEA liability when terminating older employees. More than 90 percent of the cases brought under the ADEA have involved terminations. This is particularly true during economic recessions, when many companies lay off or terminate large numbers of workers.

## *Disability*

The Americans with Disabilities Act (ADA) prohibits discrimination against a qualified individual on the basis of disability. An employer may not treat a qualified individual with a disability unfavorably because of the individual's disability.

A disability under the ADA means, with respect to an individual:

- a physical or mental impairment that substantially limits one or more major life activities of such individual,
- a record of such an impairment, or
- being regarded as having such impairment.

Major life activities include, among others, caring for oneself, performing manual tasks, seeing, hearing, sleeping, walking, standing, lifting, bending, speaking, breathing, learning, reading, concentrating, thinking, communicating and working. A major life activity also includes the operation of a major bodily function, such as functions of the immune system, digestive, bowel, bladder, brain, respiratory, circulatory, endocrine, and reproductive systems.

The ADA states that, mitigating factors, such as medication, prosthetics, hearing aids, etc. shall not be considered in determining whether someone has a disability. For example, an employer cannot conclude that just because someone wears a hearing aid they are not disabled. However, the statute excludes ordinary eyeglasses and contact lenses from the mitigating factors that must be ignored. (So, if you are wearing ordinary eyeglasses or contact lenses to read this, you cannot claim that your poor eyesight is a disability.)

An impairment that is episodic (for example seizures) or in remission (such as cancer) is a disability if it would substantially limit a major activity when active.

For someone to be regarded as having an impairment that substantially limits a major life activity, they do not have to show that the employer perceived them that way. All the individual has to prove is that he or she was subjected to an action prohibited by the ADA (for example, rejected for a job or a promotion) based on an impairment that is not minor or transitory.

The ADA states that this definition of disability shall be construed in favor of broad coverage of individuals to the maximum extent permitted by the statute.

Employers are required to provide reasonable accommodation to an applicant or an employee with a disability, unless doing so would cause an undue hardship to the employer, which under the ADA means imposing significant difficulty or expense. According to the EEOC, "a reasonable accommodation is any change in the work environment (or in the way things are usually done) to help a person with a disability apply for a job, perform the duties of a job, or enjoy the benefits and privileges of employment." Examples of reasonable accommodation include modifying facilities, equipment, examinations, or other job requirements or working conditions. The duty to accommodate may involve providing readers or interpreters, or restructuring jobs. Individuals who are covered only under the "regarded as" part of the definition of disability are not entitled to reasonable accommodation. (They do not really need it.)

The ADA forbids using qualification standards, employments tests, or other selection criteria that tend to screen out individuals with disabilities, unless the practice is job related and consistent with business necessity.

The ADA prohibits employers from asking medical questions or requiring a medical exam before a job offer is made. The employer cannot ask an applicant if he or she has a disability or the extent of the disability. The EEOC tells employers that they "may ask job applicants whether they can perform the job and how they would perform the job, with or without a reasonable accommodation."

Employers may condition a job offer on passing a medical exam if it is job related and consistent with business necessity. This is allowed only if it is required of all employees regardless of disability.

The following case involves both the nondiscrimination and accommodation aspects of the ADA.

## EEOC *v.* DOLGENCORP, LLC DBA DOLLAR GENERAL CORPORATION

Sixth Circuit U.S. Court of Appeals
899 F.3d 428 (2018)

Linda Atkins (Atkins) began working as a sales associate at Dolgencorp, LLC dba Dollar General (Dollar General) in 2009, and was promoted in 2012 to lead associate, a position that put her in charge of handling the cash in the store. She suffered from type II diabetes, a chronic condition caused by dysfunction of the endocrine system. She monitored her blood sugar level daily to ensure that it was sufficiently high. She occasionally suffered from low blood sugar (hypoglycemia) which required her to respond by quickly consuming glucose to avoid the risk of a seizure or of passing out. When she asked her manager if she could keep orange juice at her cash register in case of an emergency, the manager refused. When she was forced in an emergency to resort to juice from the checkout counter—which she paid for immediately—she was fired for violating the store's "anti-grazing" policy. The EEOC and Atkins sued Dollar General, claiming her termination was the result of disability discrimination in violation of the Americans With Disabilities Act (ADA). The jury awarded Atkins $27,565 in back pay and $250,000 in compensatory damages. The District Court judge further awarded Atkins lawyers $445,332 in attorney's fees and $1,677 in expenses. Dollar General appealed, and the United States Court of Appeals for the Sixth Circuit affirmed. The following is the Court of Appeals opinion.

## *Sutton, Circuit Judge*

Dollar General challenges this judgment on [the] grounds: Dollar General should win as a matter of law on the plaintiffs' reasonable accommodation claim; [and] Dollar General should win as a matter of law on the discriminatory discharge claim.

*Reasonable Accommodation.* Dollar General claims that the jury erred in finding that it discriminated against Atkins by failing to provide her with a reasonable accommodation for her disability. The company faces a steep hill. We may grant judgment as a matter of law only if, after reading the evidence in the light most favorable to Atkins, there is no material fact issue for the jury to decide.

Dollar General claims that it had no duty to accommodate Atkins because Teresa Thayer, her nurse, testified that Atkins could treat hypoglycemia in other ways. Thayer mentioned several equally effective treatment options to address hypoglycemia, including glucose tablets or gels, honey, candy, and peanut butter crackers. Given these options, Dollar General maintains, it had no obligation to let Atkins keep orange juice at the register.

But these options do not make the jury's verdict unreasonable. The company's "Personal Appearance" policy states that employees "should not chew gum or eat/drink, except during breaks (which should not be taken on the sales floor, at registers, etc.)." Just as the jury could find that the company prohibited employees from drinking orange juice at the register, so too could it find that it prohibited them from consuming glucose tablets, cough drops, candy, and honey packets at the register.

The policy's disclaimer, it is true, states that "[r]eligious and/or disability-related exceptions may be permitted depending on the circumstances." But Atkins asked for such an exception and got nowhere. When she asked her store manager if she could keep orange juice at her register because of her diabetic condition, the manager told her "it's against company policy" and to "[b]e careful of the cameras."

Once Atkins requested this reasonable accommodation, the employer had a duty to explore the nature of the employee's limitations, if and how those limitations affected her work, and what types of accommodations could be made. Had Dollar General followed this route, it might well have told Atkins that she could consume glucose pills at the register and perhaps that would have resolved the matter. But that's not what it did. The store manager categorically denied Atkins' request, failed to explore any alternatives, and never related the matter to a superior. That was Dollar General's problem, not Atkins'—or at least a reasonable jury could so conclude.

*Discriminatory Discharge.* Dollar General also claims that the jury went astray when it found that it discriminated against Atkins by terminating her because of her disability. Boiled to its essence, Dollar General's claim is that it had a legitimate nondiscriminatory reason for firing Atkins, namely the company anti-grazing policy.

But a company may not illegitimately deny an employee a reasonable accommodation to a general policy and use that same policy as a neutral basis for firing him. Imagine a school that lacked an elevator to accommodate a teacher with mobility problems. It could not refuse to assign him to classrooms on the first floor, then turn around and fire him for being late to class after he took too long to climb the stairs between periods. In the same way, Atkins never would have had a reason to buy the store's orange juice during a medical emergency if Dollar General had allowed her to keep her own orange juice at the register or worked with her to find another solution.

Happily for us, doctrine lines up with common sense in this setting. A defendant may use a legitimate, nondiscriminatory rationale as a shield against *indirect* or *circumstantial* evidence of discrimination. But a neutral policy is of no moment when an employee presents *direct* evidence of discrimination. And failing to provide a protected employee a reasonable accommodation constitutes direct evidence of discrimination.

Dollar General adds that the verdict cannot stand because Atkins never produced evidence of animus towards the disabled. But the Act speaks in terms of causation, not animus. An employer violates the Act whenever it discharges an employee "on the basis of disability" (a necessary requirement for liability), not only when it harbors ill will (a sufficient way of establishing liability). Imagine a company that fired a visually impaired employee to save itself the minimal expense of buying special software for her. Without more, that would constitute termination "on the basis of disability," even if all the evidence showed that cost-savings, not animus towards the blind, motivated the company.

We affirm.

**Business Application:** What should an employer do when an employee asks for an accommodation for his or her disability?

## *Genetic Information*

The Genetic Information Nondiscrimination Act (GINA) prohibits employers from discriminating on the basis of genetic information. GINA restricts the collection and disclosure of genetic information. The law's reach extends to applicants, employees, and their family members.

Genetic information means information about an individual's genetic tests, the tests of his or her family members, and the manifestation of a disease or disorder in the person's family members. However, under GINA, information about a person's sex or age is not considered genetic information.

According to the EEOC, which enforces GINA, "An employer may never use genetic information to make an employment decision because genetic information is not relevant to an individual's current ability to work."

There are six narrow exceptions to GINA's prohibitions. They are when genetic information is acquired:

1. Inadvertently
2. As part of a voluntary wellness program
3. As part of certifying leave under the Family and Medical Leave Act
4. Through commercially or publicly available documents (for example, newspapers and websites), so long as the employer was not intentionally searching for genetic information
5. As part of legally required biological monitoring of the workplace for toxic substance exposure, and the program is voluntary
6. From DNA testing for the law enforcement purpose of identifying human remains and the genetic information is used only for quality control to detect sample contamination.

## ENFORCEMENT OF EQUAL EMPLOYMENT OPPORTUNITY LAWS

Table 8-2 summarizes the enforcement scheme of the major civil rights laws.

Title VII, the ADA, and the ADEA have similar enforcement provisions. All require victims to file charges of violations with the EEOC and their state employment discrimination agencies if they exist. The EEOC is allowed time to investigate the charges and to try informally to resolve the dispute. The EEOC or the individual victims can sue to correct the violations.

Title VII, the ADA, and the ADEA differ in their timing of the enforcement process. Under Title VII, and the ADA, the charge must be filed with the EEOC within 180 days following the discriminatory act if it arises in a state that does not have an antidiscrimination agency. If the state has an antidiscrimination agency, the charge must be filed first with the state agency. The charge may be filed with the EEOC after the state agency has had it for 60 days or has terminated proceedings, whichever occurs first. The charge must be filed within 300 days following the discriminatory act.

Individuals cannot file Title VII or ADA lawsuits until the EEOC notifies them of their right to sue. This EEOC notice is called a **right-to-sue letter.** If the EEOC's investigation of the charge discloses no reasonable cause to believe a Title VII violation occurred, the EEOC dismisses the charge and issues a right-to-sue letter. The EEOC's dismissal does not prohibit the charging party from suing.

If the EEOC finds reasonable cause, it issues a determination letter. The EEOC attempts to conciliate the dispute. If conciliation efforts fail, it issues a right-to-sue letter. In all cases, suit must be filed within 90 days after receipt of the right-to-sue letter.

Under the ADEA, the charging party can file charges with the state antidiscrimination agency and the EEOC in any order. The charging party is not required to file with the state first. The 180- and 300-day time limits for filing with the EEOC apply to the ADEA. The charging party need not receive a right-to-sue letter to file suit. He or she can sue anytime after the EEOC has had the charge for 60 days. ADEA lawsuits must be filed within 90 days following a right-to-sue letter.

### TABLE 8-2 EEO Enforcement

| *Law* | *Who Enforces* | *Jury Trial* | *Punitive Damages* |
|---|---|---|---|
| ADA, Title VII | EEOC and private plaintiffs | Yes | Yes, for actual malice or reckless disregard for victim's rights; maximum recovery \$50,000–\$200,000, depending on size of employer |
| ADEA,EPA | EEOC and private plaintiffs | Yes | Double damages for willful violations |
| 1866 Civil Rights Act | Private plaintiffs | Yes | Yes, with no monetary limits |
| E.O. 11246 | Federal agencies | No | No |

# CHAPTER PROBLEMS

1. Define the following terms:
    *a.* Disparate treatment
    *b.* Disparate impact
    *c.* Mixed motive cases
    *d.* Standard deviation
    *e.* Bona fide occupational qualification
    *f.* Validation
    *g.* Bona fide seniority system
    *h.* Hostile work environment
    *i.* Bona fide employee benefit plan
    *j.* Right-to-sue letter

## *Business Application*

2. Rysy, Inc. is a janitorial company in Chicago. It advertised in a Spanish-language newspaper that it was looking to hire 15 men and 15 women. Applicants were to apply at the company's office in Chicago. Jean saw the ad and told her friend Natalie about it. Both Jean and Natalie are African-American.

    When Jean went to Rysy's office, there was another applicant who was Hispanic filling out an application. When the Hispanic woman turned in her application, she was asked to stay for an interview. The receptionist would not give Jean an application and told her that she needed a birth certificate to apply. Jean went home and came back with her birth certificate. She was then told that the company did not have any more applications. When Jean gave Rysy her resume, the receptionist told her that Rysy would call her if it was interested in her. The next day, Natalie went to Rysy's office, and had a similar experience. The receptionist took her application and told her that someone would call her if Rysy was interested in her. While she was there, she saw four Hispanic women and one Hispanic man filled out applications. All five of the other applicants were asked to stay for an interview. Rysy did not call either Jean or Natalie for an interview afterward.

    According to Rysy's human resources manager, Rysy's president told the HR manager that Rysy was a Polish company, and that she needed to recruit more Europeans and not African-Americans. The HR manager also said that when the HR manager recruited from an African-American community, she was reprimanded by the president. According to the HR manager, the president of Rysy told the HR manager that she was hiring too many N-word and then fired the HR manager shortly after that.

    Do the above facts provide a reasonable basis for believing that Title VII has been violated? Why or why not? Explain fully.

3. An insurance company has found that black people are more likely to buy insurance if approached by a black agent, while white people are more receptive to a white agent. The company plans to assign its black agents to offices in predominantly black neighborhoods and its white agents to offices in predominantly white neighborhoods. Is the practice legal? Why or why not?

4. The All African-American Co. (AAA), a real estate firm, hires only African-Americans, because its owner is African-American and the owner wants to promote the economic opportunities of African-Americans. Is AAA's practice legal? Explain fully.

5. The Vita Company has a job opening for a financial analyst. It advertises its position as requiring that the applicant possess an accounting undergraduate degree. Three applicants apply. Bob Bender, an African-American male, possesses an undergraduate business degree from a large state university, with an accounting major. Wilma Wood, a white female, possesses an undergraduate degree from a small private college, with three years of job experience. Joe Goodbar, a white male, possesses an MBA from an Ivy League college and an undergraduate accounting degree from a state university.

   All three candidates are interviewed by members of the management team at Vita Company. Each member of the management team fills out an evaluation form. One management team member responds that "Wilma is cute but dumb." Another states that Bob "won't be able to get into the right clubs." All of the team members agree that Joe is preferable because his MBA provides flexibility for future promotions and work assignments beyond the financial analyst job. Who should be hired? Why?

6. An employer's hiring policy requires that all of its employees have a college degree, even for jobs such as receptionist and file clerk, which as recently as seven years ago were filled by employees who did not have a college education. If the employer's policy would result in a significantly disproportionate exclusion of racial minorities, will adopting the requirement violate any equal employment opportunity laws? Explain fully.

7. Zugspitze Parking, Inc. manages parking facilities nationwide. It uses an Internet website to accept applications for all its job vacancies. If an applicant answers "yes" to the question, "Have you ever been convicted of a crime?" the system terminates the process with a screen telling the applicant that the application cannot be processed at that time. Is this selection practice legal? Explain fully.

8. A real estate management company manages an office building and employs a receptionist in the building lobby. The company requires the receptionist to wear a uniform that is a low-cut, tight-fitting body suit. The top of the receptionist's breasts are visible. Her legs and thighs are covered only by black fishnet stockings. Every day various people entering the building have whistled and stared at her and made cat calls, and a few have pinched her or put their arms around her. Does Title VII require the company to change the uniform? Explain.

9. Zulphia, who is from Jordan and a Muslim, wears a hijab, a headscarf that covers the head and neck but leaves the face clear. She applied for a job as a retail sales clerk at Great Gable Hardware. Gus Gable is concerned that if Zulphia wears the hijab, the store's customers, employees, and suppliers will be unnerved. What should Gus Gable do? Explain fully.

10. Ernest Employer provides medical insurance to its employees, who share in paying the premium. The employer also maintains a wellness program for employees, providing them with health care coaching, nutritional counseling, fitness activities, etc. Employer sends the employees an email notifying them that if they go to the wellness program's website and complete a questionnaire entitled *Personal Health & Well-Being Assessment (PHA)*, they will earn a $360 premium credit and have a choice of several medical plans. If they have a spouse/same-sex domestic partner on the medical plan, the employee will earn an additional $120 premium credit. If they do not complete the *PHA*, they will be able to enroll in only one of the medical plans, which carries the highest premium. The *PHA* asks for the employee to provide information about the employee's medical history as well as the medical history of his or her family members. For example, a question asks if the employee or anyone in the employee's immediate family (parents, brother, sisters) have experienced such medical conditions as hypertension (high blood pressure). Is Ernest Employer in violation of GINA? Explain.

# GLOSSARY

**Abusive discharge** A tort, recognized in some states, committed when an employer discharges an employee in violation of a clear expression of public policy.

**Acceleration clause** A provision in a credit agreement that allows the creditor to demand full payment of the debt if the debtor does not make timely payments or otherwise fails to comply with the terms of the agreement.

**Acceptance** The offeree's assent to the terms of an offer to enter into a contract.

**Act of state doctrine** Principle preventing judicial examination of certain acts of a foreign government.

**Action** A suit brought in a court.

**Actionable** A term used to show that acts provide a basis or legal reason for a lawsuit.

**Adequate protection** Usually an amount of money paid by the trustee in bankruptcy to a secured creditor to compensate for depreciation or other loss to property in which the secured creditor has a security interest.

**Adjudication** The determination of a controversy and pronouncement of a judgment or decree in a case.

**Administrative agency** An agency of the government charged with administering particular legislation.

**Administrative law judge** An officer who presides at the initial hearing on matters litigated before an administrative agency. He or she is independent of the agency staff.

**Administrative Procedure Act** A statute establishing the procedural rules governing how federal agencies operate.

**Affectation doctrine** A doctrine, developed by the Supreme Court in interpreting the Commerce Clause of the Constitution of the United States, whereby Congress has the power to regulate any activity that has an appreciable effect on interstate commerce.

**Affidavit** A written declaration or statement of facts, sworn before a person who has the authority to administer such an oath.

**Affirm** To agree with. An appellate court affirms a lower court decision when it declares the decision valid.

**Affirmative action** The aggressive search to hire qualified minorities or those underrepresented in the workplace. An obligation undertaken by federal contractors to make special efforts to hire women and minorities. It is also a remedy which a court may decree under Title VII of the Civil Rights Act of 1964 and which the National Labor Relations Board is authorized to make under the National Labor Relations Act to effectuate the policies of those statutes.

**Affirmative defense** An assertion that, if true, relieves a defendant of liability or limits a plaintiff's recovery.

**Agent** One who acts for a principal.

**Allegation** In a pleading, a declaration or statement by a party to a suit.

**Allege** To make a statement of fact, an assertion, or a charge.

**Amicus curiae** Latin, "Friend of the court." An individual or corporation that, because of strong interest in a case, petitions the court for permission to file a brief.

**Answer** A pleading of the defendant which responds to a complaint by either admitting or denying the allegations contained in the complaint.

**Antitakeover statutes** Statutes that benefit incumbent management of a corporation in the event of a corporate takeover attempt.

**Apparent authority** A doctrine whereby an agent binds a principal to a third party because the principal invests the agent with the appearance of authority, even though actual authority is absent.

**Appeal** The process by which a party asks a higher court to review alleged errors made by a lower court or an agency.

**Appellant** The party that takes an appeal from one court to another.

**Appellate court** A court having jurisdiction of appeal and review.

**Appellee** The party in a case who responds to an appeal.

**Appraisal rights** Rights of minority shareholders to have their interests appraised and sold to the corporation at the appraised value.

**Arbitrary and capricious standard of review** The standard of judicial review of agency action whereby a court sets aside agency action if the agency failed to consider relevant evidence or made a clear error in judgment.

**Arbitration** A process wherein a dispute is submitted to a mutually acceptable person or board, each party to the dispute having agreed beforehand to comply with the decision.

**Arguendo** For the sake of the purposes of argument. A statement or observation made as a matter of argument or hypothetical illustration.

**Arraignment** A proceeding wherein the accused is formally informed of the charge(s) and is asked to plead guilty, not guilty, or nolo contendere.

**Articles of Confederation** The name of the document embodying the compact made among the 13 original states of the Union, before the adoption of the present Constitution.

**Assault** The intentional tort of causing another person to be apprehensive of a battery.

**Assumption of the risk** An affirmative defense raised by the defendant that defeats the plaintiff's recovery because the plaintiff knowingly and voluntarily exposed himself or herself to the danger that caused the injury.

**Attachment** The act or process of taking, apprehending, or seizing persons or property by virtue of a judicial process for the purpose of securing satisfaction of a judgment.

**Attempt** In criminal law, an effort to accomplish a crime, amounting to more than mere preparation or planning for it, which, if not prevented, would have resulted in the full consummation of the attempted act, but which, in fact, does not bring to pass the party's ultimate design. In civil matters, an attempt ordinarily means an intent combined with an act falling short of the thing intended.

**At-will employee** An employee who may be discharged by the employer for any reason without liability.

**Authorization cards** Cards signed by employees in favor of a particular union as their collective bargaining representative.

**Aver** To set out, assert, or allege in a formal complaint before a court of law.

**Bailment** A delivery of goods by one person (bailor) to another (bailee) in trust for the accomplishment of a specific purpose involving the goods (e.g., repair) on an express or implied contract to carry out such trust and subsequently return the goods to the bailor.

**Bailor** One who entrusts goods to another under a bailment.

**Bait and switch** A method of selling in which a seller advertises at a low price a product that the seller does not intend to sell (the bait) and then disparages that product to the prospective buyer and directs the buyer to a higher-priced product (the switch) which the seller intended to sell all along.

**Banc** French, "The full court." A court sits *en banc* when all the judges making up the court hear the case in contradistinction to having the case decided by one judge or a portion of the judges of the court.

**Bargaining order** An order of the National Labor Relations Board directing an employer to bargain with a union. A bargaining order is made to remedy employer conduct during a board conducted election to decide whether the employees want a union to be their representative. The employer's conduct must be so serious an interference with employees' free choice as to render a new election incapable of being conducted.

**Bargaining unit** The group of employees sharing a community of interest and making up a unit for purposes of union representation and collective bargaining. Barred Obstruction; subject to a hindrance that prevents legal redress or recovery.

**Battery** The intentional tort of performing an unwanted touching.

**Beneficiary** One for whose benefit a trust is created.

**Best efforts underwriting** A type of underwriting whereby an underwriter agrees to use its best efforts to sell securities of an issuer to brokers in return for a commission on the sales that it makes. Under this type of distribution the underwriter is not obligated to sell any designated quantity of securities.

**Bill** The draft of an act of the legislature before it becomes law.

**Bill of information** A formal accusation of the commission of a crime made by a prosecutor in place of a grand jury indictment.

**Bill of lading** A document issued by a person engaged in the business of shipping goods. It serves as a receipt of goods received, a memorandum of the sales contract between seller and shipper, and a document of title evidencing ownership of the goods described in the bill of lading.

**Blue sky laws** State statutes regulating the sale of securities.

**Bona fide** Latin, "In good faith." Honestly, sincerely.

**Bona fide occupational qualification** A statutory exception to employment practices that might otherwise violate equal employment laws; it allows an employer to discriminate in its hiring where religion, national origin, sex, or age is reasonably necessary to the normal operation of a business.

**Bona fide seniority system** A seniority system which applies equally to all employees regardless of membership in a protected class, was not established or maintained for the purpose of discriminating, and operates rationally in accord with the practice in the industry.

**Bond (security)** A certificate issued by a governmental body or a corporation to represent a debt owed to the bondholder as well as a promise to pay interest.

**Boycott** A conspiracy or confederation to prevent anyone from carrying on business, or to injure anyone's business, by preventing potential customers from doing business with him or her.

**Breach of contract** Failure, without legal excuse, to perform any promise which forms the whole or part of a contract.

**Bribe** Anything given in value with the corrupt intent to induce or influence a public official in the performance of his or her duties.

**Broker** An agent who bargains, carries on negotiations, and makes contracts on behalf of his or her employer for compensation; also, a dealer in securities issued by others.

**Brokerage** The compensation of a broker, including wages and commission.

**Bubble concept** The treatment of all pollution-emitting devices collectively within an area, thus permitting increased pollution from sources as long as there is an equivalent decrease in pollution from other sources under the bubble.

**Burden of proof** The necessity or duty of affirmatively proving the fact or facts in dispute on an issue raised between the parties to a suit in court.

**Business judgment rule** A rule that affords board members of a corporation wide latitude in decisionmaking.

**Canons of ethics** Standards for the professional conduct expected of a lawyer, comprising the Code of Professional Responsibility. Initially adopted by the American Bar Association, it has been enacted into law in most states.

**Capitalist model of justice** A model based on the theory of economic justice that any distribution of things of value which results from unfettered economic competition is just.

**Case law** The law as developed or laid down in decided cases, as opposed to statutes.

**Case of first impression** A case which has no precedent on which the court may rely.

**Cause of action** The facts which evidence a civil wrong, thereby giving rise to a right to judicial relief.

**Cease and desist order** An order by an agency or a court directing someone to stop doing something.

**Certiorari** A means of obtaining appellate review by petition; a writ issued by an appellate court to an inferior court commanding the record to be certified to the appellate court for judicial review.

**Charging party** A person who files a complaint with a government agency alleging that there has been a violation of law. In labor law, the person who files an unfair labor practice charge with the National Labor Relations Board is called a charging party. Also, a person who files a charge with the Equal Employment Opportunity Commission, alleging that someone has violated one of the federal employment laws prohibiting employment discrimination, is called the charging party.

**Checks and balances** A system of government whose branches provide checks and balances against each other.

**Choice-of-forum provision** A provision in a contract specifying a jurisdiction's court to which the parties agree to submit any disputes that may arise under the contract.

**Choice-of-law provision** A clause in a contract specifying the body of law the parties to the contract agree will govern their contract.

**Churning** Abuse of a customer's confidence by a broker who initiates excessive transactions for the customer for personal gain.

**Circumstantial evidence** Evidence of an indirect nature; evidence from which the existence of a fact is inferred.

**Civil law** That body of law concerned with civil or private rights. Contrast *Criminal law.*

**Claim** A cause of action.

**Class action** An action brought by one or more persons as representatives of a large group of similarly situated persons.

**Close corporation** A corporation with a small number of shareholders who are family members or otherwise related.

**Closed-end credit** Refers to specific amount of credit for a definite time with loans repaid in installments.

**Codetermination** A process of management in which employers and employees share in the decision making.

**Collateral** Property pledged as security for the satisfaction of a debt.

**Collective entity doctrine** A doctrine of constitutional law holding that the Fifth Amendment's privilege against self-incrimination is a personal right and does not apply to corporations or other collective entities.

**Collusion** An agreement between two or more persons to commit a wrongful act.

**Commerce** The exchange of goods, products, or property of any kind.

**Commercial speech** A term used in constitutional law to refer to economic speech, such as advertising.

**Commodity** A movable article of commerce, especially merchandise.

**Common carrier** One that transports persons or property for compensation, providing such services to the general public.

**Common law** The principles and rules which derive solely from custom or from the judgments and decisions of courts. It is judge-made law.

**Comparative negligence** The doctrine under which a plaintiff's negligence as a factor in his or her own injury is assigned a percentage value, and his or her recovery from the defendant is reduced proportionately. Contrast with *Contributory negligence.*

**Compensable** Capable of being compensated.

**Compensable damages** Damages which compensate the victim for a loss; damages that put the victim in the position he or she was in before the injury occurred.

**Compensable injury** Within workers' compensation statutes, compensation to an employee for injury arising out of and in the course of employment.

**Compensatory damages** Damages compensating an injured party for the injury sustained, and nothing more; such compensation as will simply make good or replace the loss caused by a wrong or injury.

**Competitive injury** An injury to competition or to a competitor.

**Complaint** The first pleading by the plaintiff in a civil case. Its purpose is to give the defendant the information on which the plaintiff relies to support its demand. In a complaint, the plaintiff sets out a cause of action, consisting of a formal allegation or charge presented to the appropriate court.

**Composition plan** A plan whereby a debtor pays a pro rata share to each creditor in satisfaction of debt.

**Concerted action** Action that has been planned, arranged, adjusted, agreed on, or settled between parties acting together pursuant to some design or scheme.

**Conciliation** The proceeding in which litigants are brought together by a third party.

**Concur** To agree.

**Concurring opinion** A printed opinion in which a judge agrees with the decision of the majority of the court for a different reason. With reference to appellate court opinions, a concurring opinion is one written by a judge who may agree with the majority opinion's conclusion, but for different reasons, and therefore writes a separate opinion.

**Confederation** A league or compact for mutual support, particularly of nations or states. Such was the colonial government during the American Revolution.

**Confirmed letter of credit** A letter of credit sent to a bank near the seller's place of business, indicating another bank representing the buyer will pay on presentation of required documents.

**Conglomerate merger** A merger among firms that operate in separate or distinct markets.

**Conscious parallelism** When a competitor copies the actions of a market leader absent contract, combination, or conspiracy.

**Consent decree** A decree entered by consent of the parties. It is not a judicial sentence, but is an agreement of the parties made under the sanction of the court.

**Consent order** An agreement by the defendant to cease activities which the government asserts are illegal. Also known as consent decree.

**Consequential damages** Damage or injury that is not a direct, immediate, or predictable result of a party's act, but is nevertheless shown to be a consequence of it.

**Consideration** Something given in exchange for a promise which makes the promise legally enforceable. Consideration consists of doing or promising to do that which the giver was not previously obligated to do or refraining from doing or promising to refrain from doing that which the giver had a legal right to do.

**Consignee** One to whom goods are consigned for sale or safekeeping.

**Consignment** Property delivered by a consignor to an agent for sale where title is held by the consignor until the property is sold.

**Consignor** One who delivers goods to another on consignment.

**Conspiracy** A combination or confederation between two or more persons formed for the purpose of committing, by their joint efforts, some unlawful or criminal act.

**Construction defect** In a product liability action, a defect which results from the negligent manufacture of a particular item rather than from a defect in its design.

**Constructive conditions** Conditions that the law implies into a contract based on the order of performance under the contract.

**Consumer credit** Credit that is extended primarily for personal, family, or household purposes.

**Consumer Product Safety Commission** A federal administrative agency which supervises and regulates consumer products.

**Consumer product safety standard** Performance or labeling standard, voluntarily assumed by product manufacturers, or imposed by the CPSC on product manufacturers.

**Contempt** A willful disregard or disobedience of a public authority.

**Contempt of court** An act which disturbs or obstructs a court or is intended to detract from its authority or dignity.

**Continuing trespass** A type of trespass that occurs over an extended period of time.

**Contract** An agreement that a court enforces.

**Contributory negligence** Conduct by the plaintiff which is a contributing factor in his or her injury, thus barring any recovery against the defendant. Contrast *Comparative negligence.*

**Conversion** An unauthorized assumption and exercise of ownership over goods belonging to another, to the alteration of their condition or the exclusion of the owner's rights.

**Conviction** The result of a criminal trial which ends in a judgment that the prisoner is guilty as charged.

**Copyright** A limited monopoly granted by the federal government to protect literary type works.

**Corporate opportunity** An opportunity that arises because of a corporation's business or situation; a doctrine which prevents corporate officials from personally appropriating an opportunity which belongs to the corporation.

**Corporation** A business organization which is a legal entity formed in compliance with statutory law whose owners enjoy limited liability.

**Corrective advertising** A remedy of the Federal Trade Commission by which one found guilty of violating the Federal Trade Commission Act with regard to unlawful advertising is ordered to correct the lasting impression of the advertising on the public by engaging in advertising that repudiates the earlier advertising.

**Cost justification defense** The justification of price discrimination under the Robinson-Patman Act based on the difference in cost.

**Counterclaim** A claim presented by a defendant which, if successful, defeats or reduces the plaintiff's recovery.

**Countervailing duties** A tax imposed by an importing country on goods to counter-act a subsidy given by the exporting country to the manufacture of the goods.

**Court judgment** The official decision of a court determining the respective rights and claims of the parties in a lawsuit.

**Credit bureau** An establishment that makes a business of collecting information relating to the credit, character, responsibility, and reputation of individuals and businesses for the purpose of furnishing the information to subscribers.

**Creditor** A person to whom a debt is owed.

**Criminal law** That body of law, commonly codified into penal codes, which declares what conduct is criminal and provides punishment for such conduct to protect society from harm. Contrast *Civil law*.

**Criminal penalty** Punishment attached to the conviction of a crime.

**Cross claim** A claim made in the course of an action by a defendant against a codefendant or by a plaintiff against a coplaintiff.

**Cross elasticity of demand** An economic measure of the relationship between price changes and demand changes for a particular good.

**Cross-examination** The examination of a witness at a trial or hearing, or on taking a deposition, by the party opposed to the one that produced said witness, on his or her evidence given in chief, to test its truth, to further develop it, or for other purposes.

**Data** Acts from which to draw a conclusion. De facto In fact; in deed; actually.

**De jure corporation** A lawfully recognized corporation.

**De minimis** Something small or trifling.

**De novo** Latin, "To begin anew." Usually refers to the necessity of a new hearing on the same facts and law previously litigated.

**Debt security** Bonds, notes, debentures, and any other corporate securities which represent a debt owed to the holder.

**Debtor** One who owes money.

**Deceit** A fraudulent misrepresentation used by one person to deceive or trick another, who is ignorant of the facts, to the damage of the latter.

**Decertify** In labor law, to decertify a union is to take away its status as the exclusive bargaining agent of the employees of an employer. Decertification occurs usually after an election is conducted by the National Labor Relations Board to determine whether the employees wish to continue to have a particular union act as their exclusive bargaining agent.

**Declaratory judgment** A judgment which simply declares the rights of the parties or expresses the opinion of the court on a question of law without ordering anything to be done.

**Defamation** The disparagement of one's reputation; the offense of injuring a person's character, fame, or reputation by oral or written publication.

**Default** Failure; omission to perform a legal or contractual duty; the failure of a party to appear in court after being properly served with process.

**Defendant** The party against which an action is brought in a civil case; the accused in a criminal case.

**Defense** An assertion offered by a defendant which, if successful, relieves him or her of liability, reduces the plaintiff's recovery, or defeats a criminal charge.

**Defined benefit plan** A retirement plan that provides specific retirement benefits based on age and length of employment.

**Defined contribution plan** A pension plan whose benefits are based on the amount in the retirement account.

**Demand** The amount of a particular good that consumers buy in a given period of time.

**Deposition** Pretrial testimony of a witness taken orally and under oath before an officer of the court (but not in open court), subject to cross-examination and reduced to writing.

**Design defect** In the law of product liability, a defect in a product resulting from its design, so that every one produced is similarly defective. Contrast with *Construction defect*.

**Dicta** Plural of *dictum*. Opinions of a judge that do not embody the resolution or determination of the court.

**Dictum** The word is generally used as an abbreviated form of obiter dictum (a remark by the way). An observation or remark made by a judge in pronouncing an opinion in a case, concerning some rule, principle, or application of law, or the solution of a question suggested by the case, but not necessarily involved in the case or essential to its determination.

**Disclosure** The act of disclosing. In several areas of government regulation of business, it refers to the act of revealing required information to consumers, investors, and employees.

**Discovery** Devices that may be used by one party to obtain information about the case from the other party in preparation for trial.

**Disparagement** An untrue or misleading statement about a competitor's business or goods made to influence, or tending to influence, the public not to buy from the competitor.

**Disparate impact** The imposition of a rule of employment which disproportionately affects a protected class.

**Disparate treatment** The treatment of one employee or prospective employee less favorably than another because of race, sex, religion, national origin, age, or handicap.

**Disposable earnings** The portion of a person's income that he or she is free to spend or invest as he or she sees fit after payment of taxes and other obligations.

**Dissenting opinion** An opinion wherein a judge disagrees with the result reached by the majority of the court. Contrast *Concurring opinion.*

**Distress sale** A "going out of business" sale in which the seller receives less for the goods than would be received under normal conditions.

**Distributive justice** Theories of justice dictating the morally proper way to distribute things of value in society.

**Diversity jurisdiction** The jurisdiction of the federal courts to hear cases in which the parties are citizens of different states or one of the parties is an alien and the amount in controversy exceeds $50,000.

**Diversity of citizenship** A phrase used with reference to the jurisdiction of the federal courts, which, under Article III, Section 2, of the Constitution of the United States, extends to cases between citizens of different states. *See diversity jurisdiction.*

**Dividend** The share allotted to each of several persons entitled to participate in a division of profits or property. Dividends are what a shareholder earns from the stock owned in a corporation.

**Draft** A written order by the first party, called the drawer, instructing a second party, called the drawee (such as a bank), to pay a third party, called the payee.

**Due diligence defense** A defense to a securities violation which requires a defendant to prove that he or she exercised ordinary prudence, but nonetheless was unaware of a material misrepresentation contained in the registration statement.

**Effluent limitation** The amount of pollutants legally dischargeable from a particular source.

**Electronic Funds Transfer Act** A federal statute that requires financial institutions to disclose the terms of electronic funds transfer services, establishes a procedure for error resolution, and specifies penalties for violations.

**Eminent domain** The power of a sovereign to take private property for public use, necessitating just compensation.

**Emission limitation** A specific rule that operators of pollutant sources must follow to reduce emissions.

**Emissions offset policy** A policy under the Clean Air Act whereby increased emissions are permitted by the applicant at a source in a nonattainment area as long as sufficient reductions in emission occur in the same area.

**Employment-at-will doctrine** The legal doctrine that holds that whenever an employment relationship is of an indefinite duration, either party—the employer or the employee—may terminate the relationship at will, for good cause or bad, in good faith or with malice.

**Enabling legislation** A term applied to any statute that enables agencies, corporations, or persons to do something they could not do before. Such statutes confer a lawful power in an agency to act on a given matter.

**Enactment** The process by which a bill becomes a statute.

**Enterprise coverage** A type of coverage of the federal Fair Labor Standards Act whereby that act covers all the employees of a firm that engages in commerce.

**Entrepreneur** Someone who organizes, manages, or assumes the risk of a business.

**Environmental impact statement** A statement that details the environmental impact of proposed administrative action. The statement must be prepared by an agency whenever it plans or engages in major federal actions significantly affecting the quality of human environment.

**Equal Credit Opportunity Act** A federal statute that prohibits discrimination in credit extension on the basis of sex, race, religion, national origin, age, and other protected statuses.

**Equitable relief** Injunction, specific performance, restraining orders, and the like, as opposed to money damages.

**Equity security** A share in a corporation, usually referred to as stock.

**Escrow** A writing, deed, stock, or property delivered to a third person, to be held by that person until the fulfillment of a condition and then delivered to its owner.

**Ethicist** One versed in the study of how moral decisions are justified.

**Ethics** The study of how moral decisions are justified.

**Ex parte** On the application of one party only. A judicial proceeding is ex pane when it is taken or granted at the request of, or for the benefit of, one party only, and without notice to, or contestation by, any person adversely interested.

**Exclusive dealing agreements** Contracts on which the buyer is obligated to purchase all of its requirements of a given commodity from the seller.

**Executive agencies** Federal agencies that are under the direct control of the president. Appointments to executive agencies do not need Senate approval.

**Executive order** An order by the chief executive of a government affecting the administration of the executive branch of government.

**Exhaustion** A doctrine requiring that a party utilize remedies provided within an agency before seeking review by a court.

**Exonerate** To exculpate; to remove a responsibility or duty.

**Experience rating provision** A rating of an employer, based on historical unemployment data, which determines the employer's state unemployment compensation tax contribution.

**Export trading company** A company that acts as an intermediary in the marketing of goods overseas.

**Express conditions** Conditions inserted in a contract by the parties that must be fulfilled before a party has a duty to perform or that when fulfilled relieve a party of a duty to perform.

**Express warranty** A warranty which the seller creates by making a representation or a promise relating to goods or by showing the buyer a sample or model of them, regardless of whether such words as guaranty or warranty are used.

**Expropriation** An act by which a foreign government takes over ownership of an American company or American property located in the foreign government.

**Expunge** To destroy; to strike out wholly. "Expungement of the record" refers to the process whereby a record of a criminal conviction is sealed or destroyed after a designated period of time.

**Extension plan** A plan whereby a debtor extends the time for payments to creditors past the due date.

**Fair Credit Reporting Act** A federal statute that regulates consumer reporting agencies.

**Fair use** A doctrine under copyright law which permits reasonable use of copyrighted works for limited purposes, such as criticism, news, reporting, teaching and research.

**False imprisonment** The intentional tort of interfering with another person's freedom of movement.

**Federal question jurisdiction** The jurisdiction of the federal courts to hear cases arising under the U.S. Constitution, acts of Congress, or treaties.

**Federal Register** A federal publication providing notice of federal rulemaking by federal agencies.

**Federalism** The relationship between the states and the federal government whereby responsibility and autonomy is divided between them.

**Fellow servant doctrine** A common-law doctrine, now abrogated by all workers' compensation acts, that an employee injured by the negligent act of a fellow employee cannot recover damages from his or her employer.

**Fiduciary** A person having a duty, created by his or her undertaking, to act primarily for another's benefit.

**Fiduciary duty** The duty which arises whenever one person is in a special relationship of trust to another, such as the duty an attorney owes to a client.

**Firm commitment underwriting** A type of underwriting of securities whereby the underwriter is obligated to purchase a designated number of shares of securities from an issuer at a specified price.

**Fixture** Personal property that has been affixed to reality in such a manner as to become part of the realty.

**Foreign corporation** A corporation doing business in any state other than the one in which it is incorporated.

**Foreign Corrupt Practices Act** A federal statute which prohibits bribing a foreign official, and establishes accounting procedures designed to discover, such briberies.

**Form 10-K** A form that must be filed with the SEC within 90 days after the end of the fiscal period and which contains current audited financial statements and information regarding the operations of the business and the status of its securities.

**Forum non conveniens, doctrine of** The power of a court to decline jurisdiction when the convenience of the parties and the ends of justice would be better served by bringing the action in another court.

**Franchise** A special privilege conferred on someone.

**Franchisee** A holder of a franchise.

**Franchisor** A party granting a franchise.

**Fungible goods** Goods of any type which are by nature considered to be the equivalent of any other good of that type.

**Garnishee** The person on whom a garnishment is served; one who has in his or her possession the property of someone who owes a debt to another person.

**Garnishment** A proceeding in which money, property, or credits of a debtor in possession of a third person, the garnishee, are applied to the payment of debts. The process is available only where it is authorized by statute.

**GATT** The abbreviation for General Agreement on Tariffs and Trade. Treaty covering the treatment of exports and imports for adopting nations.

**General intent** An intention, purpose, or design, either without a specific plan or without a particular object.

**Golden parachutes** Lucrative compensation benefits granted to corporate executives in the event they are terminated after a takeover.

**Good** Under the Uniform Commercial Code, any tangible item capable of being moved other than money, securities, and real estate.

**Good faith** An intangible quality encompassing honesty, sincerity, and the lack of intent to defraud or take advantage of another.

**Goodwill** The propensity of customers to return to a business. The patronage of a particular business. As such, it is an intangible asset of a business.

**Gratuity** A gift.

**Gross negligence** A conscious or intentional act or omission likely to result in harm to a person or property; a higher level of culpability than simple negligence.

**Group boycott** A per se violation of the Sherman Antitrust Act which amounts to a refusal to economically deal by two or more.

**Handicap** A physical or mental impairment that substantially limits one or more of life's major activities.

**Hazard communication standard** An OSHA standard requiring chemical manufacturers and importers to evaluate the hazards of all chemicals they produce or import, to develop material safety data sheets for each chemical, to label containers holding chemicals with information concerning the chemicals and their hazards, and to so advise their employees about the hazards.

**Horizontal merger** Acquisition of one company by another company producing the same product or similar product and selling it in the same geographic market.

**Horizontal restraint** An agreement between two or more competitors to avoid competing with each other.

**Hot cargo agreement** A form of a secondary boycott involving an illegal agreement that the employer will not deal with nonunion employers or that the employees need not handle nonunion goods.

**Imminent hazard** An immediate danger resulting from a product defect.

**Impeach** To challenge the credibility of a witness.

**Impleader** A procedure whereby a defendant brings a new party into an action on the basis that the new party may be liable to that party.

**Implied contract** A contract not explicitly created by the parties, but inferred, as a matter of reason and justice, from the circumstances.

**Implied warranty** A warranty which arises by operation of law although the seller does not express it; for example, that a product is fit for the purpose for which it is intended.

**In camera** In chambers; in private. A cause is said to be heard in camera either when the hearing is held before a judge or agency official in his or her private office or when all spectators are excluded from the courtroom or agency hearing room.

**Incidental damages** Damages resulting from a buyer's breach of contract, such as the costs of stopping delivery and reselling the goods; damages resulting from a seller's breach, including the expenses incurred in returning rightfully rejected goods and procuring a replacement.

**Incorporation doctrine** A doctrine developed by the Supreme Court whereby it has interpreted the Due Process Clause of the 14th Amendment of the Constitution of the United States as incorporating, or absorbing, selected provisions of the Bill of Rights (the first 10 amendments) and thus applying them to the states. Prior to the incorporation doctrine, the Bill of Rights applied only to the federal government.

**Independent contractor** One who contracts to do work for a principal and maintains the means, method, and manner of accomplishing the result.

**Independent regulatory agency** A federal agency to which appointments require Senate approval.

**Indict** *See Indictment.*

**Indictment** A formal accusation made by a grand jury which charges that a person has committed a crime.

**Information** *See Bill of information.*

**Injunction** An order of the court directing someone to do or not to do something.

**In personam jurisdiction** The power which a court has over the defendant's personas opposed to the power of a court over property.

**Insider** With respect to federal regulation of securities, an insider is anyone who has knowledge of facts not available to the general public. With regard to Section 16 of the Exchange Act of 1934, an insider is specifically defined as an officer, director, or any security holder owning at least 10 percent of the stock of a corporation.

**Inside trading** Gains derived by trading on inside information.

**Intent** A conscious and purposeful state of mind with which a person acts.

**Intentional infliction of emotional distress** An intentional tort action providing redress to the victims of outrageous conduct that causes severe psychological injury.

**Intentional torts** A category of civil wrongs giving redress to the victims of willful wrongdoing.

**Interpretive rules** Rules of a federal agency rendering interpretations of the agency's enabling legislation. Such rules are not binding on the courts. Such rules do not need to be issued according to the procedures of the federal Administrative Procedure Act.

**Interpretivism** A theory of constitutional law maintaining that the Constitution should be interpreted by resort to its literal language or the intent of the framers, as found in historical accounts of the drafting of the Constitution.

**Interrogatories** A discovery device consisting of a series of written questions directed by one party to another party.

**Interstate commerce** Commercial trading, traffic, or the transportation of persons or property from a point in one state to points in other states.

**Intervention** The act of a nonparty becoming a party to a lawsuit on his/her own initiative.

**Intrastate commerce** Commerce that is carried out wholly within the limits of a single state.

**Invasion of privacy** An intentional tort providing redress to the victims whose privacy has been unreasonably intruded on.

**Investigative consumer report** Information gathered through personal interviews with neighbors, friends, associates, or others.

**Involuntary corporate dissolution** The dissolution of a corporation by the state for noncompliance of administrative requirements.

**Irrevocable letter of credit** A letter of credit that cannot be cancelled without the agreement of both buyer and seller.

**Judgment non obstante verdicto (judgment n.o.v.)** *See Judgment notwithstanding the verdict.*

**Judgment notwithstanding the verdict** A judge's judgment that is contrary to the verdict of the jury.

**Judicial review** The process by which the Supreme Court of the United States reviews legislation and refuses to enforce those laws that it declares to be unconstitutional.

**Jurisdiction** The power of a court or a judicial officer to decide a case; the geographic area of a court's authority.

**Jurisdictional standards** Standards issued by the National Labor Relations Board for particular industries for purposes of determining whether the board will assert jurisdiction.

**Jurisprudence** The philosophy of law; the science which studies the principles of law and legal relations.

**Labeling defect** In the law of product liability, a defect in a product resulting from inadequate labeling.

**Labeling standard** A standard issued by the Consumer Product Safety Commission requiring that a warning label be attached to a product.

**Laboratory conditions** Conditions regulated by the National Labor Relations Board to ensure a fair determination of the uninhibited wishes of the employees, during an election campaign.

**Labor organization** An organization of employees organized for the purpose of dealing with their employer.

**Laissez-faire economics** A policy whereby government takes a hands-off posture toward economic planning.

**Lanham Act** A federal act that prohibits the use of any false description or representation in connection with any goods or services introduced into commerce.

**Legal relief** Money damages. Contrast *Equitable relief.*

**Legislation** The act of enacting laws; the making of laws by express decree; sometimes means a statute or statutes.

**Legislative history** The background and events leading up to the enactment of a statute; for example, committee reports and floor debates. Courts use the legislative history of a statute in determining the legislature's intent in enacting it.

**Legislative rules** Regulations issued by federal agencies pursuant to the federal Administrative Procedure Act. Such rules are binding on courts.

**Legislator** One who makes laws; a member of a legislative body.

**Legislature** The department, assembly, or body of government that makes laws for a state or nation.

**Letter of credit** A letter authorizing one person to pay money or extend credit to another on the credit of the writer.

**Libel** To defame or injure a person's reputation by a published writing.

**License** A permit granted by a government authority, person, or business to pursue some occupation or to carry on some business.

**Lien** A security interest in another's property, usually exercisable on the nonpayment of a debt.

**Like grade and quality** An element in a price discrimination offense under the Robinson-Patman Act requiring two products that are the subject of price discrimination to be of like grade and quality.

**Limited partnership** A special form of partnership whereby the business is managed by general partners and financed by limited partners who do not participate in the management and who enjoy limited liability.

**Liquidation** The act or process by which a party settles his or her debt by converting all assets into cash and making distribution to creditors. The term is also used in connection with a Chapter 7 straight bankruptcy proceeding.

**Lobbying** Attempts, including personal solicitation, to induce legislators to vote in a certain way or to introduce legislation.

**Long-arm statute** A state statute subjecting a nonresident or a foreign corporation to the state›s jurisdiction if the person or corporation has committed a tortious wrong or conducted business within the state, or has otherwise had minimal contacts within the state.

**Magistrate** A term for a public officer. Commonly, however, the term is applied to judicial officers with limited authority, such as justices of the peace.

**Magnuson-Moss Warranty Act** A federal statute that requires certain disclosures in connection with written warranties, imposes restrictions on disclaimers of implied warranties, and establishes a procedure through which consumers may more effectively enforce their warranty rights.

**Mandatory subjects of bargaining** Under the National Labor Relations Act, bargaining on wages, hours, and other terms and conditions of employment, including retirement benefits, vacations, rest periods, and work assignments.

**Marxist model of justice** A model based on the theory of economic justice: "from each according to his ability, to each according to his needs."

**Mediation** The act of a third person who attempts to persuade disputing parties to adjust their positions so as to resolve their dispute.

**Meeting competition defense** A defense to price discrimination under the Robinson-Patman Act when the seller's lower price was made in good faith to meet the equally low price of a competitor.

**Merchantable** Of good quality; of the quality fit for the purpose for which the good is intended.

**Merger** The fusion or absorption of one thing or right into another. For example, a merger occurs when one corporation becomes a part of another corporation.

**Merit model of justice** A model based on a concept of justice holding that if any distribution of things of value is based on merit, the distribution is just.

**Misrepresentation** An untrue statement that justifies the rescission of a contract.

**Modification** A change.

**Monopoly** The ownership or control of so large a part of the market supply of a given commodity as to stifle competition and ensure control over prices and competition.

**Moot** A question which is no longer a controversy because the issue involved is no longer in dispute.

**Morals** Judgments regarding what is right or wrong, good or evil.

**Mortgage** A pledge or security of particular property for the payment of a debt.

**Most-favored-nation clause** A clause found in most treaties providing that the citizens or subjects of contracting nations may enjoy the privileges accorded by either nation to those of the most favored nation.

**Motion** A request to a court or judge for a rule or order favorable to the requesting party, generally made within the course of an existing lawsuit.

**Motion for directed verdict** A request that the judge order the entry of a verdict for one party on the grounds that the opposing party has failed to present sufficient evidence for any other verdict.

**Nationalization** The act whereby a host country takes the property of an alien for a public purpose.

**Natural law** Conception of law as a system of rules and principles for the guidance of human conduct which, independently of enacted law or of the systems peculiar to any one people, might be discovered by the rational intelligence of man, and would be found to grow out of and conform to man's nature.

**Necessary and Proper Clause** Clause in U.S. Constitution which authorizes Congress to make all laws necessary and proper to carry out the enumerated powers of Congress and all other powers vested in the federal government.

**Negligence** The omission to do something that a reasonable and prudent person, guided by those considerations which ordinarily regulate human affairs, would do, or the doing of something that a reasonable and prudent person would not do.

**Negligence per se** Imputation of negligence when the defendant's violation of a statute results in injury to a person who is within the class of persons the statute is designed to protect and which injury is the type the statute is designed to protect against.

**Nolo contendere** Latin, "I will not contest it." A plea in a criminal action often having the same effect as a guilty plea, except that it may not be used against the defendant in a subsequent civil action. Also known as a no-contest plea.

**Nonattainment area** An area that has not met the national standards for air quality established under the federal Clean Air Act.

**Noninterpretivism** A theory of constitutional interpretation maintaining that the Supreme Court may make the determination of constitutionality by referring to values other than those constitutionalized by the framers.

**Non-obviousness** One of the characteristics of an invention that makes it patentable; if the state of the art at the time of the development was such that the "invention" was obvious, it will not be patentable.

**Nonpoint source** Nondiscernible and unconfined conveyance, such as overflows from irrigated agriculture.

**Nuisance** A class of torts that arise from the unreasonable, unwarrantable, or unlawful use by a person of his or her property, or from unlawful personal conduct, which obstructs or injures the rights of another.

**Obiter dictum** *See Dictum.*

**Offer** A proposal or act on the part of one person whereby he or she gives to another the legal power to create a contract.

**Offeror** Someone who makes an offer.

**Oligopolistic** A market in which a few large producers dominate.

**Open-end credit** Revolving charges and credit cards which permit the consumer to pay a part of what is owed.

**Opinion of the court** The statement by a judge or court of the decision reached in regard to a cause tried or argued before them, expounding the law as applied to the case, and detailing the reasons on which the judgment is based.

**Order** A command or direction authoritatively given.

**Order for relief** An order of a court or an administrative agency providing a remedy to someone.

**OSHRC** Occupational Safety and Health Review Commission; a federal administrative agency established under the Occupational Safety and Health Act; it hears appeals from OSH Act violations.

**Over-the-counter market** The market for securities traded off the floor of a stock exchange and usually sold through brokerage houses.

**Palming off** To impose by fraud; to pass off a product as another product by unfair means.

**Parent corporation** A company which owns over 50 percent of the voting stock of another company, known as its subsidiary.

**Parliament** The supreme legislative assembly of Great Britain.

**Parole evidence** Evidence of terms of a written contract other than the written document. When the written document is intended as the parties' final expression of their contract, parole evidence of prior agreements or representations cannot be used to vary the terms of the document.

**Partnership** An association of two or more persons to carry on as co-owners of a business for profit.

**Partnership by estoppel** A partnership arising when third parties are erroneously led to rely on the existence of a partnership.

**Patent** A limited monopoly granted by the federal government to make, use, and sell an invention.

**Pattern or practice of discrimination** A general policy of treating members of a protected class less favorably than other employees, proved by circumstantial evidence.

**Per curiam** Latin, "By the court." Used to indicate an opinion by the entire court rather than a single judge. Sometimes refers to a brief statement of the court's decision unaccompanied by any written opinion.

**Per se** Latin, "By itself." Inherently.

**Performance standard** A standard issued by the Consumer Product Safety Commission specifying minimum performance criteria for a product.

**Personal property** That property which has no fixed site and is moveable.

**Petitioner** A party that files a petition with a court, applying in writing for a court order; a party that takes an appeal from a judgment; a party that initiates an equity action.

**Plain meaning rule** A rule of statutory construction which requires that the meaning of words in a statute be assigned their plain import unless to do so would result in an absurdity.

**Plaintiff** A person who brings an action or complaint against a defendant; the party who initiates a suit.

**Plea** An answer to a complaint or to a material allegation of fact therein. In criminal procedure, the answer of the accused in response to the criminal charge.

**Pleadings** The formal allegations by the parties of their respective claims and defenses; the complaint, answer, and reply.

**Plenary** Full; entire; complete; absolute; perfect.

**Point source** Any discernible and confirmed conveyance of water, such as a pipe, ditch, well, or canal.

**Police power** The inherent power of a state over persons and property which enables the state to regulate the health, safety, and welfare of society.

**Positive Law** Law actually or specifically enacted or adopted by proper authority for the government of a society.

**Possession** The control or custody of property, for one's use and enjoyment, to the exclusion of all others.

**Post hoc** Hereafter; after this time.

**Power of Attorney** A written instrument investing an agent with authority to act for a principal.

**Precedent** A previously decided court case which serves as authority for a subsequent similar case.

**Predatory intent** An attempt to drive competitors out of business by sacrificing present revenues in the hope of recouping losses through future high prices.

**Preemption doctrine** The doctrine adopted by the U.S. Supreme Court holding that certain matters are of such a national, as opposed to local, character that federal laws take precedence over state laws. As such, a state may not pass a law inconsistent with the federal law.

**Preferential transfer** A transfer made during the 90-day period before an insolvent debtor's bankruptcy petition is filed, in which the debtor transfers to the creditor a greater percentage of the debt than would have been received under the distribution provision of the act.

**Prejudicial error** An error made during a trial which materially affects the rights of a party and thus may be grounds for a reversal of judgment or a new trial.

**Premises rule** A rule of worker's compensation law that holds that an employee who is injured while on the employer's premises may recover even though the employee was going to or coming from the work site.

**Price discrimination** Selling to one customer at a price and refusing to sell to another at the same price by someone engaged in interstate commerce.

**Price fix** The act of establishing a price; a per se violation of the Sherman Antitrust Act, as an unreasonable restraint of trade.

**Prima facie** Latin, "At first sight." A fact presumed to be true unless disproved by evidence to the contrary.

**Prima facie case** A case which has proceeded on sufficient proof to that stage at which it supports a judicial finding if evidence to the contrary is disregarded. A litigating party is said to have a prima facie case when the evidence in its favor is sufficiently strong for its opponent to be called on to answer it. A prima facie case, then, is one which is established by sufficient evidence and which can be overthrown only be rebutting evidence adduced on the other side.

**Primary-fine injury** Injury that occurs when a seller suffers damages as a result of price discrimination by a competitor.

**Principal** In agency law, the party for whom an agent acts.

**Private law** As used in contrast to public law, the term means that part of the law which is administered between citizen and citizen or which is concerned with the definition and enforcement of rights in cases where both the person in whom the right inheres and the person on whom the obligation is incident are private individuals.

**Private placement** An exemption under the Securities Act for transactions by an issuer not involving any public offering.

**Privilege** A right or advantage particular to an individual or a class.

**Privity** A mutual or successive relationship, for example, the relationship between the parties to a contract.

**Pro rata** Proportionately.

**Probable cause** Reasonable grounds for belief in the existence of facts. In criminal procedure, reasonable grounds for the belief that a person should be arrested or a warrant issued.

**Procedural justice** A form of justice that deals with the process used in deciding outcomes.

**Procedural law** The part of law which concerns the method or process of enforcing rights.

**Procedural rules** Rules adopted by an administrative agency to govern its internal procedures, such as the handling of charges, the holding of hearings, and the timing of investigations and hearings.

**Promissory estoppel** A legal theory that allows a promise to be enforced without consideration. The theory applies where the promisee reasonably relies on a promise to his or her detriment and when that reliance is foreseeable to the promisor.

**Prosecution** A criminal action. The term is also frequently used with respect to civil litigation and includes every step from commencement to final determination.

**Prospectus** A pamphlet that capsulizes the information contained in the registration statement.

**Proximate cause** Event(s) or action which, in natural and unbroken sequence, produce an injury that would not have occurred absent the event(s) or action.

**Proxy** Written authorization given by a shareholder to vote his or her shares at a shareholders' meeting.

**Proxy statement** A statement containing prescribed information that must be supplied to shareholders before proxies are solicited.

**Public law** The branch of law concerned with administrative and constitutional law.

**Publicly held corporation** A corporation whose stock is in the hands of many.

**Punitive damages** Damages awarded to a plaintiff greater than the amount necessary to compensate his or her loss. They are generally granted where the wrong involves intent, violence, fraud, malice, or other aggravated circumstances.

**Quid pro quo** The giving of one valuable thing for another.

**Real property** Land and anything that is permanently attached to land.

**Realist conception** A conception of law that holds that law is not embodied in abstract principles but in the process of deciding disputes.

**Recognition picketing** The picketing of an employer by a noncertified union to force the employer to recognize it or the employees to choose it as their representative.

**Reconstruction period** Period following the Civil War during which the states of the former Confederacy were reintegrated into the Union.

**Red herring prospectus** In securities law, an advance copy of the statement (prospectus) to be filed with the Securities and Exchange Commission preceding an issue of securities. The copy is marked in red ink, "not a solicitation, for information only."

**Redlining** The practice of denying mortgage loans to finance property located in specific neighborhoods.

**Redress** The receiving of satisfaction for an injury sustained.

**Relevant market** The geographic market composed of products that have reasonable interchangeability for purposes for which they are produced, considering their price, use, and quality. The term, in relation to a case involving an alleged violation of the Sherman Act or the Clayton Act, consists of both a product market and a geographic market.

**Reliance damages** A measure of money damages for breach of contract that places the victim of the breach in the economic position he or she would have been in had the contract not been made.

**Remand** To send back. The sending of a case back to the same court out of which it came, for the purpose of having some action taken on it.

**Reorganization** A type of bankruptcy that permits a financially disturbed business to continue while arrangements for the adjustment of debts are made with creditors.

**Res ipsa loquitur** Latin, "The thing speaks for itself." Rule of evidence whereby negligence of the defendant is inferred from the circumstances as the result of a reasonable belief that the injury could not have happened without such negligence.

**Res judicata** Latin, "A matter adjudged." A thing judicially acted on or decided; a rule that a final judgment or decree on the merits by a court of competent jurisdiction is conclusive of the rights of the parties or their privies in all later suits on points and matters determined in the former suit.

**Respondeat superior** Latin, "Let the master answer." Doctrine which provides that an employer or master is responsible for the acts of an employee or servant committed within the scope of the employment.

**Respondent** The party that contends against an appeal.

**Response costs** The costs of federal or state environmental cleanups for which the violator may be ordered to pay.

**Restatement** A book published by the American Law Institute consisting of that body's restatement of the law in one of several areas, such as torts, contracts, and agency.

**Restitution** The avoidance of unjust enrichment, accomplished by requiring the recipient of a benefit to pay the reasonable value of the benefit to the party that conferred the benefit.

**Restraining order** An injunction; a court order prohibiting a party from doing something.

**Restraint of trade** Contracts or combinations which tend, or are designed, to eliminate or stifle competition, effect a monopoly, artificially maintain prices, or otherwise obstruct commerce as it would be carried on if left to the control of natural or economic forces.

**Reverse** To overthrow, vacate, set aside, make void, annul, repeal, or revoke, as to reverse a judgment.

**Reviewability** A term addressing whether a court has the power to review an administrative agency's action.

**Revocation** The recall of some power, authority, or thing granted.

**RICO** Racketeer Influenced and Corrupt Organizations Act; a federal statute that makes it a crime to acquire or operate an enterprise by a pattern of racketeering.

**Rights model** Ethical justification holding that decisions least disruptive of human rights are to be preferred.

**Right to know provision** A provision within the superfund law requiring owners and occupiers of facilities which produce, use, and store hazardous chemicals to file with local and state officials a material safety data sheet for each hazardous chemical.

**Right to sue letter** A letter issued by the Equal Employment Opportunity Commission to a complainant after finding probable cause of discrimination and when attempts to conciliate the dispute have failed.

**Rulemaking** A function of most federal agencies that allows interested parties to comment on proposed rules of an agency before their promulgation.

**Rule of reason** A restraint against trade that has a procompetitive business purpose and a competitive restraint not beyond that business purpose.

**Rule l0b-5** An SEC rule that prohibits fraud in connection with any sale or purchase of securities.

**Sale of business doctrine** A doctrine rejected by the United States Supreme Court; it holds that the sale of 100 percent of the stock of a business is not a sale of a security for purposes of federal securities law.

**Scalping** The practice of a securities broker whereby the broker recommends the purchase of a stock for the purpose of inflating its value so that the broker, who had purchased the same stock previously, capitalizes on its sale.

**Scienter** Knowledge; intent to deceive or defraud.

**Secondary boycott** In labor law, the term refers to a refusal by union employees to work for, purchase from, or handle products of a secondary employer with whom the union has no dispute, with the object of forcing such employer to stop doing business with the primary employer with whom the union has a dispute.

**Secondary meaning** A trademark that has developed a new meaning in which it serves to identify specific goods. For example, Nantucket has a primary meaning of a geographical location; however, it has a secondary meaning-a specific manufacturer's shirts.

**Secondary-line injury** Injury that occurs when a seller discriminates in price between two competing buyers.

**Security** A stock, bond, note, investment contract, or other interest involving an investment in a common enterprise with the expectation of a profit to be derived from the efforts of someone other than the investor; an obligation given by a debtor to assure payment of a debt by providing the creditor with a resource that the creditor can use if the debtor defaults on the debt.

**Security interest** A type of interest held by a creditor in a debtor›s property such that the property could be sold on the debtor›s default to satisfy the debt.

**Seniority** By seniority, the oldest worker in point of service, ability, and fitness for the job is the first to be given a choice of jobs, is the first to be promoted within a range of jobs subject to seniority, and is the last to be laid off. This proceeding is followed down the line to the youngest worker in point of service.

**Separation of powers** A phrase referring to the division of the federal government into three departments or branches: the legislative, which is empowered to make laws; the executive, which is required to carry out the laws; and the judiciary, which is charged with interpreting the laws and adjudicating disputes under the laws. One branch is not permitted to intrude on the domain of another.

**Shareholder** A person who owns stock in a corporation.

**Shipping terms** Terms in a contract which govern the shipment of goods. Shipping terms determine such matters as when risk of loss passes and when performance is complete.

**Short-swing profits** Profits made by an insider through the sale or other disposition of the corporate stock within six months after purchase.

**Single trespass** A trespass of a single instance.

**Situs** Situation or location.

**Slander** The tort of oral defamation.

**Social audit** A report of a company's social behavior.

**Social balance sheet** A report in which a company shares information on its social behavior.

**Sole proprietorship** A business owned by one person.

**Sovereign** An independent body or state; a chief ruler with supreme power, such as a king.

**Sovereign immunity** Doctrine preventing a litigant from asserting an otherwise meritorious claim against a sovereign (government).

**Specific intent** Exercise of intelligent will to commit a crime.

**Specific performance** A remedy for breach of contract that requires the breaching party to actually perform what he or she had promised to perform in the contract.

**Squeeze out** The elimination of minority shareholders by the majority shareholders.

**Standard deviation** A statistical method of measuring the probability that a given result occurred by chance.

**Standing** A stake in a controversy sufficient to entitle a person to sue and obtain judicial resolution of the controversy.

**Stare decisis** Latin, "Let the decision stand." Doctrine under which courts stand by precedent and do not disturb a settled point. Under this doctrine, once a court has laid down a principle of law as applied to a certain state of facts, the court adheres to that principle and applies to it all future cases in which the facts are substantially the same.

**State action** In constitutional law, the term is used to designate governmental action that is necessary for purposes of bringing a constitutional challenge to such action.

**State right-to-work statute** A state statute authorized by the Taft-Hartley Act whereby an employee may lawfully refuse to join a union certified as the bargaining representative of the employer's employees.

**Status quo ante** Latin, "The state of things before."

**Statute** An act of a legislature declaring, commanding, or prohibiting something; a particular law enacted by the legislative department of government. Sometimes the word is used to designate codified law as opposed to case law.

**Statute of frauds** A statute requiring that certain contracts be supported by written memoranda.

**Statute of limitations** A statute prescribing the length of time after an event in which a suit must be brought or a criminal charge filed.

**Statutory law** Law consisting of statutes as opposed to common law, which is judge-made law.

**Stay** To stop, arrest, or forbear. To stay an order or decree means to hold it in abeyance or to refrain from enforcing it.

**Stop order** The name of a Securities and Exchange Commission order directing that the effectiveness of a registration statement be suspended. The order also suspends a security issuer's license to use the mails and warns the investing public that the SEC has found the registration statement to be unreliable.

**Strict liability** Liability without fault. A case is one of strict liability when neither care nor negligence, neither good nor bad faith, neither knowledge nor ignorance exonerate the defendant.

**Subject matter jurisdiction** A court's authority to hear a particular type of case.

**Subpoena** A writ ordering a person to appear and give testimony or to bring documents in his or her control.

**Subsidiary corporation** A corporation of whose shares at least a majority are owned by another corporation, which thus has control over it.

**Substantial evidence standard of review** The standard of judicial review of agency action whereby a court examines the administrative record to determine if substantial evidence exists to support the agency determination.

**Substantiation** A requirement imposed on advertisers by the Federal Trade Commission that they be able to substantiate the truth of their advertising claims.

**Substantive law** That part of law which creates, defines, and regulates rights, as opposed to procedural law, which prescribes the methods for enforcing the rights.

**Summary judgment** A pretrial decision reached by a trial court, after considering the pleadings, affidavits, depositions, and other documents, on the ground that no genuine issue of fact has been raised.

**Summary plan description** Under the Employee Retirement Income Security Act, a statement of any material modifications to a pension plan, annual reports including certified financial statements, and terminal and supplementary reports, if the plan is to be terminated.

**Summons** An instrument served on a defendant in a civil proceeding to give the defendant notice that he or she has been sued.

**Sunset legislation** A statute which provides that an agency's authority shall expire on a given date unless the legislative body acts to extend it.

**Supremacy Clause** A clause in the U.S. Constitution providing that all laws made by the federal government pursuant to the Constitution are the supreme law of the land and are superior to and conflicting state law.

**Takeover bid** A bid to assume control or management of a corporation; a tender offer.

**Target company** The company intended to be taken over in a takover bid.

**Tender offer** An offer to purchase shares of stock, usually made in an attempt to obtain a controlling interest in a corporation.

**Terminable at will** The normal employment relationship, absent a contract, whereby an employer may discharge an employee for any nondiscriminatory reason.

**Tie-in** When a party offers to provide one good or service only to those who agree to accept another good or service.

**Tombstone ad** An advertisement of a stock offering containing language to the effect that the announcement is neither an offer to sell nor a solicitation of an offer to buy any of the securities listed. The actual offer is made only by the prospectus.

**Tort** A civil wrong or injury, other than a breach of contract, committed against the person or property of another.

**Tortfeasor** A person who has committed a tort.

**Trade association** Organizations of competitors with common interests and business pursuits.

**Trademark** A word, name, symbol or device used by a manufacturer or merchant to identify goods and distinguish them from those manufactured by others.

**Treatise** A book that expounds on a broad area of a subject.

**Treaty** An agreement between nations.

**Treble damages** Three times actual damages. The remedy provided to a successful plaintiff in certain actions, including antitrust suits.

**Trespass** A tort action affording redress for injury committed to the plaintiff by the unauthorized entry on another's land or the interference with another's personal property.

**Trust** A legal arrangement whereby property or other assets are secured for beneficiaries by placing legal title and usually management responsibility in a trustee.

**Trustee** The person appointed to execute a trust.

**Truth in Lending Act** A federal statute that regulates consumer credit by requiring lenders to disclose certain credit terms in a standard way and regulates the cancellation of credit agreements, consumer leasing, and credit card extension and use.

**Unconscionable** So unfair or one-sided as to oppress or unfairly surprise a party.

**Unfair labor practices** Those practices contained in sections 8(a) and (b) of the NLRA that prohibit specified employer and employee practices, for example, refusing to bargain in good faith.

**Uniform Commercial Code** A comprehensive code, drafted by the National Conference of Commissioners on Uniform State Laws, which has been enacted in all of the states.

**Union certification** The process by which the National Labor Relations Board certifies a union as the exclusive bargaining representative of a unit of employees in the employer's work force.

**Utility model** Ethical justification holding that acts or rules that provide the greatest benefit to the greatest number of people are right or good.

**Validation** A statistical corroboration of a selection procedure that has an adverse impact on a protected group.

**Variance** Permission to depart from the literal requirements of an administrative regulation.

**Venue** The particular county or geographic location in which a court with jurisdiction may hear a case.

**Vertical merger** A merger between two firms that have a buyer-seller relationship.

**Vertical restraint** An agreement between two or more parties at different levels of the distribution process to restrain trade by, for example, inhibiting intrabrand competition.

**Vested** Fixed, settled, absolute. Having the character of absolute ownership. With regard to pension plan benefits, vested benefits are not contingent on the employee continuing to work for the employer.

**Veto** Latin, "I forbid." The refusal of assent by the executive officer whose assent is necessary to perfect a law which a legislative body has passed.

**Vicarious liability** *See Respondeat superior.*

**Vis-a-vis** Face to face. One of two things or persons opposite or corresponding to each other. In relation to each other.

**Void** Null; ineffectual; having no legal force.

**Warrant** A writ from a competent authority in pursuance of law which directs the doing of an act, is addressed to an officer or person competent to do the act, and affords that officer or person protection from damage if he or she does it. In particular, writs are issued by a magistrate or justice, and addressed to a sheriff, constable, or other officer, requiring the latter to arrest someone or to search someone's person or property and seize items of evidence.

**Warranty** A promise that a statement is true. In contracts, a written or verbal undertaking or stipulation that a certain statement in relation to the subject matter of the contract is or shall be as it is stated or promised to be.

**White collar exemptions** Those executive, administrative, and professional personnel, who are salaried and meet other specified requirements and who are exempt from coverage of the Fair Labor Standards Act.

**Work-product doctrine** The doctrine by which certain material prepared by an attorney in anticipation of litigation is protected from discovery.

**Work councils** Plant-level committees consisting of supervisory personnel and workers, which decide plant-level matters.

**Writ** A court order directing a person to do something.

**Wrongful discharge** *See Abusive discharge.*